Contents

Algorithm 1
   What is an Algorithm? 1
   Why Learn Data Structures and Algorithms? 4
   Asymptotic Analysis 10
   Master Theorem 14
   Divide and Conquer Algorithm 16
Data Structures 21
   Stack 21
   Queue 24
      Types of Queue 30
      Circular Queue 31
      Priority Queue 38
      Deque 45
   LinkedList 51
      Linked List Operations 54
      Types of Linked List 59
   Hash Table 63
   Heap 70
      Fibonacci Heap 77
Trees 93
   Tree Traversal 96
   Binary Tree 101
      Full Binary Tree 106
      Perfect Binary Tree 108
      Complete Binary Tree 110
      Balanced Binary Tree 115
      Binary Search Tree(BST) 117

- AVL Tree 127
- B-tree 143
  - Insertion into a B-tree 147
  - Deletion from a B-tree 152
- B+ Tree 162
  - Insertion on a B+ Tree 171
  - Deletion from a B+ Tree 173
- Red-Black Tree 179
  - Insertion in a Red-Black Tree 195
  - Deletion From a Red-Black Tree 201
- Graph 210
  - Spanning Tree 212
  - Adjacency Matrix 224
  - Adjacency List 227
  - Depth First Search 230
  - Breadth First Search 233
  - Bellman Ford's Algorithm 237
- Sorting 244
  - Bubble Sort 244
  - Selection Sort 249
  - Insertion Sort 254
  - Merge Sort 259
  - Quicksort 269
  - Counting Sort 275
  - Radix Sort 279
  - Bucket Sort 283
  - Heap Sort 288
  - Shell Sort 300
- Search 306

  Linear Search 306

  Binary Search 307

Greedy Algorithm 313

  Ford-Fulkerson Algorithm 314

  Dijkstra's Algorithm 320

  Kruskal's Algorithm 326

  Prim's Algorithm 330

  Huffman Coding 334

Dynamic Programming 341

  Floyd-Warshall Algorithm 343

  Longest Common Subsequence 348

  Backtracking Algorithm 353

  Rabin-Karp Algorithm 355

Algorithm

What is an Algorithm?

An algorithm is a set of well-defined instructions in sequence to solve a problem.

Qualities of a good algorithm
1. Input and output should be defined precisely.
2. Each step in the algorithm should be clear and unambiguous.
3. Algorithms should be most effective among many different ways to solve a problem.
4. An algorithm shouldn't include computer code. Instead, the algorithm should be written in such a way that it can be used in different programming languages.

Algorithm Examples
- Algorithm to add two numbers
- Algorithm to find the largest among three numbers
- Algorithm to find all the roots of the quadratic equation
- Algorithm to find the factorial
- Algorithm to check prime number
- Algorithm of Fibonacci series

Examples Of Algorithms In Programming

Write an algorithm to add two numbers entered by the user.
Step 1: Start
Step 2: Declare variables num1, num2 and sum.
Step 3: Read values num1 and num2.
Step 4: Add num1 and num2 and assign the result to sum.
    sum←num1+num2
Step 5: Display sum
Step 6: Stop

Write an algorithm to find the largest among three different numbers entered by the user.
Step 1: Start
Step 2: Declare variables a,b and c.
Step 3: Read variables a,b and c.
Step 4: If a > b
    If a > c
      Display a is the largest number.
    Else
      Display c is the largest number.
  Else
    If b > c
      Display b is the largest number.
    Else
      Display c is the greatest number.
Step 5: Stop

Write an algorithm to find all roots of a quadratic equation $ax^2+bx+c=0$.
Step 1: Start
Step 2: Declare variables a, b, c, D, x1, x2, rp and ip;
Step 3: Calculate discriminant
    D ← b2-4ac
Step 4: If D ≥ 0
    r1 ← (-b+√D)/2a
    r2 ← (-b-√D)/2a
    Display r1 and r2 as roots.
  Else
    Calculate real part and imaginary part
    rp ← -b/2a
    ip ← √(-D)/2a
    Display rp+j(ip) and rp-j(ip) as roots
Step 5: Stop

Write an algorithm to find the factorial of a number entered by the user.
Step 1: Start
Step 2: Declare variables n, factorial and i.
Step 3: Initialize variables
    factorial ← 1
    i ← 1

Step 4: Read value of n
Step 5: Repeat the steps until i = n
    5.1: factorial ← factorial*i
    5.2: i ← i+1
Step 6: Display factorial
Step 7: Stop

Write an algorithm to check whether a number entered by the user is prime or not.
Step 1: Start
Step 2: Declare variables n, i, flag.
Step 3: Initialize variables
    flag ← 1
    i ← 2
Step 4: Read n from the user.
Step 5: Repeat the steps until i=(n/2)
    5.1 If remainder of n÷i equals 0
        flag ← 0
        Go to step 6
    5.2 i ← i+1
Step 6: If flag = 0
      Display n is not prime
    else
      Display n is prime
Step 7: Stop

Write an algorithm to find the Fibonacci series till term≤1000.
Step 1: Start
Step 2: Declare variables first_term, second_term and temp.
Step 3: Initialize variables first_term ← 0 second_term ← 1
Step 4: Display first_term and second_term
Step 5: Repeat the steps until second_term ≤ 1000
    5.1: temp ← second_term
    5.2: second_term ← second_term + first_term
    5.3: first_term ← temp
    5.4: Display second_term
Step 6: Stop

Why Learn Data Structures and Algorithms?

What are Algorithms?
Informally, an algorithm is nothing but a mention of steps to solve a problem. They are essentially a solution.
For example, an algorithm to solve the problem of factorials might look something like this:

Problem: Find the factorial of n
Initialize fact = 1
For every value v in range 1 to n:
   Multiply the fact by v
fact contains the factorial of n

Here, the algorithm is written in English. If it was written in a programming language, we would call it to code instead. Here is a code for finding the factorial of a number in C++.
int factorial(int n) {
   int fact = 1;
   for (int v = 1; v <= n; v++) {
      fact = fact * v;
   }
   return fact;
}

Programming is all about data structures and algorithms. Data structures are used to hold data while algorithms are used to solve the problem using that data.

Data structures and algorithms (DSA) goes through solutions to standard problems in detail and gives you an insight into how efficient it is to use each one of them. It also teaches you the science of evaluating the efficiency of an algorithm. This enables you to choose the best of various choices.

Use of Data Structures and Algorithms to Make Your Code Scalable

Time is precious.
Suppose, Alice and Bob are trying to solve a simple problem of finding the sum of the first 10^{11} natural numbers. While Bob was writing the

algorithm, Alice implemented it proving that it is as simple as criticizing Donald Trump.

Algorithm (by Bob)
Initialize sum = 0
for every natural number n in range 1 to 1011 (inclusive):
    add n to sum
sum is your answer
Code (by Alice)
```
int findSum() {
    int sum = 0;
    for (int v = 1; v <= 100000000000; v++) {
        sum += v;
    }
    return sum;
}
```

Alice and Bob are feeling euphoric of themselves that they could build something of their own in almost no time. Let's sneak into their workspace and listen to their conversation.
Alice: Let's run this code and find out the sum.
Bob: I ran this code a few minutes back but it's still not showing the output. What's wrong with it?

Oops, something went wrong! A computer is the most deterministic machine. Going back and trying to run it again won't help. So let's analyze what's wrong with this simple code.

Two of the most valuable resources for a computer program are time and memory.

The time taken by the computer to run code is:
Time to run code = number of instructions * time to execute each instruction

The number of instructions depends on the code you used, and the time taken to execute each code depends on your machine and compiler.

In this case, the total number of instructions executed (let's say x) are $x = 1 + (10^{11} + 1) + (10^{11}) + 1$, which is $x = 2 * 10^{11} + 3$

Let us assume that a computer can execute $y = 10^8$ instructions in one second (it can vary subject to machine configuration). The time taken to run above code is

Time taken to run code = x/y (greater than 16 minutes)

Is it possible to optimize the algorithm so that Alice and Bob do not have to wait for 16 minutes every time they run this code?

I am sure that you already guessed the right method. The sum of first N natural numbers is given by the formula:

Sum = N * (N + 1) / 2

Converting it into code will look something like this:
```
int sum(int N) {
    return N * (N + 1) / 2;
}
```

This code executes in just one instruction and gets the task done no matter what the value is. Let it be greater than the total number of atoms in the universe. It will find the result in no time.

The time taken to solve the problem, in this case, is $1/y$ (which is 10 nanoseconds). By the way, the fusion reaction of a hydrogen bomb takes 40-50 ns, which means your program will complete successfully even if someone throws a hydrogen bomb on your computer at the same time you ran your code.

Note: Computers take a few instructions (not 1) to compute multiplication and division. I have said 1 just for the sake of simplicity.

More on Scalability
Scalability is scale plus ability, which means the quality of an algorithm/system to handle the problem of larger size.

Consider the problem of setting up a classroom of 50 students. One of the simplest solutions is to book a room, get a blackboard, a few chalks, and the problem is solved.

But what if the size of the problem increases? What if the number of students increased to 200?

The solution still holds but it needs more resources. In this case, you will probably need a much larger room (probably a theater), a projector screen and a digital pen.

What if the number of students increased to 1000?
The solution fails or uses a lot of resources when the size of the problem increases. This means, your solution wasn't scalable.

What is a scalable solution then?
Consider a site like Khanacademy, millions of students can see videos, read answers at the same time and no more resources are required. So, the solution can solve the problems of larger size under resource crunch.

If you see our first solution to find the sum of first N natural numbers, it wasn't scalable. It's because it required linear growth in time with the linear growth in the size of the problem. Such algorithms are also known as linearly scalable algorithms.

Our second solution was very scalable and didn't require the use of any more time to solve a problem of larger size. These are known as constant-time algorithms.

Memory is expensive
Memory is not always available in abundance. While dealing with code/system which requires you to store or produce a lot of data, it is critical for your algorithm to save the usage of memory wherever possible. For example: While storing data about people, you can save memory by storing only their age not the date of birth. You can always calculate it on the fly using their age and current date.

Examples of an Algorithm's Efficiency
Here are some examples of what learning algorithms and data structures enable you to do:

Example 1: Age Group Problem

Problems like finding the people of a certain age group can easily be solved with a little modified version of the binary search algorithm (assuming that the data is sorted).

The naive algorithm which goes through all the persons one by one, and checks if it falls in the given age group is linearly scalable. Whereas, binary search claims itself to be a logarithmically scalable algorithm.

This means that if the size of the problem is squared, the time taken to solve it is only doubled.

Suppose, it takes 1 second to find all the people at a certain age for a group of 1000. Then for a group of 1 million people,
- the binary search algorithm will take only 2 seconds to solve the problem
- the naive algorithm might take 1 million seconds, which is around 12 days

The same binary search algorithm is used to find the square root of a number.

Example 2: Rubik's Cube Problem

Imagine you are writing a program to find the solution of a Rubik's cube.

This cute looking puzzle has annoyingly 43,252,003,274,489,856,000 positions, and these are just positions! Imagine the number of paths one can take to reach the wrong positions.

Fortunately, the way to solve this problem can be represented by the graph data structure. There is a graph algorithm known as Dijkstra's algorithm which allows you to solve this problem in linear time. Yes, you heard it right. It means that it allows you to reach the solved position in a minimum number of states.

Example 3: DNA Problem

DNA is a molecule that carries genetic information. They are made up of smaller units which are represented by Roman characters A, C, T, and G.

Imagine yourself working in the field of bioinformatics. You are assigned the work of finding out the occurrence of a particular pattern in a DNA strand.

It is a famous problem in computer science academia. And, the simplest algorithm takes the time proportional to

(number of character in DNA strand) * (number of characters in pattern)

A typical DNA strand has millions of such units. Knuth-Morris-Pratt algorithm can get this done in time which is proportional to

(number of character in DNA strand) + (number of characters in pattern)

The * operator replaced by + makes a lot of change.

Considering that the pattern was of 100 characters, your algorithm is now 100 times faster. If your pattern was of 1000 characters, the KMP algorithm would be almost 1000 times faster. That is, if you were able to find the occurrence of pattern in 1 second, it will now take you just 1 ms. We can also put this in another way. Instead of matching 1 strand, you can match 1000 strands of similar length at the same time.

Generally, software development involves learning new technologies on a daily basis. You get to learn most of these technologies while using them in one of your projects. However, it is not the case with algorithms.

If you don't know algorithms well, you won't be able to identify if you can optimize the code you are writing right now. You are expected to know them in advance and apply them wherever possible and critical. We specifically talked about the scalability of algorithms. A software system consists of many such algorithms. Optimizing any one of them leads to a better system.

However, it's important to note that this is not the only way to make a system scalable. For example, a technique known as distributed computing allows independent parts of a program to run to multiple machines together making it even more scalable.

Asymptotic Analysis

The efficiency of an algorithm depends on the amount of time, storage and other resources required to execute the algorithm. The efficiency is measured with the help of asymptotic notations.

An algorithm may not have the same performance for different types of inputs. With the increase in the input size, the performance will change.

The study of change in performance of the algorithm with the change in the order of the input size is defined as asymptotic analysis.

Asymptotic Notations
Asymptotic notations are the mathematical notations used to describe the running time of an algorithm when the input tends towards a particular value or a limiting value.

For example: In bubble sort, when the input array is already sorted, the time taken by the algorithm is linear i.e. the best case.

But, when the input array is in reverse condition, the algorithm takes the maximum time (quadratic) to sort the elements i.e. the worst case.

When the input array is neither sorted nor in reverse order, then it takes average time. These durations are denoted using asymptotic notations.
There are mainly three asymptotic notations: Theta notation, Omega notation and Big-O notation.

Theta Notation (Θ-notation)
Theta notation encloses the function from above and below. Since it represents the upper and the lower bound of the running time of an

algorithm, it is used for analyzing the average case complexity of an algorithm.

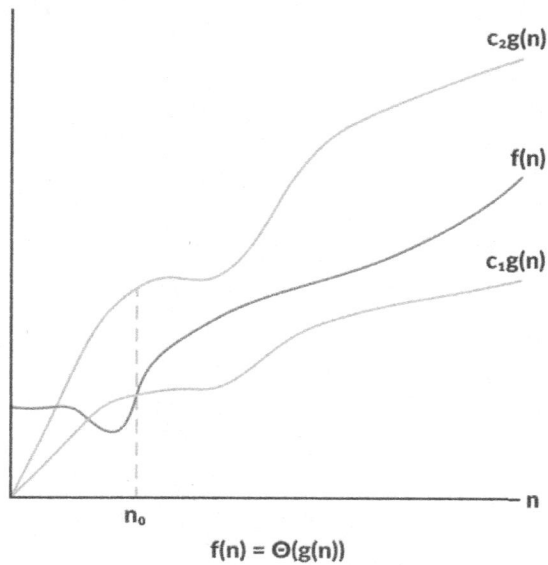

f(n) = Θ(g(n))

Theta bounds the function within constants factors

For a function g(n), Θ(g(n)) is given by the relation:

Θ(g(n)) = { f(n): there exist positive constants c_1, c_2 and n_0 such that $0 \leq c_1 g(n) \leq f(n) \leq c_2 g(n)$ for all $n \geq n_0$ }

The above expression can be described as a function f(n) belongs to the set Θ(g(n)) if there exist positive constants c_1 and c_2 such that it can be sandwiched between $c_1 g(n)$ and $c_2 g(n)$, for sufficiently large n.

If a function f(n) lies anywhere in between $c_1 g(n)$ and $c_2 > g(n)$ for all n ≥ n0, then f(n) is said to be asymptotically tight bound.

Big-O Notation (O-notation)
Big-O notation represents the upper bound of the running time of an algorithm. Thus, it gives the worst case complexity of an algorithm.

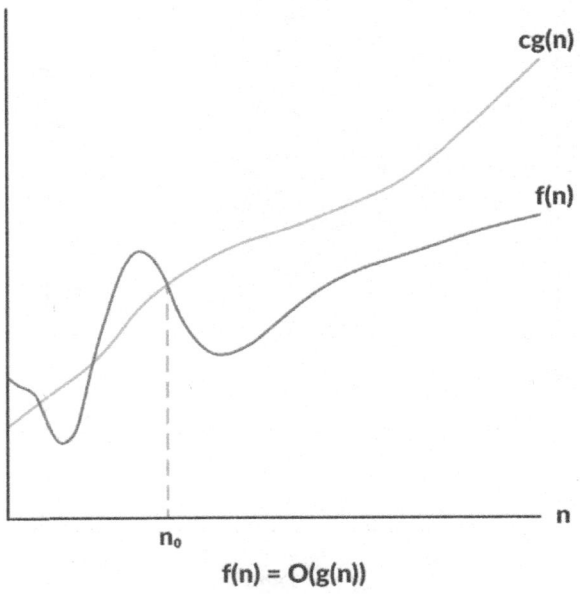

f(n) = O(g(n))

Big-O gives the upper bound of a function

$O(g(n)) = \{ f(n):$ there exist positive constants c and n_0
such that $0 \leq f(n) \leq cg(n)$ for all $n \geq n_0 \}$

The above expression can be described as a function f(n) belongs to the set O(g(n)) if there exists a positive constant c such that it lies between 0 and cg(n), for sufficiently large n.

For any value of n, the running time of an algorithm does not cross time provided by O(g(n)).

Since it gives the worst case running time of an algorithm, it is widely used to analyze an algorithm as we are always interested in the worst case scenario.

Omega Notation (Ω-notation)
Omega notation represents the lower bound of the running time of an algorithm. Thus, it provides best case complexity of an algorithm.

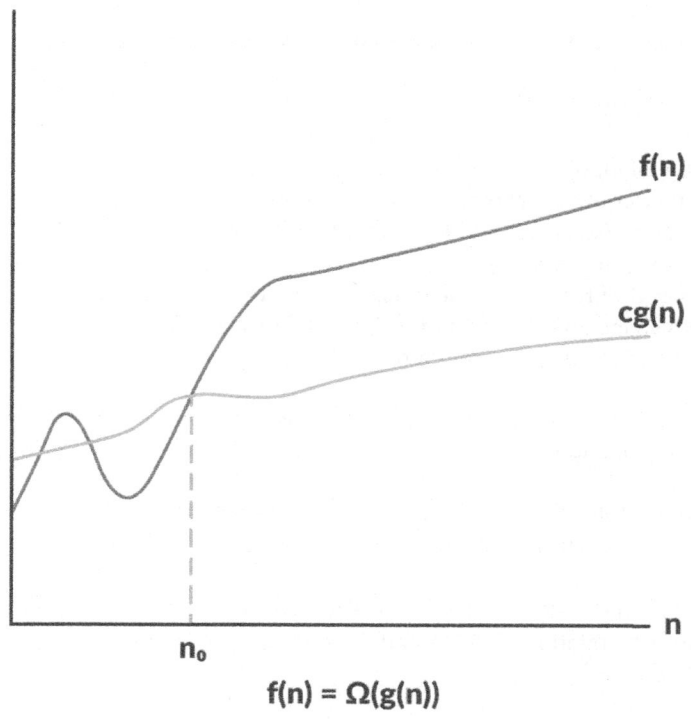

$f(n) = \Omega(g(n))$

Omega gives the lower bound of a function

$\Omega(g(n)) = \{\,f(n):$ there exist positive constants c and n_0
such that $0 \le cg(n) \le f(n)$ for all $n \ge n_0\,\}$

The above expression can be described as a function f(n) belongs to the set $\Omega(g(n))$ if there exists a positive constant c such that it lies above cg(n), for sufficiently large n.

For any value of n, the minimum time required by the algorithm is given by Omega $\Omega(g(n))$

Master Theorem

The master method is a formula for solving recurrence relations of the form:
$T(n) = aT(n/b) + f(n)$,
where,
n = size of input
a = number of subproblems in the recursion
n/b = size of each subproblem. All subproblems are assumed to have the same size.
f(n) = cost of the work done outside the recursive call, which includes the cost of dividing the problem and cost of merging the solutions

Here, $a \geq 1$ and $b > 1$ are constants, and f(n) is an asymptotically positive function.

An asymptotically positive function means that for a sufficiently large value of n, we have f(n) > 0.

Master theorem is used in calculating the time complexity of recurrence relations (divide and conquer algorithms) in a simple and quick way.

Master Theorem
If $a \geq 1$ and $b > 1$ are constants and f(n) is an asymptotically positive function, then the time complexity of a recursive relation is given by
$T(n) = aT(n/b) + f(n)$

where, T(n) has the following asymptotic bounds:

   1. If $f(n) = O(n^{\log_b a - \epsilon})$, then $T(n) = \Theta(n^{\log_b a})$.

   2. If $f(n) = \Theta(n^{\log_b a})$, then $T(n) = \Theta(n^{\log_b a} * \log n)$.

   3. If $f(n) = \Omega(n^{\log_b a + \epsilon})$, then $T(n) = \Theta(f(n))$.

$\epsilon > 0$ is a constant.

Each of the above conditions can be interpreted as:

1. If the cost of solving the sub-problems at each level increases by a certain factor, the value of f(n) will become polynomially smaller than $n^{\log_b a}$. Thus, the time complexity is oppressed by the cost of the last level ie. $n^{\log_b a}$

2. If the cost of solving the sub-problem at each level is nearly equal, then the value of f(n) will be $n^{\log_b a}$. Thus, the time complexity will be f(n) times the total number of levels ie. $n^{\log_b a} * \log n$

3. If the cost of solving the subproblems at each level decreases by a certain factor, the value of f(n) will become polynomially larger than $n^{\log_b a}$. Thus, the time complexity is oppressed by the cost of f(n).

Solved Example of Master Theorem
T(n) = 3T(n/2) + n2
Here,
a = 3
n/b = n/2
f(n) = n²

$\log_b a = \log_2 3 \approx 1.58 < 2$

ie. $f(n) < n^{\log_b a + \epsilon}$, where, ϵ is a constant.

Case 3 implies here.

Thus, T(n) = f(n) = Θ(n²)

Master Theorem Limitations
The master theorem cannot be used if:
- T(n) is not monotone. eg. T(n) = sin n
- f(n) is not a pilynomial. eg. f(n) = 2n
- a is not a constant. eg. a = 2n
- a < 1

Divide and Conquer Algorithm

A divide and conquer algorithm is a strategy of solving a large problem by
1. breaking the problem into smaller sub-problems
2. solving the sub-problems, and
3. combining them to get the desired output.

To use divide and conquer algorithms, recursion is used. Learn about recursion in different programming languages:
- Recursion in Java
- Recursion in Python
- Recursion in C++

How Divide and Conquer Algorithms Work?
Here are the steps involved:
1. Divide : Divide the given problem into sub-problems using recursion.
2. Conquer: Solve the smaller sub-problems recursively. If the subproblem is small enough, then solve it directly.
3. Combine: Combine the solutions of the sub-problems which is part of the recursive process to get the solution to the actual problem.

Let us understand this concept with the help of an example.
Here, we are going to sort an array using the divide and conquer approach (ie. merge sort).

Let the given array be:

Array for merge sort

Divide the array into two halves.

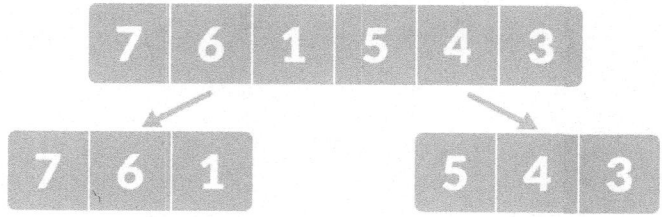

Divide the array into two subparts

Again, divide each subpart recursively into two halves until you get individual elements.

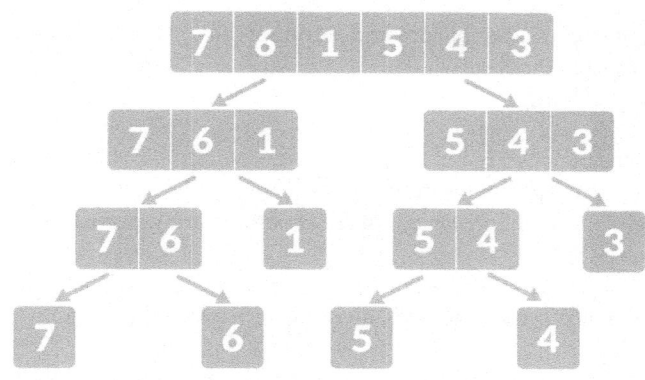

Divide the array into smaller subparts

Now, combine the individual elements in a sorted manner. Here, conquer and combine steps go side by side.

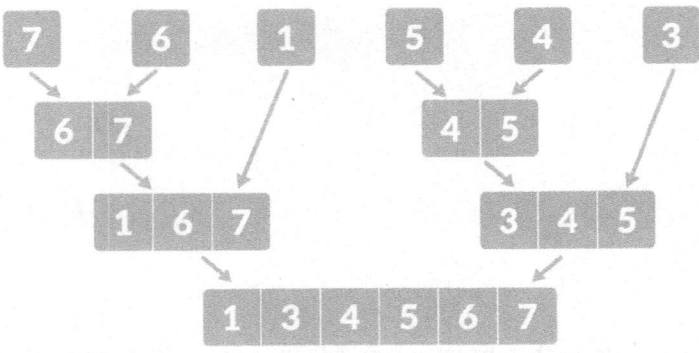

Combine the subparts

Complexity

The complexity of the divide and conquer algorithm is calculated using the master theorem.
$T(n) = aT(n/b) + f(n)$,
where,
n = size of input
a = number of subproblems in the recursion
n/b = size of each subproblem. All subproblems are assumed to have the same size.
f(n) = cost of the work done outside the recursive call, which includes the cost of dividing the problem and cost of merging the solutions

Let us take an example to find the time complexity of a recursive problem.

For a merge sort, the equation can be written as:
$T(n) = aT(n/b) + f(n)$
$\quad\ = 2T(n/2) + O(n)$

Where,
a = 2 (each time, a problem is divided into 2 subproblems)
n/b = n/2 (size of each sub problem is half of the input)
f(n) = time taken to divide the problem and merging the subproblems
$T(n/2) = O(n \log n)$ (To understand this, please refer to the master theorem.)

Now, T(n) = 2T(n log n) + O(n)
   ≈ O(n log n)

Divide and Conquer vs Dynamic approach

The divide and conquer approach divides a problem into smaller subproblems, these subproblems are further solved recursively. The result of each subproblem is not stored for future reference, whereas, in a dynamic approach, the result of each subproblem is stored for future reference.

Use the divide and conquer approach when the same subproblem is not solved multiple times. Use the dynamic approach when the result of a subproblem is to be used multiple times in the future.

Let us understand this with an example. Suppose we are trying to find the Fibonacci series. Then,

Divide and Conquer approach:
fib(n)
   If n < 2, return 1
   Else , return f(n - 1) + f(n -2)

Dynamic approach:
mem = [ ]
fib(n)
   If n in mem: return mem[n]
   else,
      If n < 2, f = 1
      else , f = f(n - 1) + f(n -2)
      mem[n] = f
      return f

In a dynamic approach, mem stores the result of each subproblem.

Advantage of Divide and Conquer Algorithm
- The complexity for the multiplication of two matrices using the naive method is $O(n^3)$, whereas using the divide and conquer approach (ie. Strassen's matrix multiplication) is $O(n^{2.8074})$. Other problems such as the Tower of Hanoi are also simplified by this approach.
- This approach is suitable for multiprocessing systems.

- It makes efficient use of memory caches.

Divide and Conquer Application
- Binary Search
- Merge Sort
- Quick Sort
- Strassen's Matrix multiplication
- Karatsuba Algorithm

Data Structures

Stack

A stack is a useful data structure in programming. It is just like a pile of plates kept on top of each other.

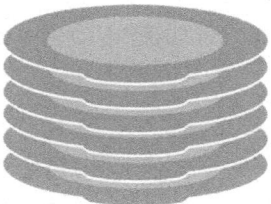

Stack representation similar to a pile of plate

Think about the things you can do with such a pile of plates
- Put a new plate on top
- Remove the top plate

If you want the plate at the bottom, you have to first remove all the plates on top. Such an arrangement is called Last In First Out - the last item that was placed is the first item to go out.

LIFO Principle of Stack
In programming terms, putting an item on top of the stack is called "push" and removing an item is called "pop".

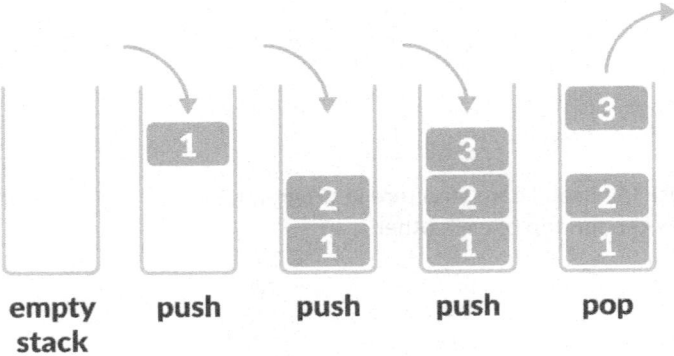

empty stack   push   push   push   pop

Stack Push and Pop Operations

In the above image, although item 2 was kept last, it was removed first - so it follows the Last In First Out(LIFO) principle.

Basic Operations of Stack

A stack is an object or more specifically an abstract data structure(ADT) that allows the following operations:
- Push: Add an element to the top of a stack
- Pop: Remove an element from the top of a stack
- IsEmpty: Check if the stack is empty
- IsFull: Check if the stack is full
- Peek: Get the value of the top element without removing it

Working of Stack Data Structure

The operations work as follows:
1. A pointer called TOP is used to keep track of the top element in the stack.
2. When initializing the stack, we set its value to -1 so that we can check if the stack is empty by comparing TOP == -1.
3. On pushing an element, we increase the value of TOP and place the new element in the position pointed to by TOP.
4. On popping an element, we return the element pointed to by TOP and reduce its value.
5. Before pushing, we check if the stack is already full
6. Before popping, we check if the stack is already empty

22

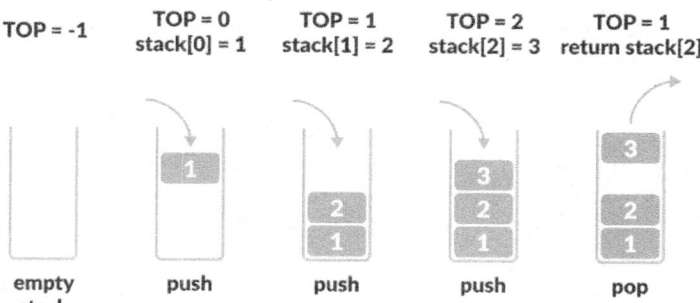

Working of Stack Data Structure

Stack Implementations in Python

```python
# Stack implementation in python


# Creating a stack
def create_stack():
    stack = []
    return stack


# Creating an empty stack
def check_empty(stack):
    return len(stack) == 0


# Adding items into the stack
def push(stack, item):
    stack.append(item)
    print("pushed item: " + item)


# Removing an element from the stack
def pop(stack):
    if (check_empty(stack)):
        return "stack is empty"

    return stack.pop()


stack = create_stack()
push(stack, str(1))
push(stack, str(2))
push(stack, str(3))
push(stack, str(4))
print("popped item: " + pop(stack))
```

```
print("stack after popping an element: " + str(stack))
```

Output
```
pushed item: 1
pushed item: 2
pushed item: 3
pushed item: 4
popped item: 4
stack after popping an element: ['1', '2', '3']
```

Stack Time Complexity
For the array-based implementation of a stack, the push and pop operations take constant time i.e. O(1) because there is only a movement of the pointer in both the cases.

Applications of Stack Data Structure
Although stack is a simple data structure to implement, it is very powerful. The most common uses of a stack are:
- To reverse a word - Put all the letters in a stack and pop them out. Because of the LIFO order of stack, you will get the letters in reverse order.
- In compilers - Compilers use the stack to calculate the value of expressions like 2 + 4 / 5 * (7 - 9) by converting the expression to prefix or postfix form.
- In browsers - The back button in a browser saves all the URLs you have visited previously in a stack. Each time you visit a new page, it is added on top of the stack. When you press the back button, the current URL is removed from the stack and the previous URL is accessed.

Queue

A queue is a useful data structure in programming. It is similar to the ticket queue outside a cinema hall, where the first person entering the queue is the first person who gets the ticket.

Queue follows the First In First Out(FIFO) rule - the item that goes in first is the item that comes out first too.

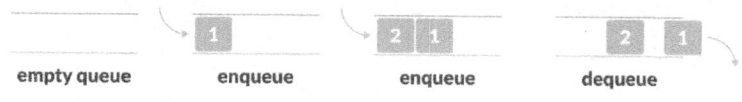

empty queue   enqueue   enqueue   dequeue

FIFO Representation of Queue

In the above image, since 1 was kept in the queue before 2, it was the first to be removed from the queue as well. It follows the FIFO rule.

In programming terms, putting an item in the queue is called an "enqueue" and removing an item from the queue is called "dequeue".

Basic Operations of Queue

A queue is an object or more specifically an abstract data structure(ADT) that allows the following operations:

- Enqueue: Add an element to the end of the queue
- Dequeue: Remove an element from the front of the queue
- IsEmpty: Check if the queue is empty
- IsFull: Check if the queue is full
- Peek: Get the value of the front of the queue without removing it

Working of Queue

Queue operations work as follows:

- two pointers FRONT and REAR
- FRONT track the first element of the queue
- REAR track the last elements of the queue
- initially, set value of FRONT and REAR to -1

Enqueue Operation

- check if the queue is full
- for the first element, set value of FRONT to 0
- increase the REAR index by 1
- add the new element in the position pointed to by REAR

Dequeue Operation

- check if the queue is empty
- return the value pointed by FRONT
- increase the FRONT index by 1

- for the last element, reset the values of FRONT and REAR to -1

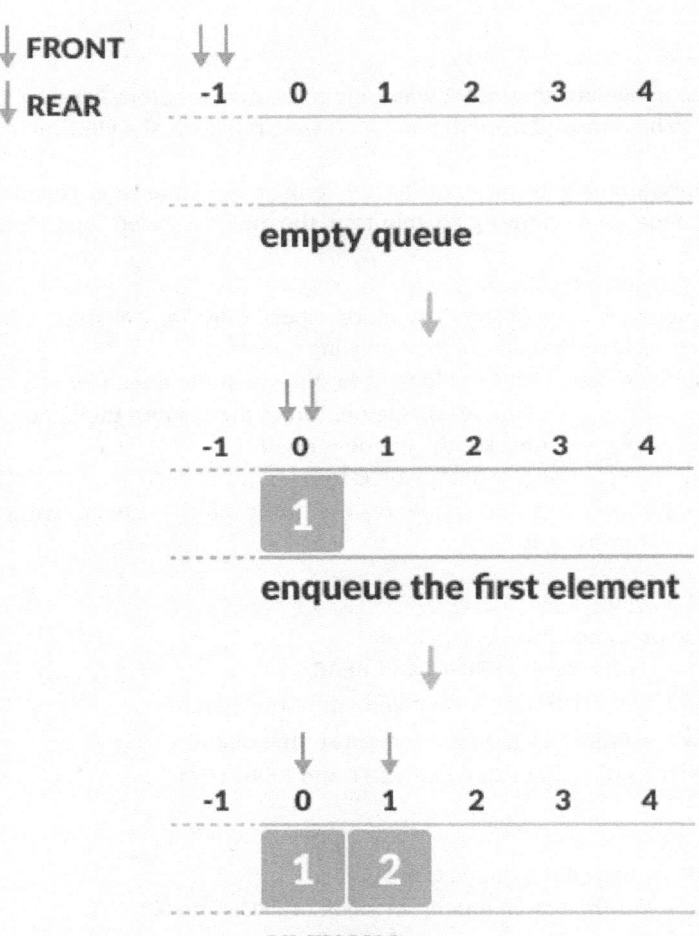

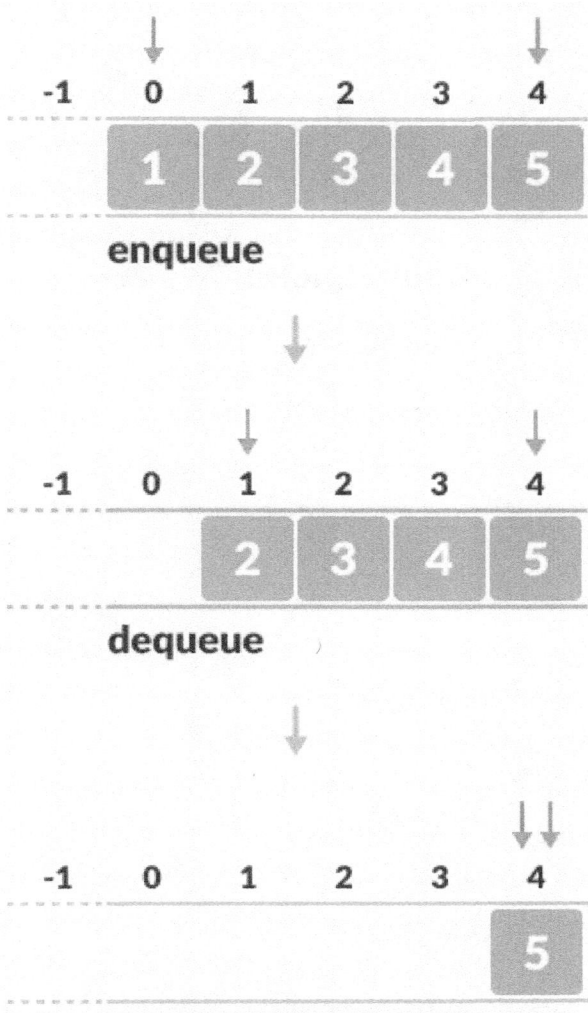

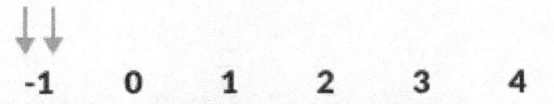

empty queue

Enqueue and Dequeu Operations

Queue Implementations in Python

```python
# Queue implementation in Python

class Queue:

    def __init__(self):
        self.queue = []

    # Add an element
    def enqueue(self, item):
        self.queue.append(item)

    # Remove an element
    def dequeue(self):
        if len(self.queue) < 1:
            return None
        return self.queue.pop(0)

    # Display  the queue
    def display(self):
        print(self.queue)

    def size(self):
        return len(self.queue)


q = Queue()
q.enqueue(1)
q.enqueue(2)
q.enqueue(3)
q.enqueue(4)
q.enqueue(5)

q.display()

q.dequeue()
```

```
print("After removing an element")
q.display()
```

Output
```
[1, 2, 3, 4, 5]
After removing an element
[2, 3, 4, 5]
```

Limitation of Queue
As you can see in the image below, after a bit of enqueuing and dequeuing, the size of the queue has been reduced.

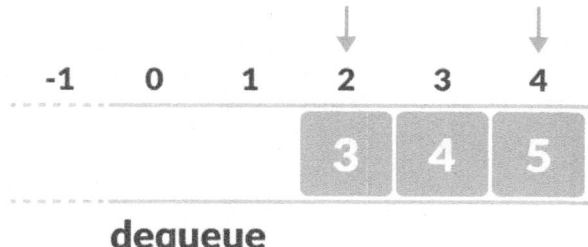

Limitation of a queue

The indexes 0 and 1 can only be used after the queue is reset when all the elements have been dequeued.

After REAR reaches the last index, if we can store extra elements in the empty spaces (0 and 1), we can make use of the empty spaces. This is implemented by a modified queue called the circular queue.

Complexity Analysis
The complexity of enqueue and dequeue operations in a queue using an array is O(1).

Applications of Queue Data Structure
- CPU scheduling, Disk Scheduling
- When data is transferred asynchronously between two processes.The queue is used for synchronization. eg: IO Buffers, pipes, file IO, etc
- Handling of interrupts in real-time systems.

- Call Center phone systems use Queues to hold people calling them in an order

Types of Queue

A queue is a useful data structure in programming. It is similar to the ticket queue outside a cinema hall, where the first person entering the queue is the first person who gets the ticket.

There are four different types of queue in data structure. Let's discuss them below.

Simple Queue
In a simple queue, insertion takes place at the rear and removal occurs at the front. It strictly follows FIFO rule.

Simple Queue Representation

Circular Queue
In a circular queue, the last element points to the first element making a circular link.

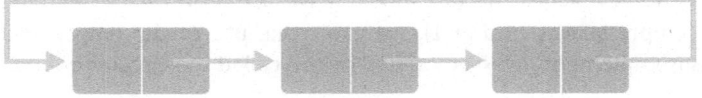

Circular Queue Representation

The main advantage of a circular queue over a simple queue is better memory utilization. If the last position is full and the first position is empty then, an element can be inserted in the first position. This action is not possible in a simple queue.

Priority Queue

A priority queue is a special type of queue in which each element is associated with a priority and is served according to its priority. If elements with the same priority occur, they are served according to their order in the queue.

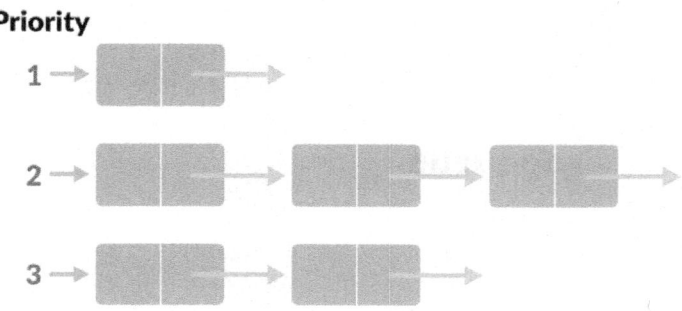

Priority Queue Representation

Insertion occurs based on the arrival of the values and removal occurs based on priority.

Deque (Double Ended Queue)
Double Ended Queue is a type of queue in which insertion and removal of elements can be performed from either from the front or rear. Thus, it does not follow FIFO rule (First In First Out).

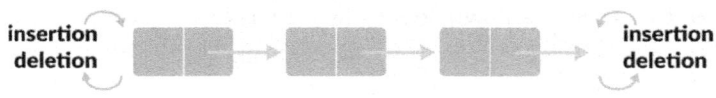

Deque Representation

Circular Queue

Circular queue avoids the wastage of space in a regular queue implementation using arrays.

31

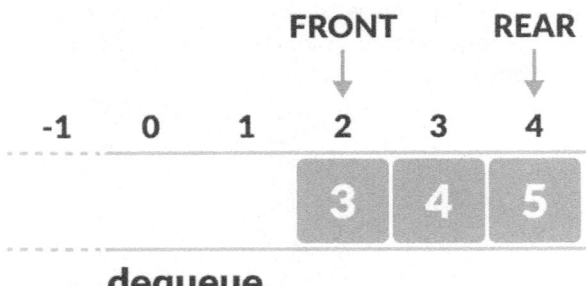

dequeue

Limitation of the regular Queue

As you can see in the above image, after a bit of enqueuing and dequeuing, the size of the queue has been reduced.

The indexes 0 and 1 can only be used after the queue is reset when all the elements have been dequeued.

How Circular Queue Works
Circular Queue works by the process of circular increment i.e. when we try to increment the pointer and we reach the end of the queue, we start from the beginning of the queue. Here, the circular increment is performed by modulo division with the queue size. That is,

if REAR + 1 == 5 (overflow!), REAR = (REAR + 1)%5 = 0 (start of queue)

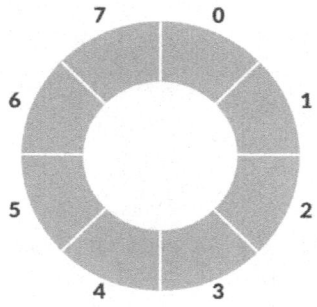

Circular queue representation

Circular Queue Operations
The circular queue work as follows:
- two pointers FRONT and REAR
- FRONT track the first element of the queue
- REAR track the last elements of the queue
- initially, set value of FRONT and REAR to -1

1. Enqueue Operation
- check if the queue is full
- for the first element, set value of FRONT to 0
- circularly increase the REAR index by 1 (i.e. if the rear reaches the end, next it would be at the start of the queue)
- add the new element in the position pointed to by REAR

2. Dequeue Operation
- check if the queue is empty
- return the value pointed by FRONT
- circularly increase the FRONT index by 1
- for the last element, reset the values of FRONT and REAR to -1

However, the check for full queue has a new additional case:
- Case 1: FRONT = 0 && REAR == SIZE - 1
- Case 2: FRONT = REAR + 1

The second case happens when REAR starts from 0 due to circular increment and when its value is just 1 less than FRONT, the queue is full.

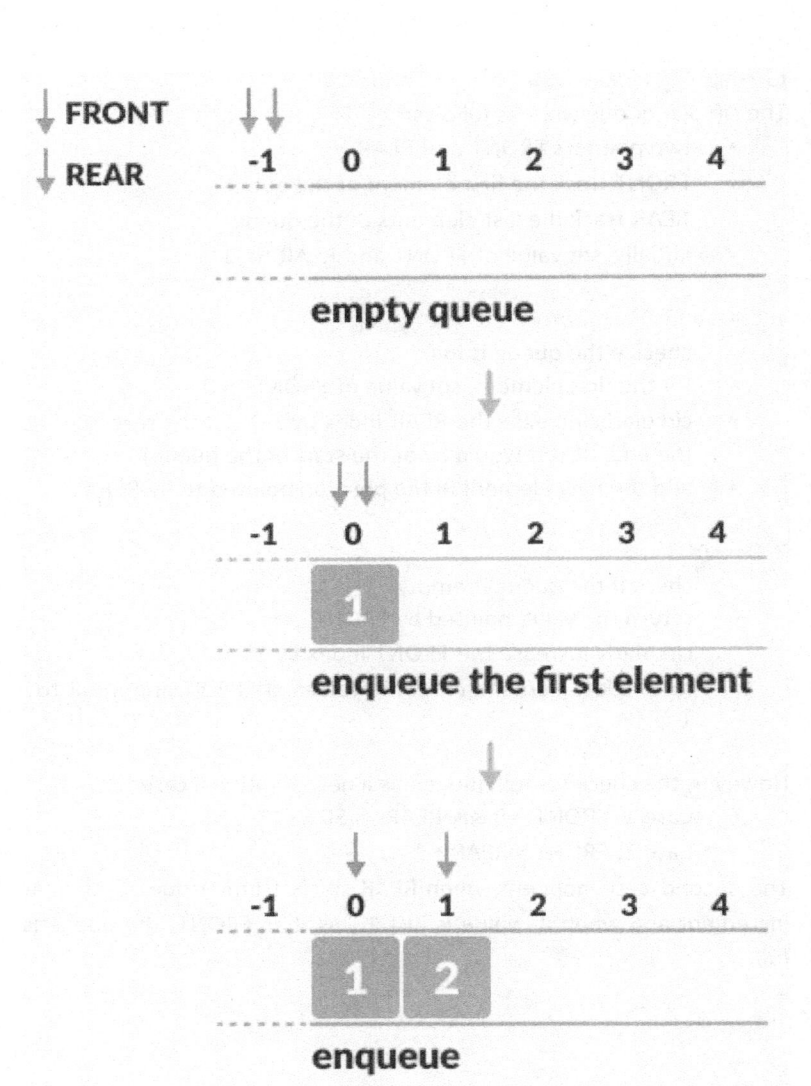

↓ FRONT   ↓↓
↓ REAR   -1   0   1   2   3   4

empty queue

↓

↓↓
-1   0   1   2   3   4
     1

enqueue the first element

↓

↓   ↓
-1   0   1   2   3   4
     1   2

enqueue

-1	0	1	2	3	4
	1	2	3	4	5

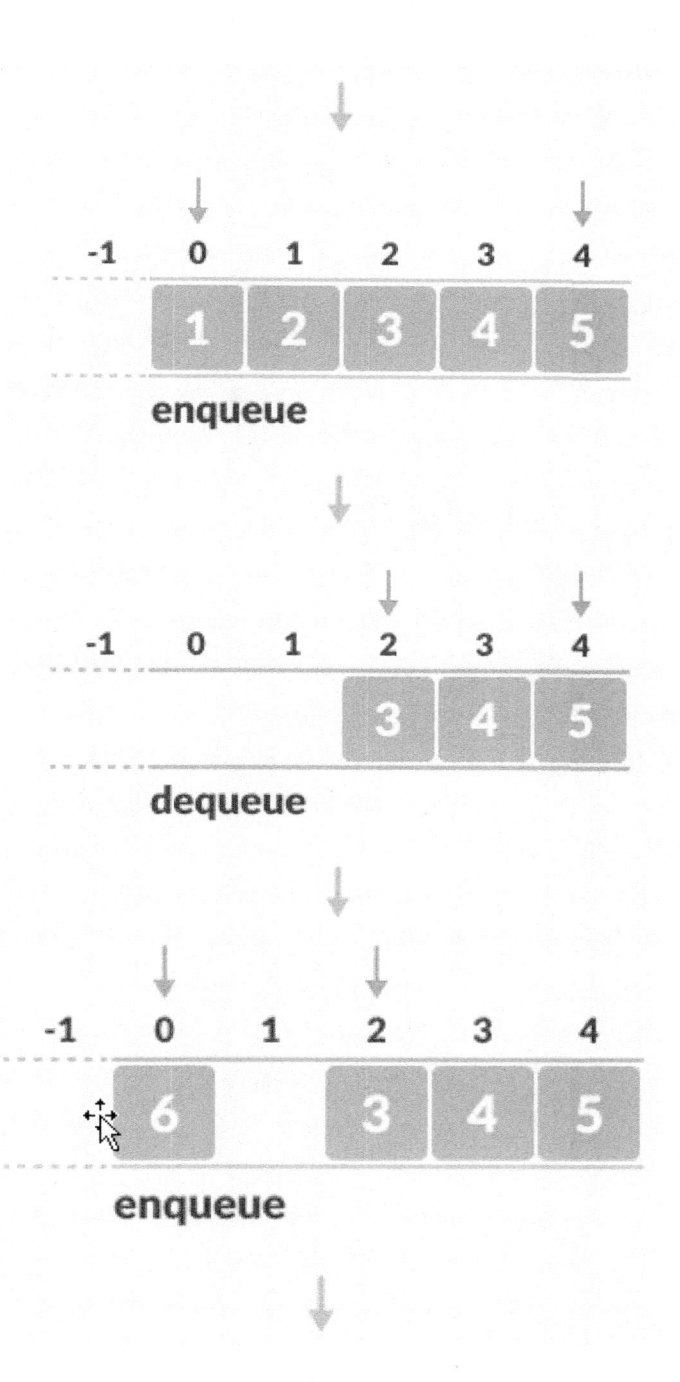

enqueue

-1	0	1	2	3	4
			3	4	5

dequeue

-1	0	1	2	3	4
	6		3	4	5

enqueue

-1	0	1	2	3	4
	6	7	3	4	5

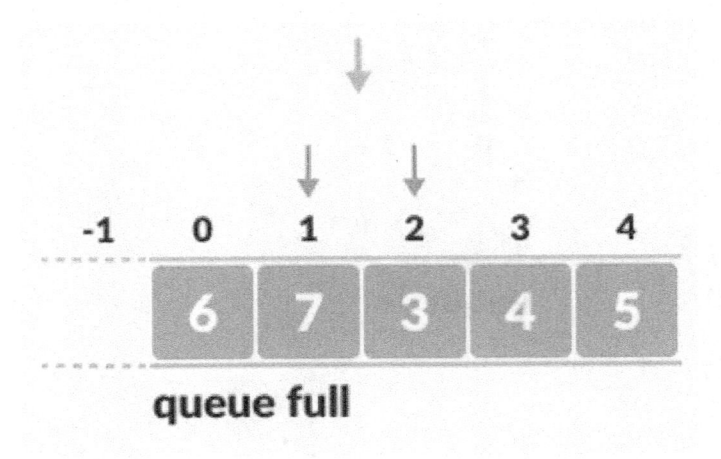

queue full

Enque and Deque Operations

Circular Queue Implementations in Python

```python
# Circular Queue implementation in Python


class MyCircularQueue():

    def __init__(self, k):
        self.k = k
        self.queue = [None] * k
        self.head = self.tail = -1

    # Insert an element into the circular queue
    def enqueue(self, data):

        if ((self.tail + 1) % self.k == self.head):
            print("The circular queue is full\n")

        elif (self.head == -1):
            self.head = 0
            self.tail = 0
            self.queue[self.tail] = data
        else:
            self.tail = (self.tail + 1) % self.k
            self.queue[self.tail] = data

    # Delete an element from the circular queue
    def dequeue(self):
```

```python
        if (self.head == -1):
            print("The circular queue is empty\n")

        elif (self.head == self.tail):
            temp = self.queue[self.head]
            self.head = -1
            self.tail = -1
            return temp
        else:
            temp = self.queue[self.head]
            self.head = (self.head + 1) % self.k
            return temp

    def printCQueue(self):
        if(self.head == -1):
            print("No element in the circular queue")

        elif (self.tail >= self.head):
            for i in range(self.head, self.tail + 1):
                print(self.queue[i], end=" ")
            print()
        else:
            for i in range(self.head, self.k):
                print(self.queue[i], end=" ")
            for i in range(0, self.tail + 1):
                print(self.queue[i], end=" ")
            print()


# Your MyCircularQueue object will be instantiated and call
ed as such:
obj = MyCircularQueue(5)
obj.enqueue(1)
obj.enqueue(2)
obj.enqueue(3)
obj.enqueue(4)
obj.enqueue(5)
print("Initial queue")
obj.printCQueue()

obj.dequeue()
print("After removing an element from the queue")
obj.printCQueue()
```

Output
```
Initial queue
1 2 3 4 5
After removing an element from the queue
2 3 4 5
```

Circular Queue Complexity Analysis
The complexity of the enqueue and dequeue operations of a circular queue is O(1) for (array implementations).

Applications of Circular Queue
- CPU scheduling
- Memory management
- Traffic Management

Priority Queue

A priority queue is a special type of queue in which each element is associated with a priority and is served according to its priority. If elements with the same priority occur, they are served according to their order in the queue.

Generally, the value of the element itself is considered for assigning the priority.

For example, The element with the highest value is considered as the highest priority element. However, in other cases, we can assume the element with the lowest value as the highest priority element. In other cases, we can set priorities according to our needs.

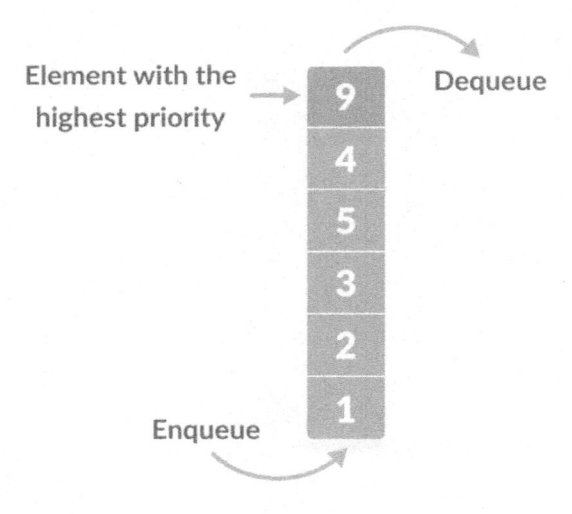

Removing Highest Priority Element

Difference between Priority Queue and Normal Queue

In a queue, the first-in-first-out rule is implemented whereas, in a priority queue, the values are removed on the basis of priority. The element with the highest priority is removed first.

Implementation of Priority Queue

Priority queue can be implemented using an array, a linked list, a heap data structure, or a binary search tree. Among these data structures, heap data structure provides an efficient implementation of priority queues.

Hence, we will be using the heap data structure to implement the priority queue in this tutorial. A max-heap is implement is in the following operations. If you want to learn more about it, please visit max-heap and mean-heap.

A comparative analysis of different implementations of priority queue is given below.

Operations	peek	insert	delete
Linked List	O(1)	O(n)	O(1)
Binary Heap	O(1)	O(log n)	O(log n)
Binary Search Tree	O(1)	O(log n)	O(log n)

Priority Queue Operations

Basic operations of a priority queue are inserting, removing, and peeking elements.

Before studying the priority queue, please refer to the heap data structure for a better understanding of binary heap as it is used to implement the priority queue in this article.

1. Inserting an Element from the Priority Queue

Inserting an element into a priority queue (max-heap) is done by the following steps.

Insert the new element at the end of the tree.

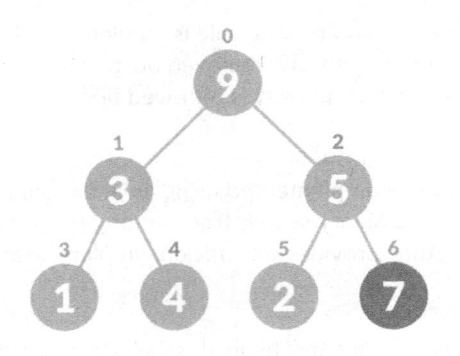

Insert an element at the end of the queue

Heapify the tree.

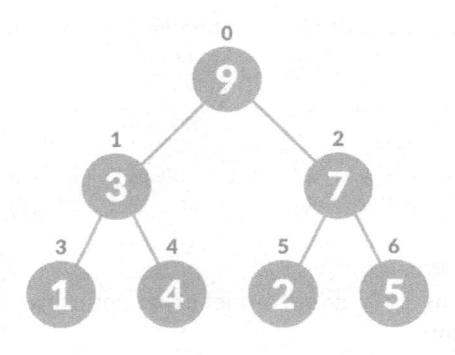

Heapify after insertion

Algorithm for insertion of an element into priority queue (max-heap)

If there is no node,
  create a newNode.
else (a node is already present)
  insert the newNode at the end (last node from left to right.)

heapify the array

For Min Heap, the above algorithm is modified so that `parentNode` is always smaller than `newNode`.

2. Deleting an Element from the Priority Queue

Deleting an element from a priority queue (max-heap) is done as follows:

Select the element to be deleted.

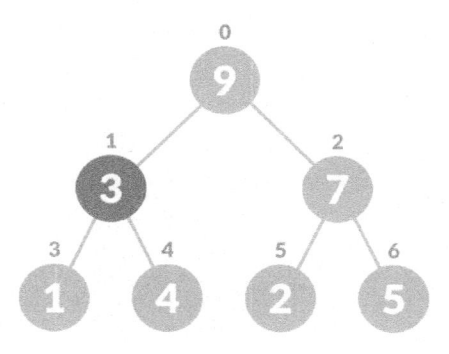

Select the element to be deleted

Swap it with the last element.

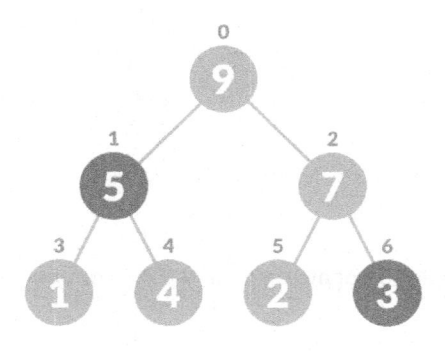

Swap with the last leaf node element

Remove the last element.

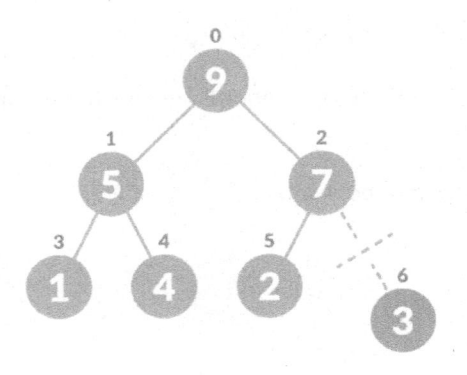

Remove the last element leaf

Heapify the tree.

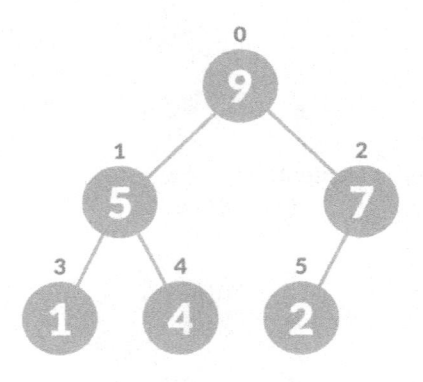

Heapify the priority queue

Algorithm for deletion of an element in the priority queue (max-heap)

If nodeToBeDeleted is the leafNode
　remove the node
Else swap nodeToBeDeleted with the lastLeafNode
　remove noteToBeDeleted

heapify the array

For Min Heap, the above algorithm is modified so that the both childNodes are smaller than currentNode.

3. Peeking from the Priority Queue (Find max/min)
Peek operation returns the maximum element from Max Heap or minimum element from Min Heap without deleting the node.

For both Max heap and Min Heap
return rootNode

4. Extract-Max/Min from the Priority Queue
Extract-Max returns the node with maximum value after removing it from a Max Heap whereas Extract-Min returns the node with minimum value after removing it from Min Heap.

Priority Queue Implementations in Python

```python
# Priority Queue implementation in Python


# Function to heapify the tree
def heapify(arr, n, i):
    # Find the largest among root, left child and right child
    largest = i
    l = 2 * i + 1
    r = 2 * i + 2

    if l < n and arr[i] < arr[l]:
        largest = l

    if r < n and arr[largest] < arr[r]:
        largest = r

    # Swap and continue heapifying if root is not largest
    if largest != i:
        arr[i], arr[largest] = arr[largest], arr[i]
        heapify(arr, n, largest)


# Function to insert an element into the tree
def insert(array, newNum):
    size = len(array)
    if size == 0:
        array.append(newNum)
    else:
        array.append(newNum)
        for i in range((size // 2) - 1, -1, -1):
            heapify(array, size, i)
```

```python
# Function to delete an element from the tree
def deleteNode(array, num):
    size = len(array)
    i = 0
    for i in range(0, size):
        if num == array[i]:
            break

    array[i], array[size - 1] = array[size - 1], array[i]

    array.remove(size - 1)

    for i in range((len(array) // 2) - 1, -1, -1):
        heapify(array, len(array), i)

arr = []

insert(arr, 3)
insert(arr, 4)
insert(arr, 9)
insert(arr, 5)
insert(arr, 2)

print ("Max-Heap array: " + str(arr))

deleteNode(arr, 4)
print("After deleting an element: " + str(arr))
```

Output
Max-Heap array: [9, 5, 4, 3, 2]
After deleting an element: [9, 5, 2, 3]

Priority Queue Applications
Some of the applications of a priority queue are:
- Dijkstra's algorithm
- for implementing stack
- for load balancing and interrupt handling in an operating system
- for data compression in Huffman code

Deque

Deque or Double Ended Queue is a type of queue in which insertion and removal of elements can be performed from either from the front or rear. Thus, it does not follow FIFO rule (First In First Out).

Representation of Deque

Types of Deque

- Input Restricted Deque

In this deque, input is restricted at a single end but allows deletion at both the ends.

- Output Restricted Deque

In this deque, output is restricted at a single end but allows insertion at both the ends.

Operations on a Deque

Below is the circular array implementation of deque. In a circular array, if the array is full, we start from the beginning.

But in a linear array implementation, if the array is full, no more elements can be inserted. In each of the operations below, if the array is full, "overflow message" is thrown.

Before performing the following operations, these steps are followed.
Take an array (deque) of size n.

Set two pointers at the first position and set front = -1 and rear = 0.

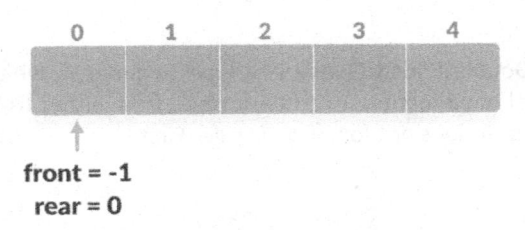

Initialize an array and pointers for deque

1. Insert at the Front
This operation adds an element at the front.

Check the position of front.

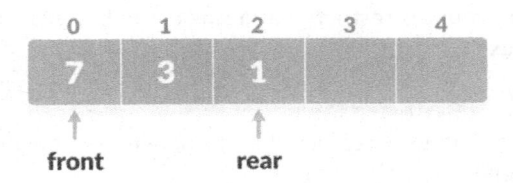

Check the position of front

If front < 1, reinitialize front = n-1 (last index).

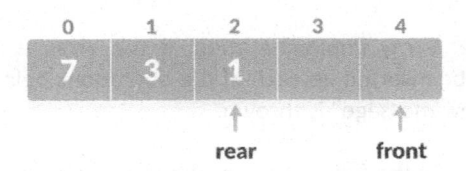

Shift front to the end

Else, decrease front by 1.

Add the new key 5 into array[front].

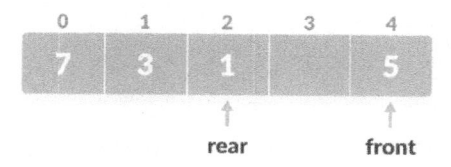

```
   0    1    2    3    4
[  7 |  3 |  1 |    |  5 ]
          ↑         ↑
         rear      front
```

Insert the element at Front

2. Insert at the Rear

This operation adds an element to the rear.

Check if the array is full.

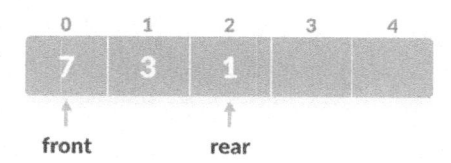

```
   0    1    2    3    4
[  7 |  3 |  1 |    |    ]
   ↑         ↑
 front      rear
```

Check if deque is full

If the deque is full, reinitialize rear = 0.

Else, increase rear by 1.

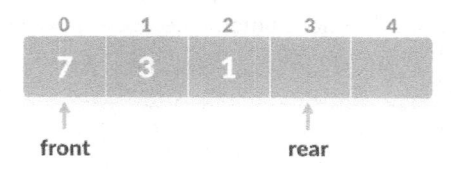

```
   0    1    2    3    4
[  7 |  3 |  1 |    |    ]
   ↑              ↑
 front           rear
```

Increase the rear

Add the new key 5 into array[rear].

	0	1	2	3	4
	7	3	1	5	

↑ front   ↑ rear

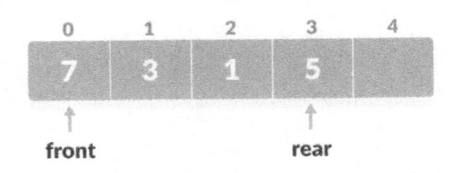

Insert the element at rear

3. Delete from the Front

The operation deletes an element from the front.

Check if the deque is empty.

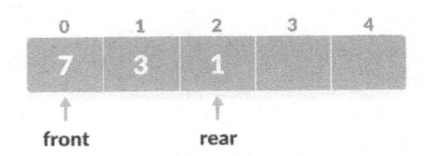

	0	1	2	3	4
	7	3	1		

↑ front   ↑ rear

Check if deque is empty

If the deque is empty (i.e. front = -1), deletion cannot be performed (underflow condition).

If the deque has only one element (i.e. front = rear), set front = -1 and rear = -1.

Else if front is at the end (i.e. front = n - 1), set go to the front front = 0.
Else, front = front + 1.

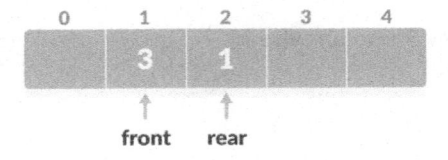

	0	1	2	3	4
		3	1		

↑ front ↑ rear

Increase the front

4. Delete from the Rear

48

This operation deletes an element from the rear.

Check if the deque is empty.

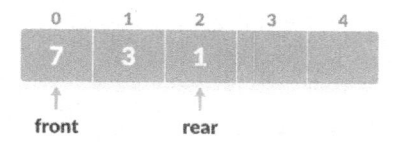

Check if deque is empty

If the deque is empty (i.e. front = -1), deletion cannot be performed (underflow condition).

If the deque has only one element (i.e. front = rear), set front = -1 and rear = -1, else follow the steps below.

If rear is at the front (i.e. rear = 0), set go to the front rear = n - 1. Else, rear = rear - 1.

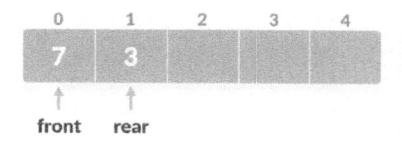

Decrease the rear

5. Check Empty

This operation checks if the deque is empty. If front = -1, the deque is empty.

6. Check Full
This operation checks if the deque is full. If front = 0 and rear = n - 1 OR front = rear + 1, the deque is full.

Deque Implementation in Python

```
# Deque implementaion in python
```

```python
class Deque:
    def __init__(self):
        self.items = []

    def isEmpty(self):
        return self.items == []

    def addFront(self, item):
        self.items.append(item)

    def addRear(self, item):
        self.items.insert(0, item)

    def removeFront(self):
        return self.items.pop()

    def removeRear(self):
        return self.items.pop(0)

    def size(self):
        return len(self.items)

d = Deque()
print(d.isEmpty())
d.addRear(8)
d.addRear(5)
d.addFront(7)
d.addFront(10)
print(d.size())
print(d.isEmpty())
d.addRear(11)
print(d.removeRear())
print(d.removeFront())
d.addFront(55)
d.addRear(45)
print(d.items)
```

Output
True
4
False
11
10
[45, 5, 8, 7, 55]

Time Complexity
The time complexity of all the above operations is constant i.e. O(1).

Applications of Deque Data Structure
- In undo operations on software.
- To store history in browsers.

- For implementing both stacks and queues.

LinkedList

A linked list data structure includes a series of connected nodes. Here, each node store the data and the address of the next node. For example,

Linkedin Data Structure

You have to start somewhere, so we give the address of the first node a special name called HEAD.

Also, the last node in the linked list can be identified because its next portion points to NULL.

You might have played the game Treasure Hunt, where each clue includes the information about the next clue. That is how the linked list operates.

Representation of LinkedList
Let's see how each node of the LinkedList is represented. Each node consists:
- A data item
- An address of another node

We wrap both the data item and the next node reference in a struct as:

```
struct node
{
  int data;
  struct node *next;
};
```

51

Understanding the structure of a linked list node is the key to having a grasp on it.

Each struct node has a data item and a pointer to another struct node. Let us create a simple Linked List with three items to understand how this works.

```
/* Initialize nodes */
struct node *head;
struct node *one = NULL;
struct node *two = NULL;
struct node *three = NULL;

/* Allocate memory */
one = malloc(sizeof(struct node));
two = malloc(sizeof(struct node));
three = malloc(sizeof(struct node));

/* Assign data values */
one->data = 1;
two->data = 2;
three->data=3;

/* Connect nodes */
one->next = two;
two->next = three;
three->next = NULL;

/* Save address of first node in head */
head = one;
```

In just a few steps, we have created a simple linked list with three nodes.

HEAD → | 1 | next | → | 2 | next | → | 3 | next | → NULL

LinkedList Representation

The power of LinkedList comes from the ability to break the chain and rejoin it. E.g. if you wanted to put an element 4 between 1 and 2, the steps would be:
- Create a new struct node and allocate memory to it.
- Add its data value as 4
- Point its next pointer to the struct node containing 2 as the data value
- Change the next pointer of "1" to the node we just created.

Doing something similar in an array would have required shifting the positions of all the subsequent elements.

Linked List Utility
Apart from that, linked lists are a great way to learn how pointers work. By practicing how to manipulate linked lists, you can prepare yourself to learn more advanced data structures like graphs and trees.

Linked List Implementations in Python

```python
# Linked list implementation in Python


class Node:
    # Creating a node
    def __init__(self, item):
        self.item = item
        self.next = None


class LinkedList:

    def __init__(self):
        self.head = None


if __name__ == '__main__':

    linked_list = LinkedList()

    # Assign item values
    linked_list.head = Node(1)
    second = Node(2)
    third = Node(3)

    # Connect nodes
    linked_list.head.next = second
    second.next = third

    # Print the linked list item
```

```
while linked_list.head != None:
    print(linked_list.head.item, end=" ")
    linked_list.head = linked_list.head.next
```

Output
1 2 3

Linked List Complexity

Time Complexity

	Worst case	Average Case
Search	O(n)	O(n)
Insert	O(1)	O(1)
Deletion	O(1)	O(1)

Space Complexity: O(n)

Linked List Applications
- Dynamic memory allocation
- Implemented in stack and queue
- In undo functionality of softwares
- Hash tables, Graphs

Linked List Operations
Now that you have got an understanding of the basic concepts behind linked list and their types, it's time to dive into the common operations that can be performed.

Two important points to remember:
- `head` points to the first node of the linked list
- `next` pointer of the last node is `NULL`, so if the next current node is `NULL`, we have reached the end of the linked list.

In all of the examples, we will assume that the linked list has three nodes `1 --->2 --->3` with node structure as below:

struct node
{
  int data;

```
    struct node *next;
};
```

How to Traverse a Linked List

Displaying the contents of a linked list is very simple. We keep moving the temp node to the next one and display its contents.

When temp is NULL, we know that we have reached the end of the linked list so we get out of the while loop.

```
struct node *temp = head;
printf("\n\nList elements are - \n");
while(temp != NULL)
{
    printf("%d --->",temp->data);
    temp = temp->next;
}
```

The output of this program will be:
List elements are -
1 --->2 --->3 --->

How to Add Elements to a Linked List

You can add elements to either the beginning, middle or end of the linked list.

Add to the beginning
- Allocate memory for new node
- Store data
- Change next of new node to point to head
- Change head to point to recently created node

```
struct node *newNode;
newNode = malloc(sizeof(struct node));
newNode->data = 4;
newNode->next = head;
head = newNode;
```

Add to the End
- Allocate memory for new node

- Store data
- Traverse to last node
- Change next of last node to recently created node

```
struct node *newNode;
newNode = malloc(sizeof(struct node));
newNode->data = 4;
newNode->next = NULL;

struct node *temp = head;
while(temp->next != NULL){
 temp = temp->next;
}

temp->next = newNode;
```

Add to the Middle
- Allocate memory and store data for new node
- Traverse to node just before the required position of new node
- Change next pointers to include new node in between

```
struct node *newNode;
newNode = malloc(sizeof(struct node));
newNode->data = 4;

struct node *temp = head;

for(int i=2; i < position; i++) {
   if(temp->next != NULL) {
      temp = temp->next;
   }
}
newNode->next = temp->next;
temp->next = newNode;
```

How to Delete from a Linked List
You can delete either from the beginning, end or from a particular position.

Delete from beginning
- Point head to the second node

head = head->next;

Delete from end
- Traverse to second last element
- Change its next pointer to null

```
struct node* temp = head;
while(temp->next->next!=NULL){
  temp = temp->next;
}
temp->next = NULL;
```

Delete from middle
- Traverse to element before the element to be deleted
- Change next pointers to exclude the node from the chain

```
for(int i=2; i< position; i++) {
  if(temp->next!=NULL) {
    temp = temp->next;
  }
}

temp->next = temp->next->next;
```

Implementing LinkedList Operations in Python

```python
# Linked list operations in Python


# Create a node
class Node:
    def __init__(self, item):
        self.item = item
        self.next = None


class LinkedList:

    def __init__(self):
```

```python
        self.head = None

    # Insert at the beginning
    def insertAtBeginning(self, data):
        new_node = Node(data)

        new_node.next = self.head
        self.head = new_node

    # Insert after a node
    def insertAfter(self, node, data):

        if node is None:
            print("The given previous node must inLinkedList.")
            return

        new_node = Node(data)
        new_node.next = node.next
        node.next = new_node

    # Insert at the end
    def insertAtEnd(self, data):
        new_node = Node(data)

        if self.head is None:
            self.head = new_node
            return

        last = self.head
        while (last.next):
            last = last.next

        last.next = new_node

    # Deleting a node
    def deleteNode(self, position):

        if self.head == None:
            return

        temp_node = self.head

        if position == 0:
            self.head = temp_node.next
            temp_node = None
            return

        # Find the key to be deleted
        for i in range(position - 1):
            temp_node = temp_node.next
            if temp_node is None:
                break

        # If the key is not present
```

```
            if temp_node is None:
                return

            if temp_node.next is None:
                return

            next = temp_node.next.next
            temp_node.next = None
            temp_node.next = next

    def printList(self):
        temp_node = self.head
        while (temp_node):
            print(str(temp_node.item) + " ", end="")
            temp_node = temp_node.next

if __name__ == '__main__':

    llist = LinkedList()
    llist.insertAtEnd(1)
    llist.insertAtBeginning(2)
    llist.insertAtBeginning(3)
    llist.insertAtEnd(4)
    llist.insertAfter(llist.head.next, 5)

    print('Linked list:')
    llist.printList()

    print("\nAfter deleting an element:")
    llist.deleteNode(3)
    llist.printList()
```

Output
Linked list:
3 2 5 1 4
After deleting an element:
3 2 5 4

Types of Linked List
There are three common types of Linked List.
1. Singly Linked List
2. Doubly Linked List
3. Circular Linked List

Singly Linked List
It is the most common. Each node has data and a pointer to the next node.

59

HEAD → data next → data next → data next → NULL

Singly linked list

Node is represented as:

```
struct node {
   int data;
   struct node *next;
}
```

A three-member singly linked list can be created as:

```
/* Initialize nodes */
struct node *head;
struct node *one = NULL;
struct node *two = NULL;
struct node *three = NULL;

/* Allocate memory */
one = malloc(sizeof(struct node));
two = malloc(sizeof(struct node));
three = malloc(sizeof(struct node));

/* Assign data values */
one->data = 1;
two->data = 2;
three->data = 3;

/* Connect nodes */
one->next = two;
two->next = three;
three->next = NULL;

/* Save address of first node in head */
head = one;
```

Doubly Linked List

We add a pointer to the previous node in a doubly-linked list. Thus, we can go in either direction: forward or backward.

Doubly linked list

A node is represented as

```
struct node {
   int data;
   struct node *next;
   struct node *prev;
}
```

A three-member doubly linked list can be created as

```
/* Initialize nodes */
struct node *head;
struct node *one = NULL;
struct node *two = NULL;
struct node *three = NULL;

/* Allocate memory */
one = malloc(sizeof(struct node));
two = malloc(sizeof(struct node));
three = malloc(sizeof(struct node));

/* Assign data values */
one->data = 1;
two->data = 2;
three->data = 3;

/* Connect nodes */
one->next = two;
one->prev = NULL;

two->next = three;
```

two->prev = one;

three->next = NULL;
three->prev = two;

/* Save address of first node in head */
head = one;

Circular Linked List

A circular linked list is a variation of a linked list in which the last element is linked to the first element. This forms a circular loop.

Circular linked list

A circular linked list can be either singly linked or doubly linked.
- for singly linked list, next pointer of last item points to the first item
- In the doubly linked list, prev pointer of the first item points to the last item as well.

A three-member circular singly linked list can be created as:

```
/* Initialize nodes */
struct node *head;
struct node *one = NULL;
struct node *two = NULL;
struct node *three = NULL;

/* Allocate memory */
one = malloc(sizeof(struct node));
two = malloc(sizeof(struct node));
three = malloc(sizeof(struct node));

/* Assign data values */
one->data = 1;
two->data = 2;
```

```
three->data = 3;

/* Connect nodes */
one->next = two;
two->next = three;
three->next = one;

/* Save address of first node in head */
head = one;
```

Hash Table

Hash table is a data structure that represents data in the form of key-value pairs. Each key is mapped to a value in the hash table. The keys are used for indexing the values/data. A similar approach is applied by an associative array.

Data is represented in a key value pair with the help of keys as shown in the figure below. Each data is associated with a key. The key is an integer that point to the data.

| key | data |

1. Direct Address Table
Direct address table is used when the amount of space used by the table is not a problem for the program. Here, we assume that
- the keys are small integers
- the number of keys is not too large, and
- no two data have the same key

A pool of integers is taken called universe U = {0, 1, ..., n-1}. Each slot of a direct address table T[0...n-1] contains a pointer to the element that corresponds to the data.

The index of the array T is the key itself and the content of T is a pointer to the set [key, element]. If there is no element for a key then, it is left as NULL.

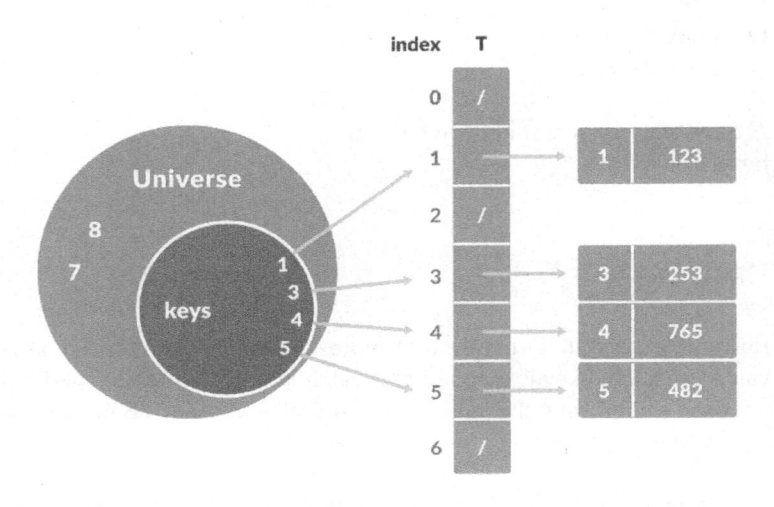

Sometimes, the key itself is the data.

Pseudocode for operations

```
directAddressSearch(T, k)
  return T[k]
directAddressInsert(T, x)
  T[x.key] = x
directAddressDelete(T, x)
  T[x.key] = NIL
```

Limitations of a Direct Address Table
- The value of the key should be small.
- The number of keys must be small enough so that it does not cross the size limit of an array.

2. Hash Table

In a hash table, the keys are processed to produce a new index that maps to the required element. This process is called hashing. Let h(x) be a hash function and k be a key. h(k) is calculated and it is used as an index for the element.

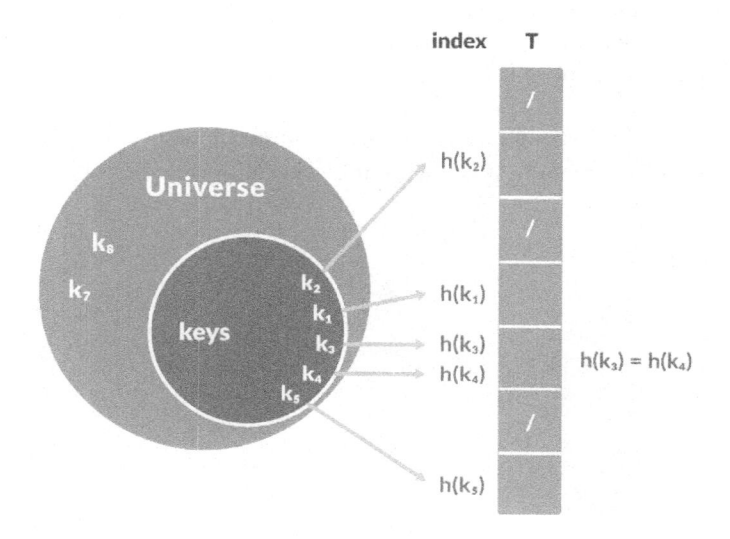

Limitations of a Hash Table

If the same index is produced by the hash function for multiple keys then, conflict arises. This situation is called collision.

To avoid this, a suitable hash function is chosen. But, it is impossible to produce all unique keys because |U|>m. Thus a good hash function may not prevent the collisions completely however it can reduce the number of collisions.

However, we have other techniques to resolve collision.

Advantages of hash table over direct address table:
The main issues with direct address table are the size of the array and the possibly large value of a key. The hash function reduces the range of index and thus the size of the array is also reduced.

For example, If k = 9845648451321, then h(k) = 11 (by using some hash function). This helps in saving the memory wasted while providing the index of 9845648451321 to the array

Collision resolution by chaining

In this technique, if a hash function produces the same index for multiple elements, these elements are stored in the same index by using a doubly linked list.

If j is the slot for multiple elements, it contains a pointer to the head of the list of elements. If no element is present, j contains NIL.

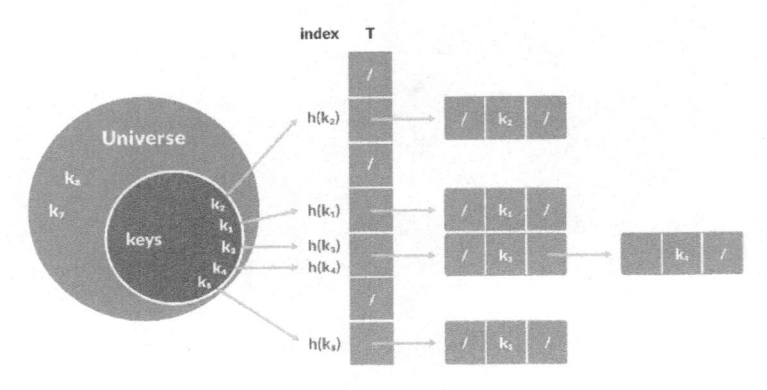

Pseudocode for operations

chainedHashSearch(T, k)
 return T[h(k)]
chainedHashInsert(T, x)
 T[h(x.key)] = x //insert at the head
chainedHashDelete(T, x)
 T[h(x.key)] = NIL

```python
# Python program to demonstrate working of HashTable

hashTable = [[],] * 10

def checkPrime(n):
    if n == 1 or n == 0:
        return 0

    for i in range(2, n//2):
        if n % i == 0:
            return 0

    return 1
```

```
def getPrime(n):
    if n % 2 == 0:
        n = n + 1

    while not checkPrime(n):
        n += 2

    return n

def hashFunction(key):
    capacity = getPrime(10)
    return key % capacity

def insertData(key, data):
    index = hashFunction(key)
    hashTable[index] = [key, data]

def removeData(key):
    index = hashFunction(key)
    hashTable[index] = 0

insertData(123, "apple")
insertData(432, "mango")
insertData(213, "banana")
insertData(654, "guava")

print(hashTable)

removeData(123)

print(hashTable)
```

Output
[[], [], [123, 'apple'], [432, 'mango'], [213, 'banana'], [654, 'guava'], [], [], [], []]
[[], [], 0, [432, 'mango'], [213, 'banana'], [654, 'guava'], [], [], [], []]

Good Hash Functions
A good hash function has the following characteristics.
1. It should not generate keys that are too large and the bucket space is small. Space is wasted.
2. The keys generated should be neither very close nor too far in range.
3. The collision must be minimized as much as possible.

Some of the methods used for hashing are:

Division Method

If k is a key and m is the size of the hash table, the hash function h() is calculated as:

h(k) = k mod m

For example, If the size of a hash table is 10 and k = 112 then h(k) = 112 mod 10 = 2. The value of m must not be the powers of 2. This is because the powers of 2 in binary format are 10, 100, 1000, …. When we find k mod m, we will always get the lower order p-bits.

if m = 2², k = 17, then h(k) = 17 mod 2² = 10001 mod 100 = 01
if m = 2³, k = 17, then h(k) = 17 mod 2² = 10001 mod 100 = 001
if m = 2⁴, k = 17, then h(k) = 17 mod 2² = 10001 mod 100 = 0001
if m = 2p, then h(k) = p lower bits of m

Multiplication Method

h(k) = ⌊m(kA mod 1)⌋

where,

- kA mod 1 gives the fractional part kA,
- ⌊ ⌋ gives the floor value
- A is any constant. The value of A lies between 0 and 1. But, an optimal choice will be ≈ (√5-1)/2 suggested by Knuth.

Universal Hashing

In Universal hashing, the hash function is chosen at random independent of keys.

Open Addressing

Multiple values can be stored in a single slot in a normal hash table. By using open addressing, each slot is either filled with a single key or left NIL. All the elements are stored in the hash table itself.

Unlike chaining, multiple elements cannot be fit into the same slot. Open addressing is basically a collision resolving technique. Some of the methods used by open addressing are:

Linear Probing
In linear probing, collision is resolved by checking the next slot.
$h(k, i) = (h'(k) + i) \mod m$

where,
- $i = \{0, 1, ...\}$
- $h'(k)$ is a new hash function

If a collision occurs at $h(k, 0)$, then $h(k, 1)$ is checked. In this way, the value of i is incremented linearly.

The problem with linear probing is that a cluster of adjacent slots is filled. When inserting a new element, the entire cluster must be traversed. This adds to the time required to perform operations on the hash table.

Quadratic Probing
In quadratic probing, the spacing between the slots is increased (greater than one) by using the following relation.

$h(k, i) = (h'(k) + c_1 i + c_2 i^2) \mod m$

where,
- c_1 and c_2 are positive auxiliary constants,
- $i = \{0, 1, ...\}$

Double Hashing
If a collision occurs after applying a hash function $h(k)$, then another hash function is calculated for finding the next slot.

$h(k, i) = (h_1(k) + i h_2(k)) \mod m$

Hash Table Applications
Hash tables are implemented where
- constant time lookup and insertion is required
- cryptographic applications
- indexing data is required

69

Heap

Heap data structure is a complete binary tree that satisfies the heap property. It is also called as a binary heap. A complete binary tree is a special binary tree in which every level, except possibly the last, is filled
all the nodes are as far left as possible

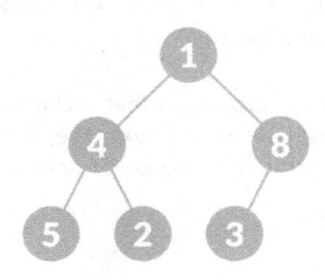

Heap Property is the property of a node in which

- (for max heap) key of each node is always greater than its child node/s and the key of the root node is the largest among all other nodes;

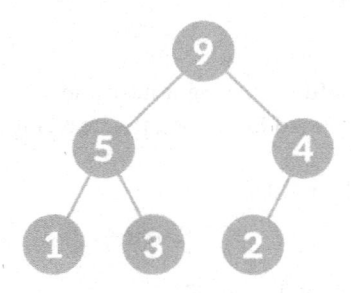

- (for min heap) key of each node is always smaller than the child node/s and the key of the root node is the smallest among all other nodes.

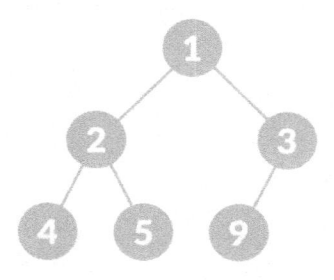

Heap Operations
Some of the important operations performed on a heap are described below along with their algorithms.

Heapify
Heapify is the process of creating a heap data structure from a binary tree. It is used to create a Min-Heap or a Max-Heap.

Let the input array be

3	9	2	1	4	5
0	1	2	3	4	5

Create a complete binary tree from the array

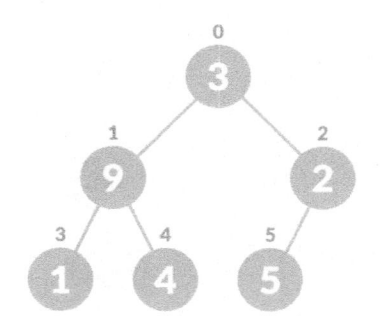

Start from the first index of non-leaf node whose index is given by n/2 - 1.

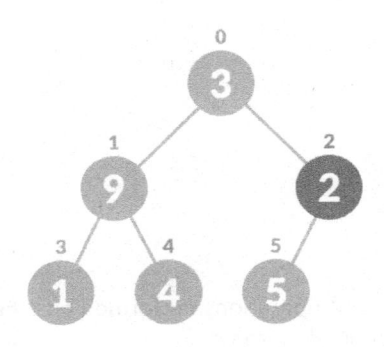

Set current element i as largest.

The index of left child is given by 2i + 1 and the right child is given by 2i + 2.

If leftChild is greater than currentElement (i.e. element at ith index), set leftChildIndex as largest.

If rightChild is greater than element in largest, set rightChildIndex as largest.

Swap largest with currentElement

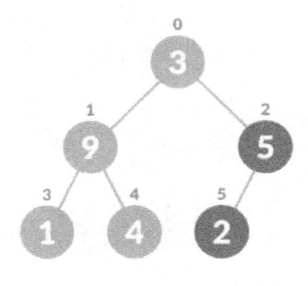

Repeat steps 3-7 until the subtrees are also heapified.

Algorithm

```
Heapify(array, size, i)
  set i as largest
  leftChild = 2i + 1
  rightChild = 2i + 2

  if leftChild > array[largest]
    set leftChildIndex as largest
  if rightChild > array[largest]
    set rightChildIndex as largest

  swap array[i] and array[largest]
```

To create a Max-Heap:

```
MaxHeap(array, size)
  loop from the first index of non-leaf node down to zero
    call heapify
```

For Min-Heap, both leftChild and rightChild must be smaller than the parent for all nodes.

Insert Element into Heap
Algorithm for insertion in Max Heap

```
If there is no node,
  create a newNode.
else (a node is already present)
  insert the newNode at the end (last node from left to right.)

heapify the array
```

Insert the new element at the end of the tree.

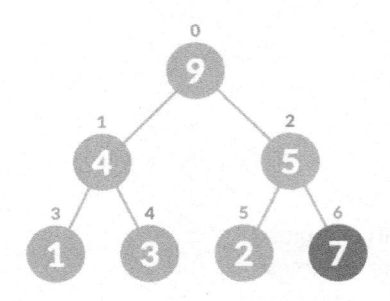

Heapify the tree.

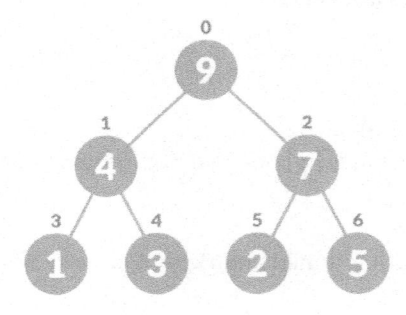

For Min Heap, the above algorithm is modified so that `parentNode` is always smaller than `newNode`.

Delete Element from Heap
Algorithm for deletion in Max Heap

```
If nodeToBeDeleted is the leafNode
  remove the node
Else swap nodeToBeDeleted with the lastLeafNode
  remove noteToBeDeleted

heapify the array
```

Select the element to be deleted.

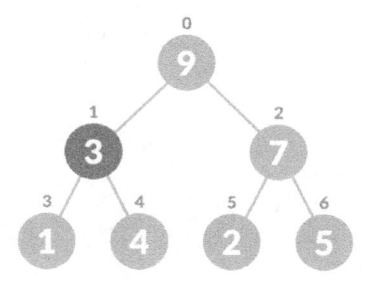

Swap it with the last element.

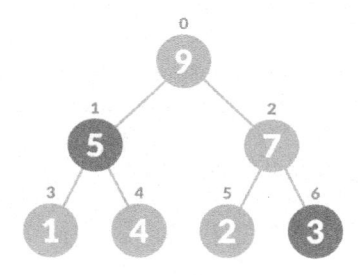

Remove the last element.

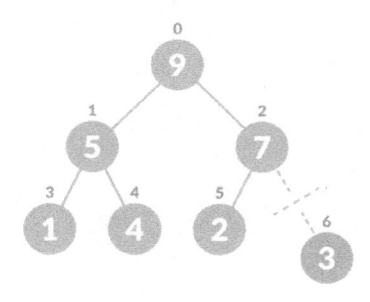

Heapify the tree.

75

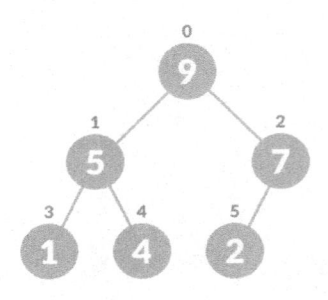

For Min Heap, above algorithm is modified so that both childNodes are greater smaller than currentNode.

Peek (Find max/min)
Peek operation returns the maximum element from Max Heap or minimum element from Min Heap without deleting the node.

For both Max heap and Min Heap
return rootNode

Extract-Max/Min
Extract-Max returns the node with maximum value after removing it from a Max Heap whereas Extract-Min returns the node with minimum after removing it from Min Heap.

```python
# Max-Heap data structure in Python
def heapify(arr, n, i):
    largest = i
    l = 2 * i + 1
    r = 2 * i + 2

    if l < n and arr[i] < arr[l]:
        largest = l

    if r < n and arr[largest] < arr[r]:
        largest = r

    if largest != i:
        arr[i],arr[largest] = arr[largest],arr[i]
        heapify(arr, n, largest)

def insert(array, newNum):
    size = len(array)
    if size == 0:
```

```
            array.append(newNum)
        else:
            array.append(newNum);
            for i in range((size//2)-1, -1, -1):
                heapify(array, size, i)
def deleteNode(array, num):
    size = len(array)
    i = 0
    for i in range(0, size):
        if num == array[i]:
            break

    array[i], array[size-1] = array[size-1], array[i]

    array.remove(size-1)

    for i in range((len(array)//2)-1, -1, -1):
        heapify(array, len(array), i)
arr = []
insert(arr, 3)
insert(arr, 4)
insert(arr, 9)
insert(arr, 5)
insert(arr, 2)

print ("Max-Heap array: " + str(arr))

deleteNode(arr, 4)
print("After deleting an element: " + str(arr))
```

Output
Max-Heap array: [9, 5, 4, 3, 2]
After deleting an element: [9, 5, 2, 3]

Heap Data Structure Applications
- Heap is used while implementing a priority queue.
- Dijkstra's Algorithm
- Heap Sort

Fibonacci Heap

Fibonacci heap is a modified form of a binomial heap with more efficient heap operations than that supported by the binomial and binary heaps.

Unlike binary heap, a node can have more than two children. The fibonacci heap is called a fibonacci heap because the trees are constructed in a way such that a tree of order n has at least Fn+2 nodes in it, where Fn+2 is the (n + 2)nd Fibonacci number.

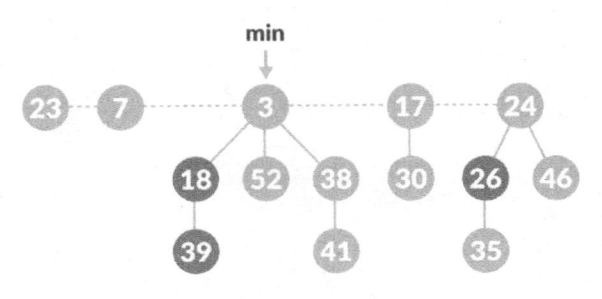

Fibonacci Heap

Properties of a Fibonacci Heap
Important properties of a Fibonacci heap are:
1. It is a set of min heap-ordered trees. (i.e. The parent is always smaller than the children.)
2. A pointer is maintained at the minimum element node.
3. It consists of a set of marked nodes. (Decrease key operation)
4. The trees within a Fibonacci heap are unordered but rooted.

Memory Representation of the Nodes in a Fibonacci Heap
The roots of all the trees are linked together for faster access. The child nodes of a parent node are connected to each other through a circular doubly linked list as shown below.

There are two main advantages of using a circular doubly linked list.
1. Deleting a node from the tree takes O(1) time.
2. The concatenation of two such lists takes O(1) time.

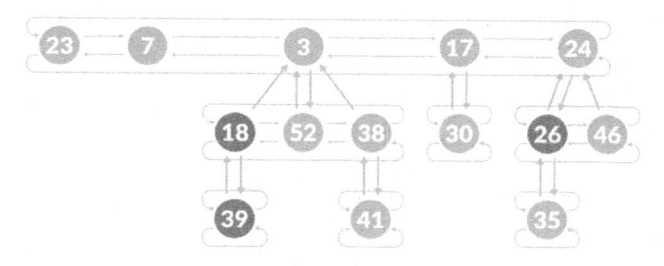

Fibonacci Heap Structure

Operations on a Fibonacci Heap

Insertion

Algorithm

```
insert(H, x)
   degree[x] = 0
   p[x] = NIL
   child[x] = NIL
   left[x] = x
   right[x] = x
   mark[x] = FALSE
   concatenate the root list containing x with root list H
   if min[H] == NIL or key[x] < key[min[H]]
      then min[H] = x
   n[H] = n[H] + 1
```

Inserting a node into an already existing heap follows the steps below.
1. Create a new node for the element.
2. Check if the heap is empty.
3. If the heap is empty, set the new node as a root node and mark it min.
4. Else, insert the node into the root list and update min.

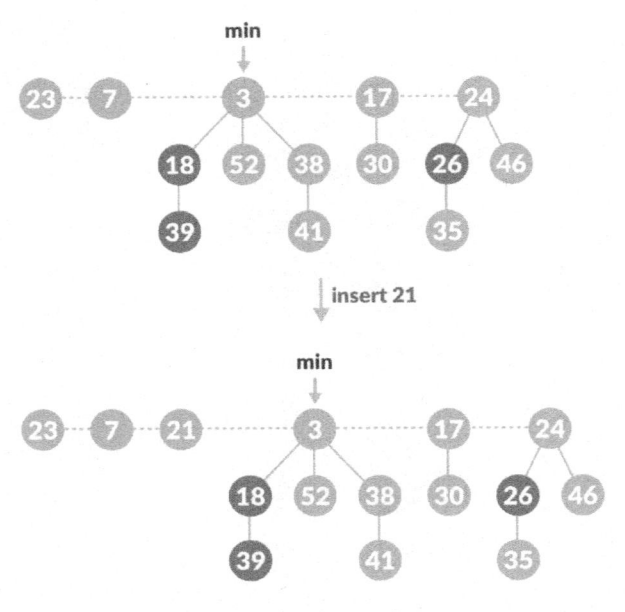

Insertion Example

Find Min
The minimum element is always given by the min pointer.

Union
Union of two fibonacci heaps consists of following steps.
1. Concatenate the roots of both the heaps.
2. Update min by selecting a minimum key from the new root lists.

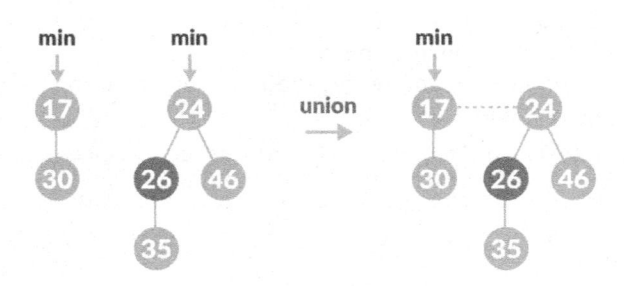

Union of two heaps

80

Extract Min

It is the most important operation on a fibonacci heap. In this operation, the node with minimum value is removed from the heap and the tree is re-adjusted.

The following steps are followed:
1. Delete the min node.
2. Set the min-pointer to the next root in the root list.
3. Create an array of size equal to the maximum degree of the trees in the heap before deletion.
4. Do the following (steps 5-7) until there are no multiple roots with the same degree.
5. Map the degree of current root (min-pointer) to the degree in the array.
6. Map the degree of next root to the degree in array.
7. If there are more than two mappings for the same degree, then apply union operation to those roots such that the min-heap property is maintained (i.e. the minimum is at the root).

An implementation of the above steps can be understood in the example below.

We will perform an extract-min operation on the heap below.

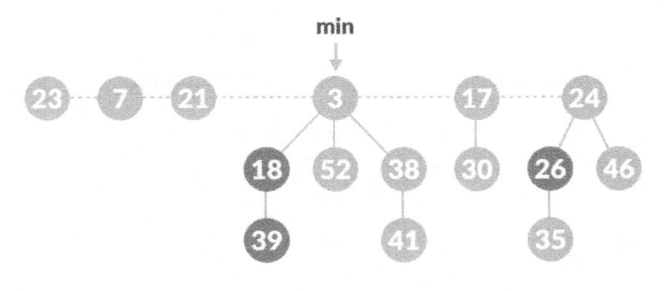

Fibonacci Heap

Delete the min node, add all its child nodes to the root list and set the min-pointer to the next root in the root list.

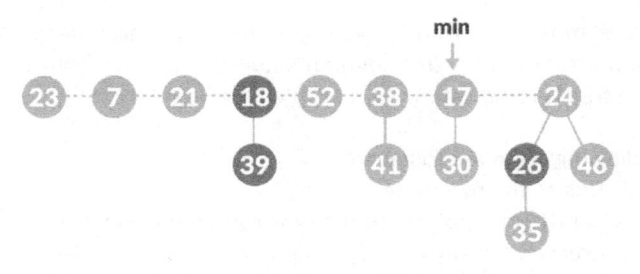

Delete the min node

The maximum degree in the tree is 3. Create an array of size 4 and map degree of the next roots with the array.

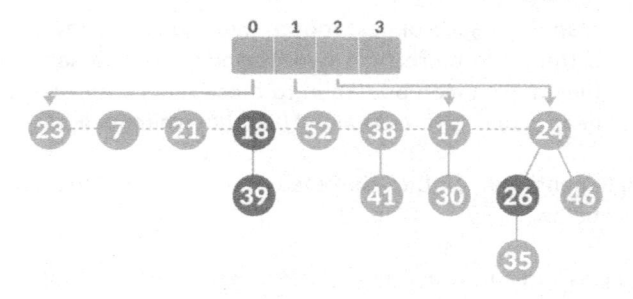

Create an array

Here, 23 and 7 have the same degrees, so unite them.

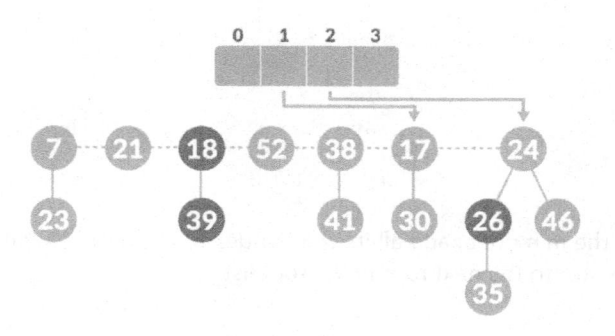

Unite those having the same degrees

Again, 7 and 17 have the same degrees, so unite them as well.

82

Unite those having the same degrees

Again 7 and 24 have the same degree, so unite them.

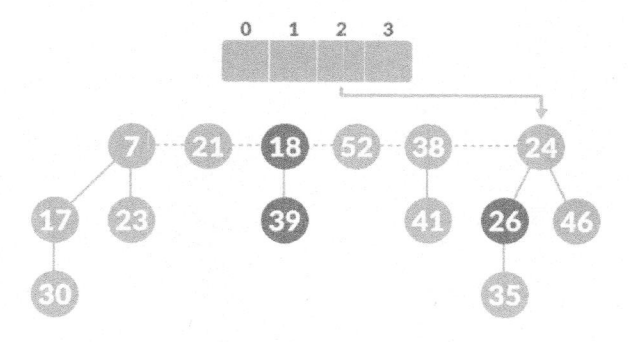

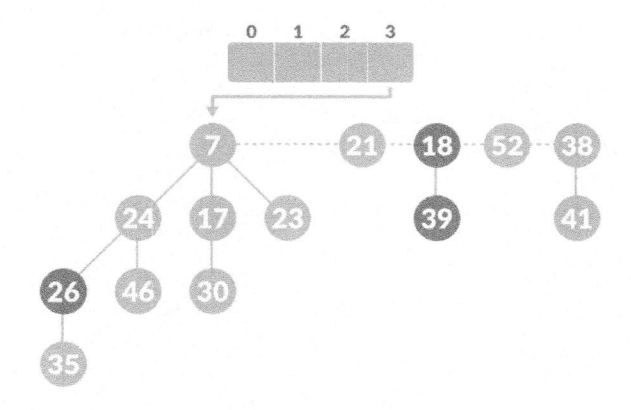

Unite those having the same degrees

Map the next nodes.

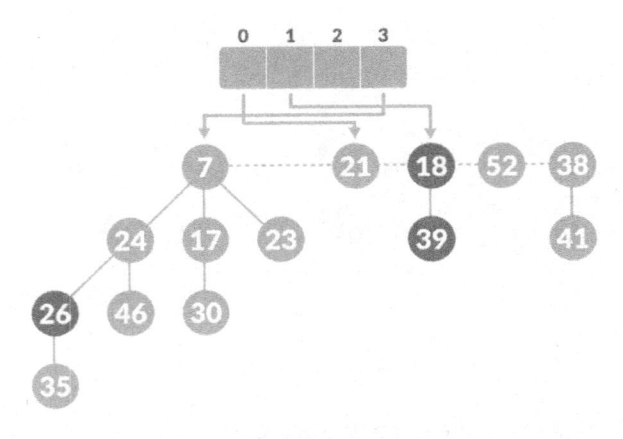

Map the remaining nodes

Again, 52 and 21 have the same degree, so unite them

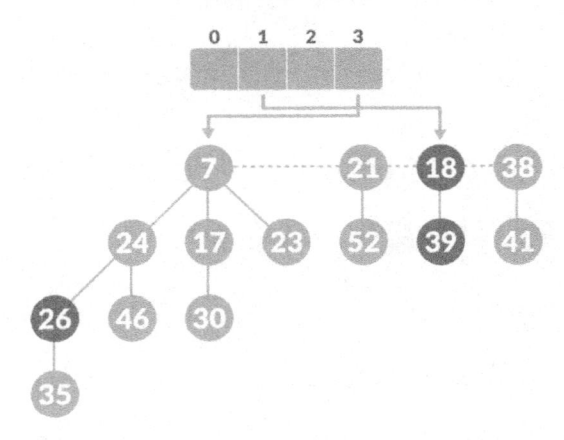

Unite those having the same degrees

Similarly, unite 21 and 18.

84

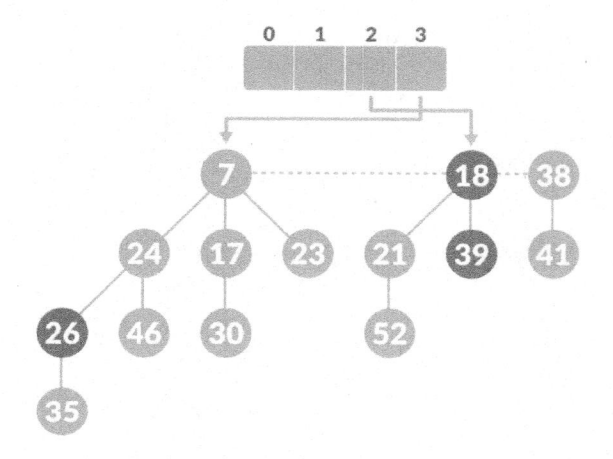

Unite those having the same degrees

Map the remaining root.

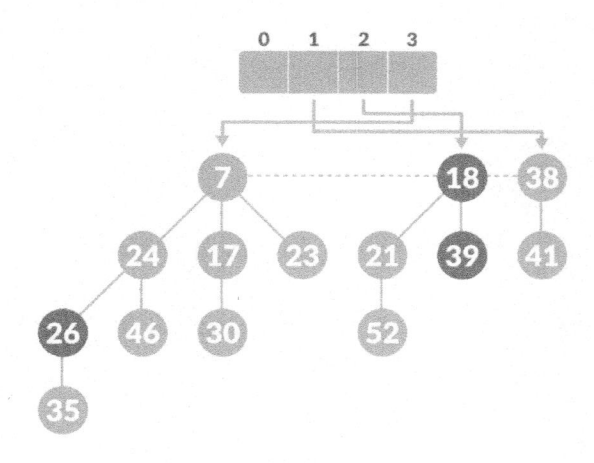

Map the remaining nodes

The final heap is.

85

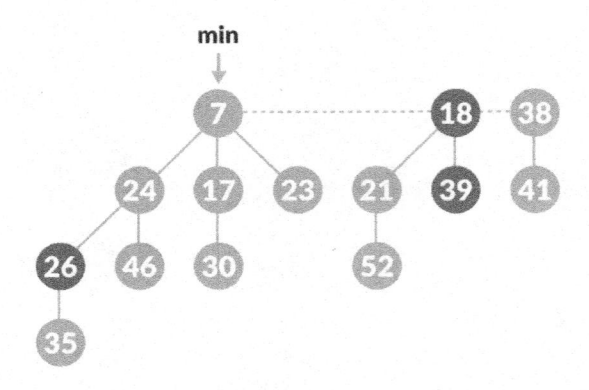

Final fibonacci heap

```python
# Fibonacci Heap in python

import math

# Creating fibonacci tree
class FibonacciTree:
    def __init__(self, value):
        self.value = value
        self.child = []
        self.order = 0

    # Adding tree at the end of the tree
    def add_at_end(self, t):
        self.child.append(t)
        self.order = self.order + 1


# Creating Fibonacci heap
class FibonacciHeap:
    def __init__(self):
        self.trees = []
        self.least = None
        self.count = 0

    # Insert a node
    def insert_node(self, value):
        new_tree = FibonacciTree(value)
        self.trees.append(new_tree)
        if (self.least is None or value < self.least.value)
:
            self.least = new_tree
        self.count = self.count + 1

    # Get minimum value
    def get_min(self):
```

86

```python
        if self.least is None:
            return None
        return self.least.value

    # Extract the minimum value
    def extract_min(self):
        smallest = self.least
        if smallest is not None:
            for child in smallest.child:
                self.trees.append(child)
            self.trees.remove(smallest)
            if self.trees == []:
                self.least = None
            else:
                self.least = self.trees[0]
                self.consolidate()
            self.count = self.count - 1
        return smallest.value

    # Consolidate the tree
    def consolidate(self):
        aux = (floor_log(self.count) + 1) * [None]

        while self.trees != []:
            x = self.trees[0]
            order = x.order
            self.trees.remove(x)
            while aux[order] is not None:
                y = aux[order]
                if x.value > y.value:
                    x, y = y, x
                x.add_at_end(y)
                aux[order] = None
                order = order + 1
            aux[order] = x

        self.least = None
        for k in aux:
            if k is not None:
                self.trees.append(k)
                if (self.least is None
                        or k.value < self.least.value):
                    self.least = k


def floor_log(x):
    return math.frexp(x)[1] - 1


fibonacci_heap = FibonacciHeap()

fibonacci_heap.insert_node(7)
fibonacci_heap.insert_node(3)
fibonacci_heap.insert_node(17)
fibonacci_heap.insert_node(24)
```

```
print('the minimum value of the fibonacci heap: {}'.format(
fibonacci_heap.get_min()))

print('the minimum value removed: {}'.format(fibonacci_heap
.extract_min()))
```

Output
```
the minimum value of the fibonacci heap: 3
the minimum value removed: 3
```

Complexities

Insertion	O(1)
Find Min	O(1)
Union	O(1)
Extract Min	O(log n)
Decrease Key	O(1)
Delete Node	O(log n)

Fibonacci Heap Applications
- To improve the asymptotic running time of Dijkstra's algorithm.

Decrease Key and Delete Node Operations on a Fibonacci Heap

Decreasing a Key
In decreasing a key operation, the value of a key is decreased to a lower value. Following functions are used for decreasing the key.

Decrease-Key
1. Select the node to be decreased, x, and change its value to the new value k.
2. If the parent of x, y, is not null and the key of parent is greater than that of the k then call Cut(x) and Cascading-Cut(y) subsequently.
3. If the key of x is smaller than the key of min, then mark x as min.

Cut
1. Remove x from the current position and add it to the root list.

88

2. If x is marked, then mark it as false.

Cascading-Cut
1. If the parent of y is not null then follow the following steps.
2. If y is unmarked, then mark y.
3. Else, call Cut(y) and Cascading-Cut(parent of y).

Decrease Key Example
The above operations can be understood in the examples below.

Example: Decreasing 46 to 15.

Decrease the value 46 to 15.

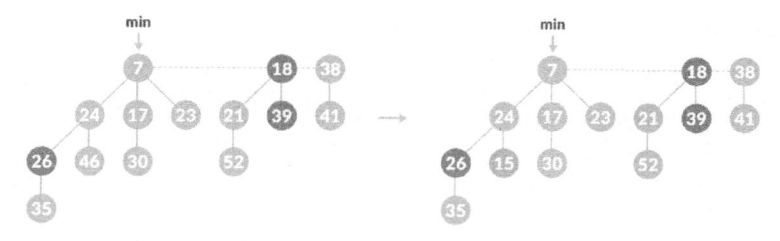

Decrease 46 to 15

Cut part: Since 24 ≠ nill and 15 < its parent, cut it and add it to the root list. Cascading-Cut part: mark 24.

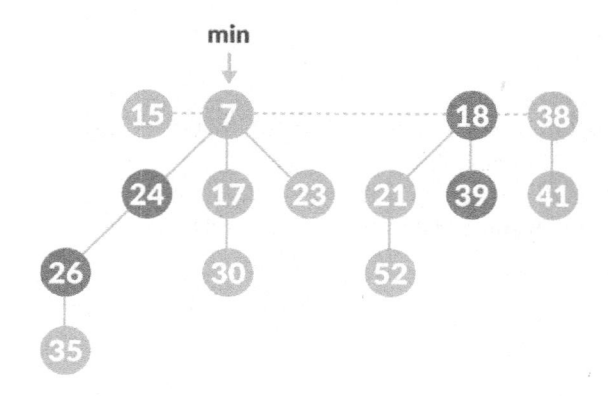

Add 15 to root list and mark 24

Example: Decreasing 35 to 5

Decrease the value 35 to 5.

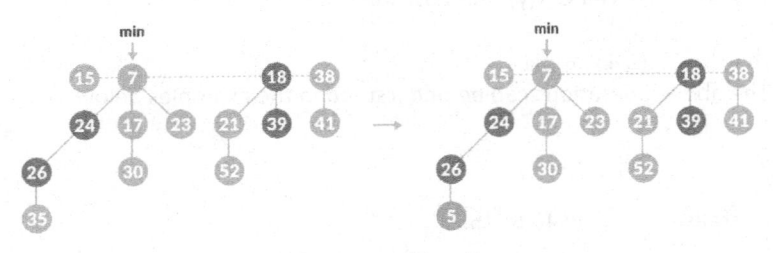

Decrease 35 to 5

Cut part: Since 26 ≠ nill and 5<its parent, cut it and add it to the root list.

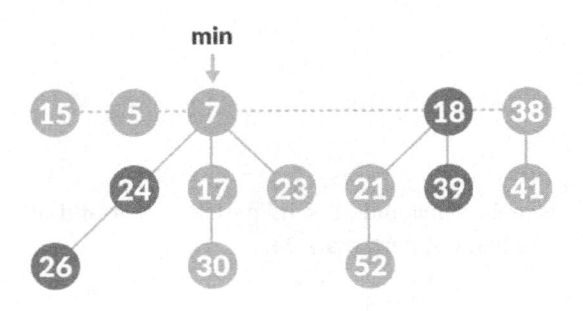

Cut 5 and add it to root list

Cascading-Cut part: Since 26 is marked, the flow goes to Cut and Cascading-Cut.

Cut(26): Cut 26 and add it to the root list and mark it as false.

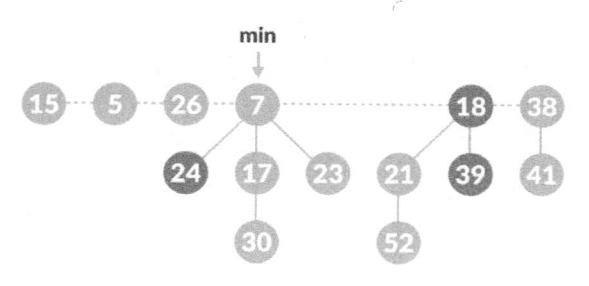

Cut 26 and add it to root list

Cascading-Cut(24):

Since the 24 is also marked, again call Cut(24) and Cascading-Cut(7). These operations result in the tree below.

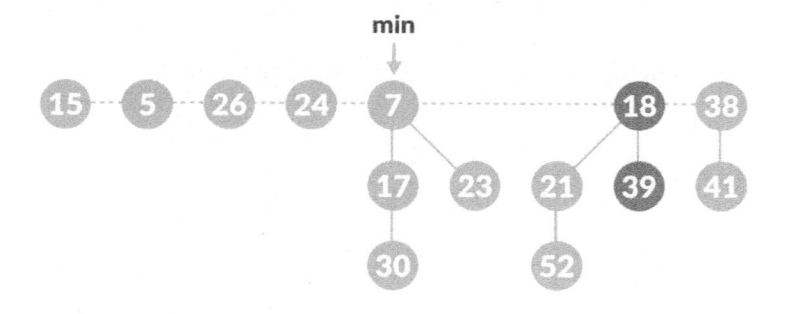

Cut 24 and add it to root list

Since 5 < 7, mark 5 as min.

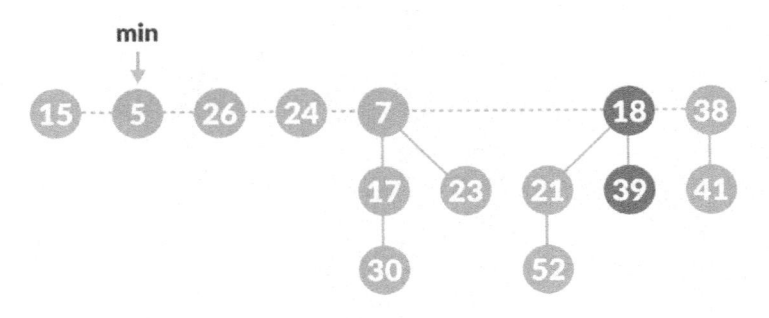

Mark 5 as min

Deleting a Node
This process makes use of decrease-key and extract-min operations. The following steps are followed for deleting a node.
1. Let k be the node to be deleted.
2. Apply decrease-key operation to decrease the value of k to the lowest possible value (i.e. $-\infty$).
3. Apply extract-min operation to remove this node.

Complexities

Decrease Key	O(1)
Delete Node	O(log n)

Trees

A tree is a nonlinear hierarchical data structure that consists of nodes connected by edges.

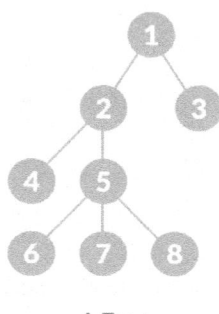

A Tree

Why Tree Data Structure?
Other data structures such as arrays, linked list, stack, and queue are linear data structures that store data sequentially. In order to perform any operation in a linear data structure, the time complexity increases with the increase in the data size. But, it is not acceptable in today's computational world.

Different tree data structures allow quicker and easier access to the data as it is a non-linear data structure.

Tree Terminologies

Node
A node is an entity that contains a key or value and pointers to its child nodes.
T
he last nodes of each path are called leaf nodes or external nodes that do not contain a link/pointer to child nodes.
The node having at least a child node is called an internal node.

Edge
It is the link between any two nodes.

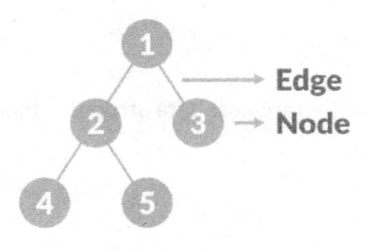

Nodes and edges of a tree

Root
It is the topmost node of a tree.

Height of a Node
The height of a node is the number of edges from the node to the deepest leaf (ie. the longest path from the node to a leaf node).

Depth of a Node
The depth of a node is the number of edges from the root to the node.

Height of a Tree
The height of a Tree is the height of the root node or the depth of the deepest node.

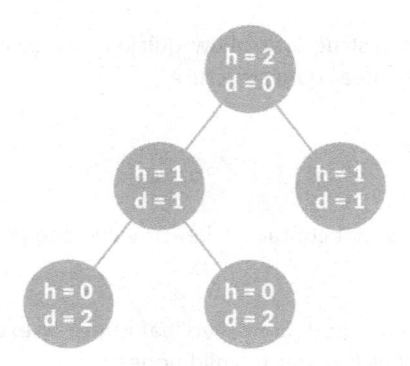

Height and depth of each node in a tree

Degree of a Node
The degree of a node is the total number of branches of that node.

Forest
A collection of disjoint trees is called a forest.

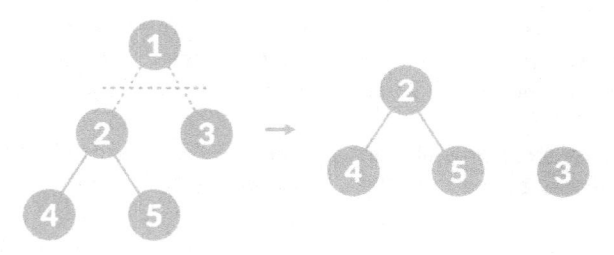

Creating forest from a tree

You can create a forest by cutting the root of a tree.

Types of Tree
1. Binary Tree
2. Binary Search Tree
3. AVL Tree
4. B-Tree

Tree Traversal
In order to perform any operation on a tree, you need to reach to the specific node. The tree traversal algorithm helps in visiting a required node in the tree.

Tree Applications
- Binary Search Trees (BSTs) are used to quickly check whether an element is present in a set or not.
- Heap is a kind of tree that is used for heap sort.
- A modified version of a tree called Tries is used in modern routers to store routing information.
- Most popular databases use B-Trees and T-Trees, which are variants of the tree structure we learned above to store their data
- Compilers use a syntax tree to validate the syntax of every program you write.

Tree Traversal

Traversing a tree means visiting every node in the tree. You might, for instance, want to add all the values in the tree or find the largest one. For all these operations, you will need to visit each node of the tree.

Linear data structures like arrays, stacks, queues, and linked list have only one way to read the data. But a hierarchical data structure like a tree can be traversed in different ways.

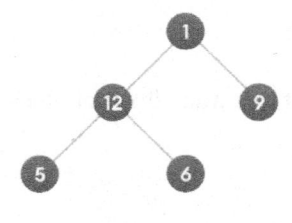

Tree traversal

Let's think about how we can read the elements of the tree in the image shown above.

Starting from top, Left to right
1 -> 12 -> 5 -> 6 -> 9

Starting from bottom, Left to right
5 -> 6 -> 12 -> 9 -> 1

Although this process is somewhat easy, it doesn't respect the hierarchy of the tree, only the depth of the nodes.

Instead, we use traversal methods that take into account the basic structure of a tree i.e.

```
struct node {
    int data;
    struct node* left;
    struct node* right;
}
```

The struct node pointed to by left and right might have other left and right children so we should think of them as sub-trees instead of sub-nodes.

According to this structure, every tree is a combination of
- A node carrying data
- Two subtrees

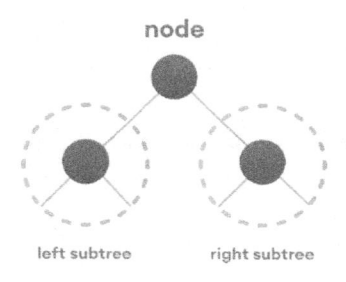

Left and Right Subtree

Remember that our goal is to visit each node, so we need to visit all the nodes in the subtree, visit the root node and visit all the nodes in the right subtree as well.

Depending on the order in which we do this, there can be three types of traversal.

Inorder traversal
1. First, visit all the nodes in the left subtree
2. Then the root node
3. Visit all the nodes in the right subtree

inorder(root->left)
display(root->data)
inorder(root->right)

Preorder traversal
1. Visit root node
2. Visit all the nodes in the left subtree
3. Visit all the nodes in the right subtree

97

display(root->data)
preorder(root->left)
preorder(root->right)

Postorder traversal
Visit all the nodes in the left subtree
Visit all the nodes in the right subtree
Visit the root node

postorder(root->left)
postorder(root->right)
display(root->data)

Let's visualize in-order traversal. We start from the root node.

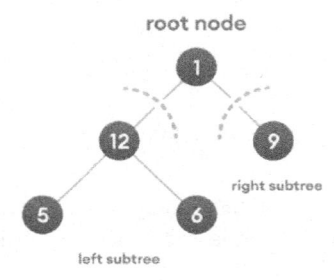

Left and Right Subtree

We traverse the left subtree first. We also need to remember to visit the root node and the right subtree when this tree is done.

Let's put all this in a stack so that we remember.

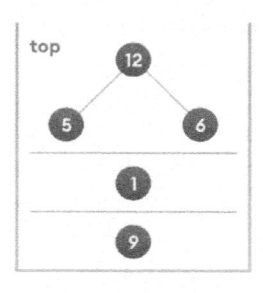

Stack

98

Now we traverse to the subtree pointed on the TOP of the stack.

Again, we follow the same rule of inorder
Left subtree -> root -> right subtree

After traversing the left subtree, we are left with

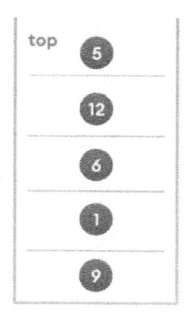

Final Stack

Since the node "5" doesn't have any subtrees, we print it directly. After that we print its parent "12" and then the right child "6".

Putting everything on a stack was helpful because now that the left-subtree of the root node has been traversed, we can print it and go to the right subtree.

After going through all the elements, we get the inorder traversal as
5 -> 12 -> 6 -> 1 -> 9

We don't have to create the stack ourselves because recursion maintains the correct order for us.

```
# Tree traversal in Python

class Node:
    def __init__(self, item):
        self.left = None
        self.right = None
        self.val = item

def inorder(root):

    if root:
```

```python
        # Traverse left
        inorder(root.left)
        # Traverse root
        print(str(root.val) + "->", end='')
        # Traverse right
        inorder(root.right)

def postorder(root):

    if root:
        # Traverse left
        postorder(root.left)
        # Traverse right
        postorder(root.right)
        # Traverse root
        print(str(root.val) + "->", end='')

def preorder(root):

    if root:
        # Traverse root
        print(str(root.val) + "->", end='')
        # Traverse left
        preorder(root.left)
        # Traverse right
        preorder(root.right)

root = Node(1)
root.left = Node(2)
root.right = Node(3)
root.left.left = Node(4)
root.left.right = Node(5)

print("Inorder traversal ")
inorder(root)

print("\nPreorder traversal ")
preorder(root)

print("\nPostorder traversal ")
postorder(root)
```

Output
```
Inorder traversal
4->2->5->1->3->
Preorder traversal
1->2->4->5->3->
Postorder traversal
4->5->2->3->1->
```

Binary Tree

A binary tree is a tree data structure in which each parent node can have at most two children.

For example: In the image below, each element has at most two children.

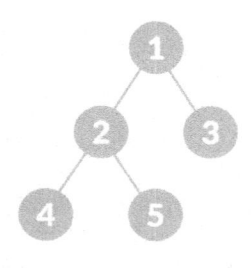

Binary Tree

Types of Binary Tree

Full Binary Tree
A full Binary tree is a special type of binary tree in which every parent node/internal node has either two or no children.

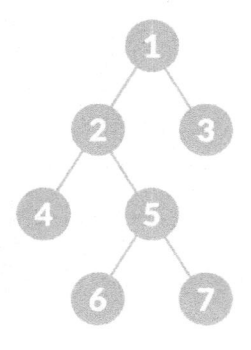

Full Binary Tree

Perfect Binary Tree
A perfect binary tree is a type of binary tree in which every internal node has exactly two child nodes and all the leaf nodes are at the same level.

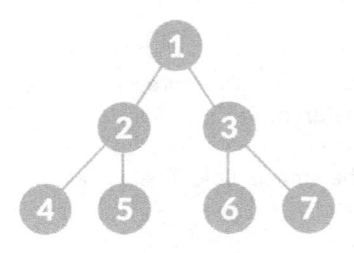

Perfect Binary Tree

Complete Binary Tree
A complete binary tree is just like a full binary tree, but with two major differences
1. Every level must be completely filled
2. All the leaf elements must lean towards the left.
3. The last leaf element might not have a right sibling i.e. a complete binary tree doesn't have to be a full binary tree.

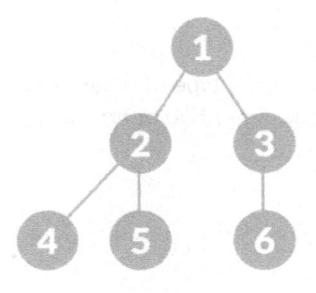

Complete Binary Tree

Degenerate or Pathological Tree
A degenerate or pathological tree is the tree having a single child either left or right.

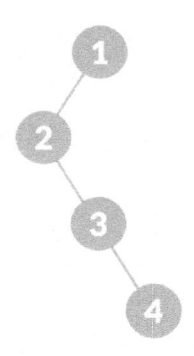

Degenerate Binary Tree

Skewed Binary Tree
A skewed binary tree is a pathological/degenerate tree in which the tree is either dominated by the left nodes or the right nodes. Thus, there are two types of skewed binary tree: left-skewed binary tree and right-skewed binary tree.

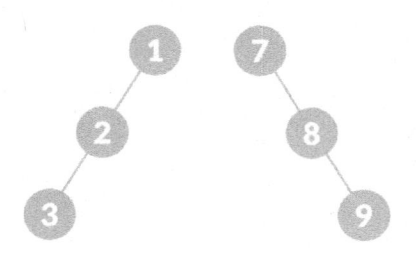

Skewed Binary Tree

Balanced Binary Tree
It is a type of binary tree in which the difference between the left and the right subtree for each node is either 0 or 1.

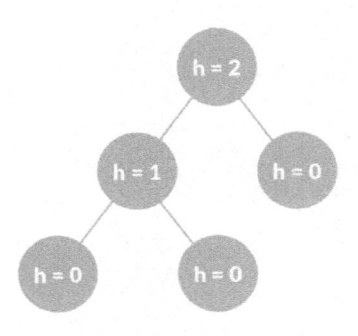

Balanced Binary Tree

Binary Tree Representation
A node of a binary tree is represented by a structure containing a data part and two pointers to other structures of the same type.

```
struct node
{
 int data;
 struct node *left;
 struct node *right;
};
```

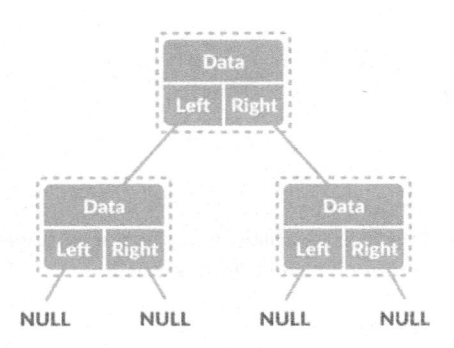

Binary Tree Representation

```
# Binary Tree in Python

class Node:
```

104

```python
    def __init__(self, key):
        self.left = None
        self.right = None
        self.val = key

    # Traverse preorder
    def traversePreOrder(self):
        print(self.val, end=' ')
        if self.left:
            self.left.traversePreOrder()
        if self.right:
            self.right.traversePreOrder()

    # Traverse inorder
    def traverseInOrder(self):
        if self.left:
            self.left.traverseInOrder()
        print(self.val, end=' ')
        if self.right:
            self.right.traverseInOrder()

    # Traverse postorder
    def traversePostOrder(self):
        if self.left:
            self.left.traversePostOrder()
        if self.right:
            self.right.traversePostOrder()
        print(self.val, end=' ')


root = Node(1)

root.left = Node(2)
root.right = Node(3)

root.left.left = Node(4)

print("Pre order Traversal: ", end="")
root.traversePreOrder()
print("\nIn order Traversal: ", end="")
root.traverseInOrder()
print("\nPost order Traversal: ", end="")
root.traversePostOrder()
```

Output
Pre order Traversal: 1 2 4 3
In order Traversal: 4 2 1 3
Post order Traversal: 4 2 3 1

Binary Tree Applications
- For easy and quick access to data
- In router algorithms
- To implement heap data structure

- Syntax tree

Full Binary Tree

A full Binary tree is a special type of binary tree in which every parent node/internal node has either two or no children. It is also known as a proper binary tree.

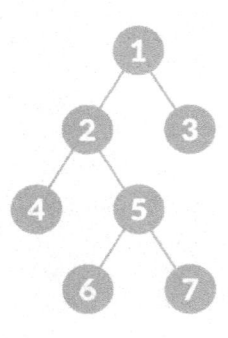

Full Binary Tree

Full Binary Tree Theorems
Let, i = the number of internal nodes
   n = be the total number of nodes
   l = number of leaves
   λ = number of levels

1. The number of leaves is i + 1.
2. The total number of nodes is 2i + 1.
3. The number of internal nodes is (n – 1) / 2.
4. The number of leaves is (n + 1) / 2.
5. The total number of nodes is 2l – 1.
6. The number of internal nodes is l – 1.
7. The number of leaves is at most $2^{\lambda-1}$.

```
# Python program to check whether given Binary tree is full
or not

# Tree node structure
class Node:

    # Constructor of the node class for creating the node
    def __init__(self , key):
        self.key = key
```

106

```python
        self.left = None
        self.right = None

# Checks if the binary tree is full or not
def isFullTree(root):

    # If empty tree
    if root is None:
        return True

    # If leaf node
    if root.left is None and root.right is None:
        return True

    # If both left and right subtress are not None and
    # left and right subtress are full
    if root.left is not None and root.right is not None:
        return (isFullTree(root.left) and isFullTree(root.right))

    # We reach here when none of the above if condiitions work
    return False

# Driver Program
root = Node(10);
root.left = Node(20);
root.right = Node(30);

root.left.right = Node(40);
root.left.left = Node(50);
root.right.left = Node(60);
root.right.right = Node(70);

root.left.left.left = Node(80);
root.left.left.right = Node(90);
root.left.right.left = Node(80);
root.left.right.right = Node(90);
root.right.left.left = Node(80);
root.right.left.right = Node(90);
root.right.right.left = Node(80);
root.right.right.right = Node(90);

if isFullTree(root):
    print("The Binary tree is full")
else:
    print("Binary tree is not full")
```

Output
The Binary tree is full

Perfect Binary Tree

A perfect binary tree is a type of binary tree in which every internal node has exactly two child nodes and all the leaf nodes are at the same level.

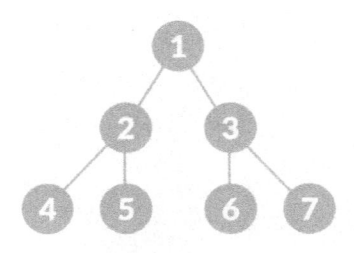

Perfect Binary Tree

All the internal nodes have a degree of 2.

Recursively, a perfect binary tree can be defined as:
1. If a single node has no children, it is a perfect binary tree of height $h = 0$,
2. If a node has $h > 0$, it is a perfect binary tree if both of its subtrees are of height $h - 1$ and are non-overlapping.

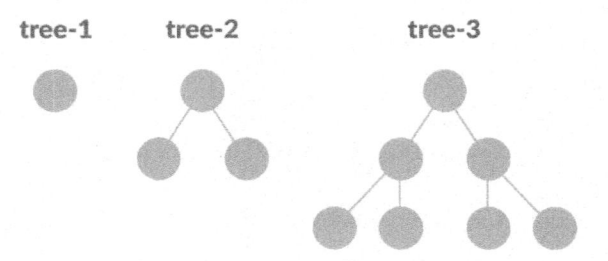

Perfect Binary Tree (Recursive Representation)

```
# Checking if a binary tree is a perfect binary tree in Python

class newNode:
    def __init__(self, k):
        self.key = k
        self.right = self.left = None
```

```python
# Calculate the depth
def calculateDepth(node):
    d = 0
    while (node is not None):
        d += 1
        node = node.left
    return d


# Check if the tree is perfect binary tree
def is_perfect(root, d, level=0):

    # Check if the tree is empty
    if (root is None):
        return True

    # Check the presence of trees
    if (root.left is None and root.right is None):
        return (d == level + 1)

    if (root.left is None or root.right is None):
        return False

    return (is_perfect(root.left, d, level + 1) and
            is_perfect(root.right, d, level + 1))

root = None
root = newNode(1)
root.left = newNode(2)
root.right = newNode(3)
root.left.left = newNode(4)
root.left.right = newNode(5)

if (is_perfect(root, calculateDepth(root))):
    print("The tree is a perfect binary tree")
else:
    print("The tree is not a perfect binary tree")
```

Output
The tree is not a perfect binary tree

Perfect Binary Tree Theorems
1. A perfect binary tree of height h has $2^{h+1} - 1$ node.
2. A perfect binary tree with n nodes has height $\log(n + 1) - 1 = \Theta(\ln(n))$.
3. A perfect binary tree of height h has 2^h leaf nodes.
4. The average depth of a node in a perfect binary tree is $\Theta(\ln(n))$.

Complete Binary Tree

A complete binary tree is a binary tree in which all the levels are completely filled except possibly the lowest one, which is filled from the left.

A complete binary tree is just like a full binary tree, but with two major differences
1. All the leaf elements must lean towards the left.
2. The last leaf element might not have a right sibling i.e. a complete binary tree doesn't have to be a full binary tree.

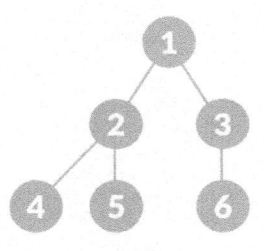

Complete Binary Tree

Full Binary Tree vs Complete Binary Tree

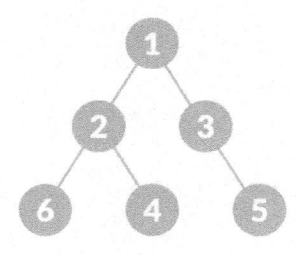

✘ Full Binary Tree
✘ Complete Binary Tree

Comparison between full binary tree and complete binary tree

✓ **Full Binary Tree**
✗ **Complete Binary Tree**

Comparison between full binary tree and complete binary tree

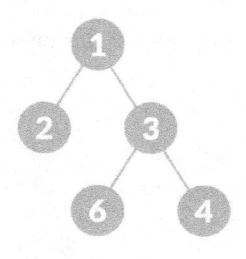

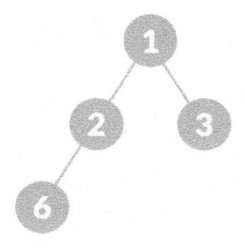

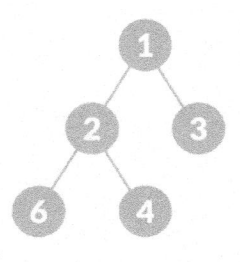

✗ **Full Binary Tree**
✓ **Complete Binary Tree**

Comparison between full binary tree and complete binary tree

✓ **Full Binary Tree**
✓ **Complete Binary Tree**

Comparison between full binary tree and complete binary tree

How a Complete Binary Tree is Created?

Select the first element of the list to be the root node. (no. of elements on level-I: 1)

Select the first element as root

Put the second element as a left child of the root node and the third element as the right child. (no. of elements on level-II: 2)

12 as a left child and 9 as a right child

Put the next two elements as children of the left node of the second level. Again, put the next two elements as children of the right node of the second level (no. of elements on level-III: 4) elements).

Keep repeating until you reach the last element.

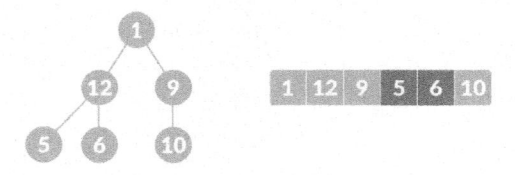

5 as a left child and 6 as a right child

```
# Checking if a binary tree is a complete binary tree

class Node:

    def __init__(self, item):
        self.item = item
        self.left = None
        self.right = None


# Count the number of nodes
```

```python
def count_nodes(root):
    if root is None:
        return 0
    return (1 + count_nodes(root.left) + count_nodes(root.right))


# Check if the tree is complete binary tree
def is_complete(root, index, numberNodes):

    # Check if the tree is empty
    if root is None:
        return True

    if index >= numberNodes:
        return False

    return (is_complete(root.left, 2 * index + 1, numberNodes)
            and is_complete(root.right, 2 * index + 2, numberNodes))


root = Node(1)
root.left = Node(2)
root.right = Node(3)
root.left.left = Node(4)
root.left.right = Node(5)
root.right.left = Node(6)

node_count = count_nodes(root)
index = 0

if is_complete(root, index, node_count):
    print("The tree is a complete binary tree")
else:
    print("The tree is not a complete binary tree")
```

Output
```
The tree is a complete binary tree
```

Relationship between array indexes and tree element

A complete binary tree has an interesting property that we can use to find the children and parents of any node.

If the index of any element in the array is i, the element in the index 2i+1 will become the left child and element in 2i+2 index will become the right child. Also, the parent of any element at index i is given by the lower bound of (i-1)/2.

Let's test it out,

Left child of 1 (index 0)
= element in (2*0+1) index
= element in 1 index
= 12

Right child of 1
= element in (2*0+2) index
= element in 2 index
= 9

Similarly,
Left child of 12 (index 1)
= element in (2*1+1) index
= element in 3 index
= 5

Right child of 12
= element in (2*1+2) index
= element in 4 index
= 6

Let us also confirm that the rules hold for finding parent of any node

Parent of 9 (position 2)
= (2-1)/2
= ½
= 0.5
~ 0 index
= 1

Parent of 12 (position 1)
= (1-1)/2
= 0 index
= 1

Complete Binary Tree Applications
- Heap-based data structures
- Heap sort

114

Balanced Binary Tree

A balanced binary tree, also referred to as a height-balanced binary tree, is defined as a binary tree in which the height of the left and right subtree of any node differ by not more than 1.

Following are the conditions for a height-balanced binary tree:
1. difference between the left and the right subtree for any node is not more than one
2. the left subtree is balanced
3. the right subtree is balanced

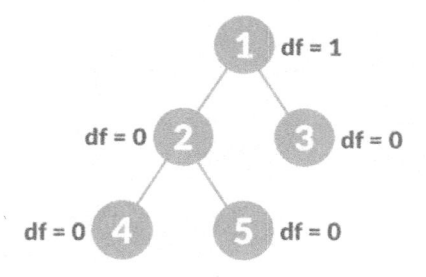

Balanced Binary Tree with depth at each level

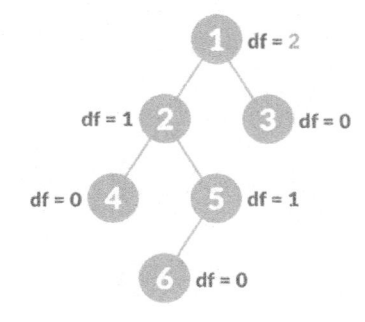

df = |height of left child - height of right child|

Unbalanced Binary Tree with depth at each level

```
# Determine if a binary tree is height-balanced in Python
```

```python
class Node:
    # Constructor to create a new Node
    def __init__(self, data):
        self.data = data
        self.left = None
        self.right = None

# function to find height of binary tree
def height(root):

    # base condition when binary tree is empty
    if root is None:
        return 0
    return max(height(root.left), height(root.right)) + 1

# function to check if tree is height-balanced or not
def isBalanced(root):

    # Base condition
    if root is None:
        return True

    # for left and right subtree height
    lh = height(root.left)
    rh = height(root.right)

    # allowed values for (lh - rh) are 1, -1, 0
    if (abs(lh - rh) <= 1) and isBalanced(
    root.left) is True and isBalanced( root.right) is True:
        return True

    # if we reach here means tree is not
    # height-balanced tree
    return False

# Driver function to test the above function
root = Node(1)
root.left = Node(2)
root.right = Node(3)
root.left.left = Node(4)
root.left.right = Node(5)
root.left.left.left = Node(8)
if isBalanced(root):
    print("Tree is balanced")
else:
    print("Tree is not balanced")
```

Output
Tree is not balanced

Balanced Binary Tree Applications
- AVL tree
- Balanced Binary Search Tree

Binary Search Tree(BST)

Binary search tree is a data structure that quickly allows us to maintain a sorted list of numbers.

- It is called a binary tree because each tree node has a maximum of two children.
- It is called a search tree because it can be used to search for the presence of a number in $O(\log(n))$ time.

The properties that separate a binary search tree from a regular binary tree is
1. All nodes of left subtree are less than the root node
2. All nodes of right subtree are more than the root node
3. Both subtrees of each node are also BSTs i.e. they have the above two properties

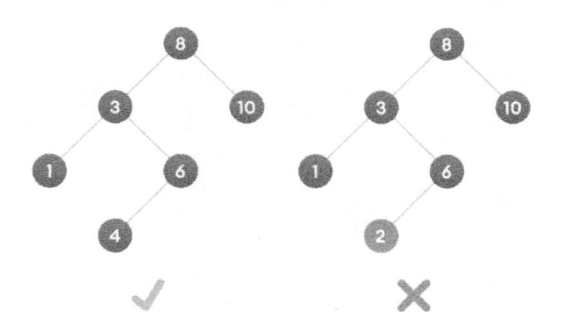

A tree having a right subtree with one value smaller than the root is shown to demonstrate that it is not a valid binary search tree

The binary tree on the right isn't a binary search tree because the right subtree of the node "3" contains a value smaller than it.

There are two basic operations that you can perform on a binary search tree:

Search Operation
The algorithm depends on the property of BST that if each left subtree has values below root and each right subtree has values above the root.

If the value is below the root, we can say for sure that the value is not in the right subtree; we need to only search in the left subtree and if the value is above the root, we can say for sure that the value is not in the left subtree; we need to only search in the right subtree.

Algorithm:
If root == NULL
   return NULL;
If number == root->data
   return root->data;
If number < root->data
   return search(root->left)
If number > root->data
   return search(root->right)

Let us try to visualize this with a diagram.

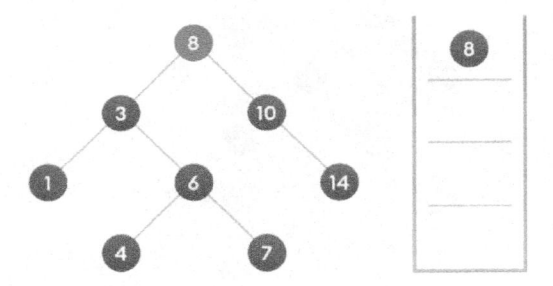

4 is not found so, traverse through the left subtree of 8

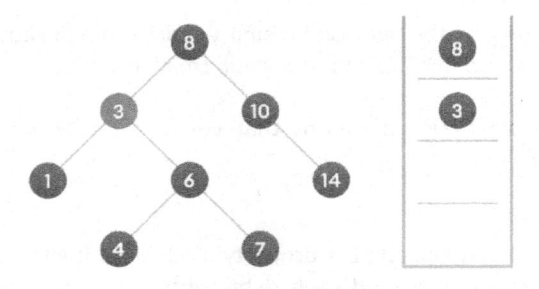

4 is not found so, traverse through the right subtree of 3

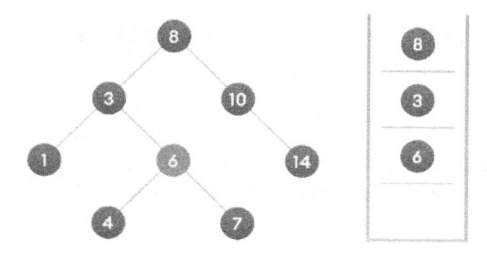

4 is not found so, traverse through the left subtree of 6

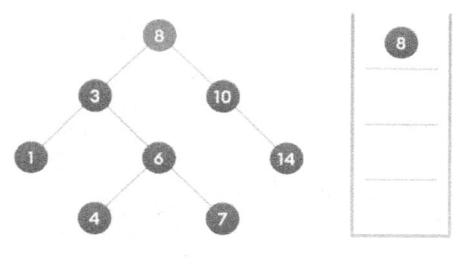

4 is found

If the value is found, we return the value so that it gets propagated in each recursion step as shown in the image below.

If you might have noticed, we have called return search(struct node*) four times. When we return either the new node or NULL, the value gets returned again and again until search(root) returns the final result.

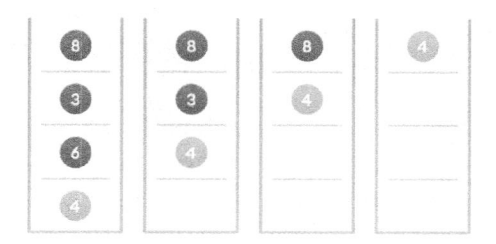

If the value is found in any of the subtrees, it is propagated up so that in the end it is returned, otherwise null is returned

If the value is not found, we eventually reach the left or right child of a leaf node which is NULL and it gets propagated and returned.

Insert Operation

Inserting a value in the correct position is similar to searching because we try to maintain the rule that the left subtree is lesser than root and the right subtree is larger than root.

We keep going to either right subtree or left subtree depending on the value and when we reach a point left or right subtree is null, we put the new node there.

Algorithm:
```
If node == NULL
    return createNode(data)
if (data < node->data)
    node->left = insert(node->left, data);
else if (data > node->data)
    node->right = insert(node->right, data);
return node;
```

The algorithm isn't as simple as it looks. Let's try to visualize how we add a number to an existing BST.

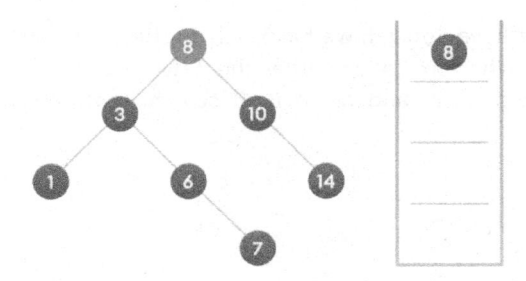

4<8 so, transverse through the left child of 8

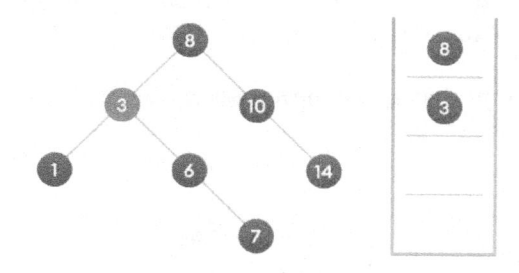

4>3 so, transverse through the right child of 8

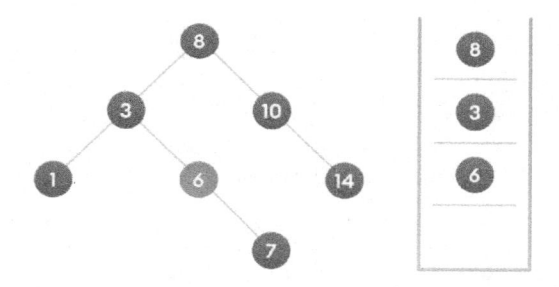

4<6 so, transverse through the left child of 6

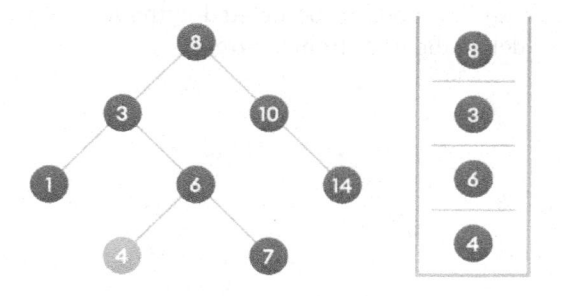

Insert 4 as a left child of 6

We have attached the node but we still have to exit from the function without doing any damage to the rest of the tree. This is where the return node; at the end comes in handy. In the case of NULL, the newly created node is returned and attached to the parent node,

121

otherwise the same node is returned without any change as we go up until we return to the root.

This makes sure that as we move back up the tree, the other node connections aren't changed.

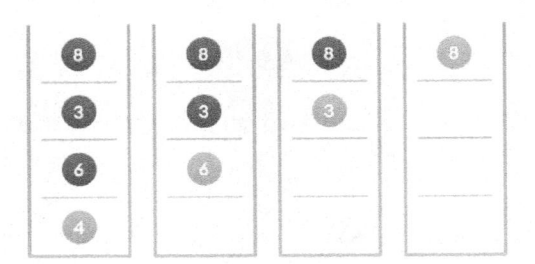

Image showing the importance of returning the root element at the end so that the elements don't lose their position during the upward recursion step.

Deletion Operation
There are three cases for deleting a node from a binary search tree.

Case I
In the first case, the node to be deleted is the leaf node. In such a case, simply delete the node from the tree.

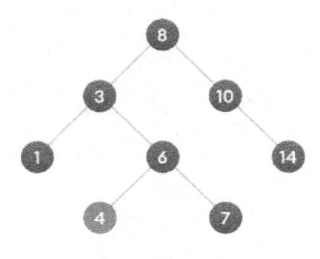

4 is to be deleted

122

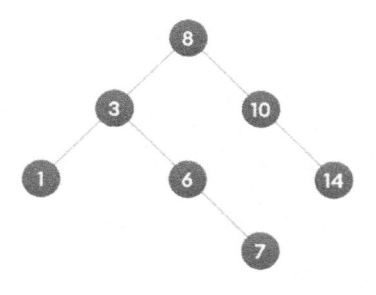

Delete the node

Case II
In the second case, the node to be deleted lies has a single child node.
In such a case follow the steps below:
1. Replace that node with its child node.
2. Remove the child node from its original position.

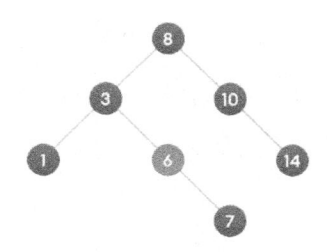

6 is to be deleted

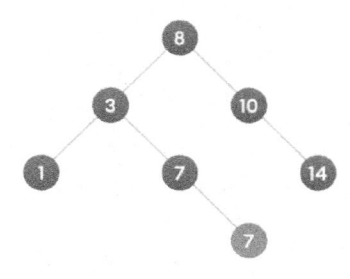

copy the value of its child to the node and delete the child

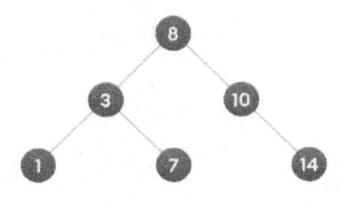

Final tree

Case III

In the third case, the node to be deleted has two children. In such a case follow the steps below:
1. Get the inorder successor of that node.
2. Replace the node with the inorder successor.
3. Remove the inorder successor from its original position.

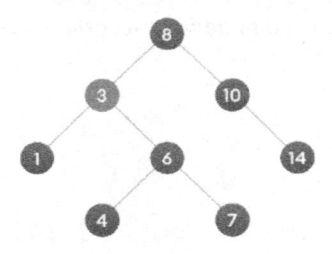

3 is to be deleted

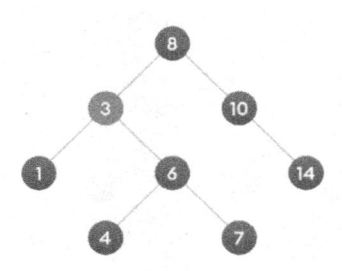

Copy the value of the inorder successor (4) to the node

124

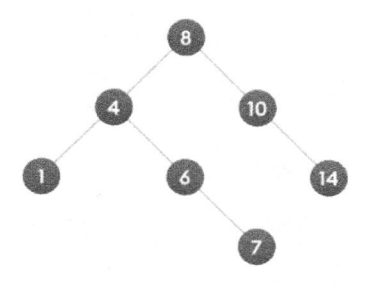

Delete the inorder successor

```python
# Binary Search Tree operations in Python

# Create a node
class Node:
    def __init__(self, key):
        self.key = key
        self.left = None
        self.right = None


# Inorder traversal
def inorder(root):
    if root is not None:
        # Traverse left
        inorder(root.left)

        # Traverse root
        print(str(root.key) + "->", end=' ')

        # Traverse right
        inorder(root.right)

# Insert a node
def insert(node, key):

    # Return a new node if the tree is empty
    if node is None:
        return Node(key)

    # Traverse to the right place and insert the node
    if key < node.key:
        node.left = insert(node.left, key)
    else:
        node.right = insert(node.right, key)

    return node

# Find the inorder successor
def minValueNode(node):
```

125

```python
    current = node

    # Find the leftmost leaf
    while(current.left is not None):
        current = current.left

    return current

# Deleting a node
def deleteNode(root, key):

    # Return if the tree is empty
    if root is None:
        return root

    # Find the node to be deleted
    if key < root.key:
        root.left = deleteNode(root.left, key)
    elif(key > root.key):
        root.right = deleteNode(root.right, key)
    else:
        # If the node is with only one child or no child
        if root.left is None:
            temp = root.right
            root = None
            return temp

        elif root.right is None:
            temp = root.left
            root = None
            return temp

        # If the node has two children,
        # place the inorder successor in position of the node to be deleted
        temp = minValueNode(root.right)

        root.key = temp.key

        # Delete the inorder successor
        root.right = deleteNode(root.right, temp.key)

    return root

root = None
root = insert(root, 8)
root = insert(root, 3)
root = insert(root, 1)
root = insert(root, 6)
root = insert(root, 7)
root = insert(root, 10)
root = insert(root, 14)
root = insert(root, 4)

print("Inorder traversal: ", end=' ')
```

```
inorder(root)

print("\nDelete 10")
root = deleteNode(root, 10)
print("Inorder traversal: ", end=' ')
inorder(root)
```

Output
```
Inorder traversal:   1-> 3-> 4-> 6-> 7-> 8-> 10-> 14->
Delete 10
Inorder traversal:   1-> 3-> 4-> 6-> 7-> 8-> 14->
```

Binary Search Tree Complexities

Time Complexity

Operation	Best Case	Average Case	Worst Case
Search	O(log n)	O(log n)	O(n)
Insertion	O(log n)	O(log n)	O(n)
Deletion	O(log n)	O(log n)	O(n)

Here, n is the number of nodes in the tree.

Space Complexity
The space complexity for all the operations is O(n).

Binary Search Tree Applications
1. In multilevel indexing in the database
2. For dynamic sorting
3. For managing virtual memory areas in Unix kernel

AVL Tree

AVL tree is a self-balancing binary search tree in which each node maintains extra information called a balance factor whose value is either -1, 0 or +1.

AVL tree got its name after its inventor Georgy Adelson-Velsky and Landis.

Balance Factor

Balance factor of a node in an AVL tree is the difference between the height of the left subtree and that of the right subtree of that node.

Balance Factor = (Height of Left Subtree - Height of Right Subtree) or (Height of Right Subtree - Height of Left Subtree)

The self balancing property of an avl tree is maintained by the balance factor. The value of balance factor should always be -1, 0 or +1.

An example of a balanced avl tree is:

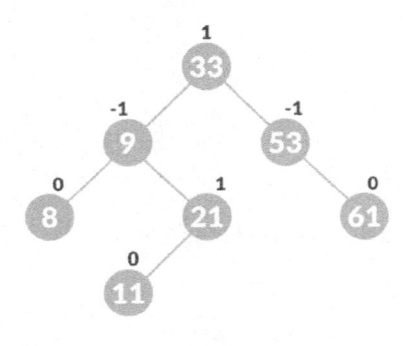

Avl tree

Operations on an AVL tree

Various operations that can be performed on an AVL tree are:

Rotating the subtrees in an AVL Tree

In rotation operation, the positions of the nodes of a subtree are interchanged.

There are two types of rotations:

Left Rotate

In left-rotation, the arrangement of the nodes on the right is transformed into the arrangements on the left node.

Algorithm

Let the initial tree be:

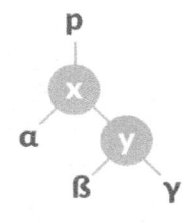

Left rotate

If y has a left subtree, assign x as the parent of the left subtree of y.

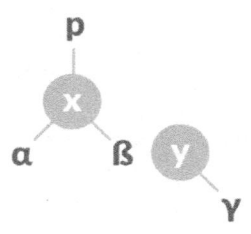

Assign x as the parent of the left subtree of y

If the parent of x is NULL, make y as the root of the tree.

Else if x is the left child of p, make y as the left child of p.

Else assign y as the right child of p.

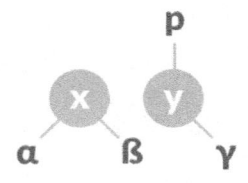

Change the parent of x to that of y

Make y as the parent of x.

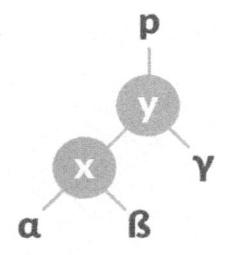

Assign y as the parent of x.

Right Rotate

In left-rotation, the arrangement of the nodes on the left is transformed into the arrangements on the right node.

Let the initial tree be:

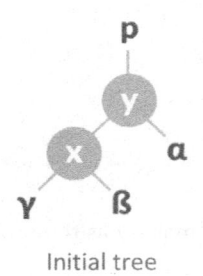

Initial tree

If x has a right subtree, assign y as the parent of the right subtree of x.

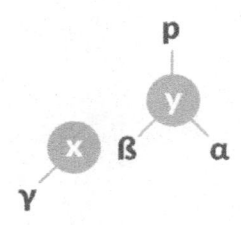

Assign y as the parent of the right subtree of x

If the parent of y is NULL, make x as the root of the tree.

Else if y is the right child of its parent p, make x as the right child of p.

Else assign x as the left child of p.

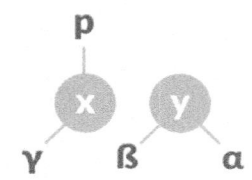

Assign the parent of y as the parent of x.

Make x as the parent of y.

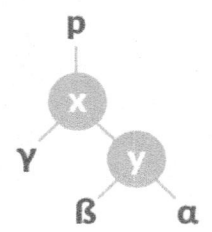

Assign x as the parent of y

Left-Right and Right-Left Rotate
In left-right rotation, the arrangements are first shifted to the left and then to the right.

Do left rotation on x-y.

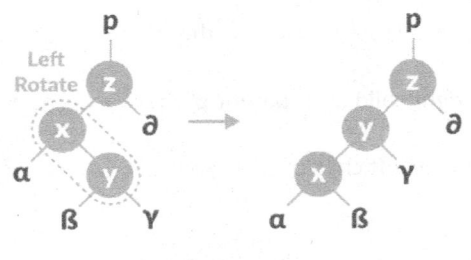

Left rotate x-y

Do right rotation on y-z.

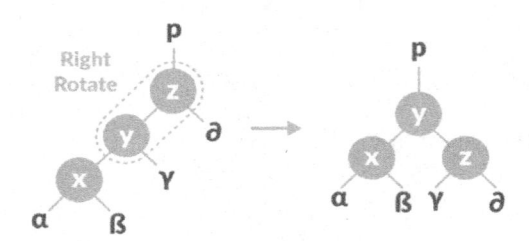

Right rotate z-y

In right-left rotation, the arrangements are first shifted to the right and then to the left.

Do right rotation on x-y.

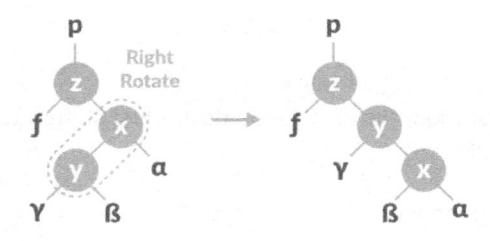

Right rotate x-y

Do left rotation on z-y.

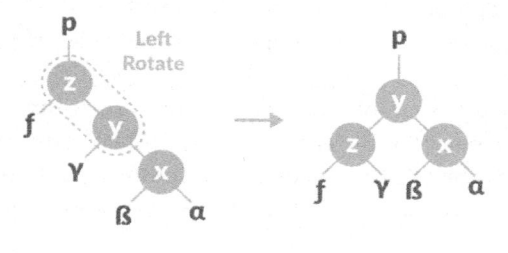

Left rotate z-y

Algorithm to insert a newNode

A `newNode` is always inserted as a leaf node with balance factor equal to 0.

Let the initial tree be:

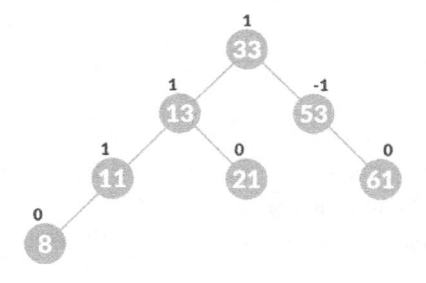

Initial tree for insertion

Let the node to be inserted be:

New node

Go to the appropriate leaf node to insert a newNode using the following recursive steps. Compare newKey with rootKey of the current tree.
- If newKey < rootKey, call insertion algorithm on the left subtree of the current node until the leaf node is reached.
- Else if newKey > rootKey, call insertion algorithm on the right subtree of current node until the leaf node is reached.
- Else, return leafNode.

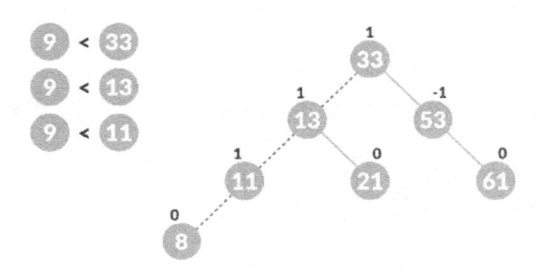

Finding the location to insert newNode

Compare leafKey obtained from the above steps with newKey:
- If newKey < leafKey, make newNode as the leftChild of leafNode.
- Else, make newNode as rightChild of leafNode.

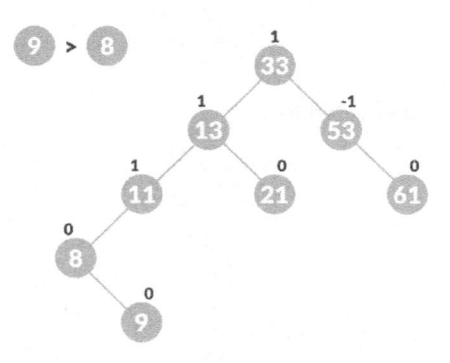

Inserting the new node

Update balanceFactor of the nodes.

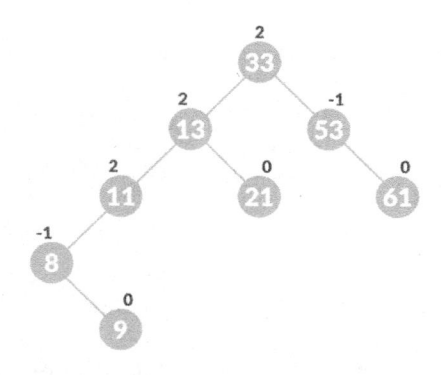

Updating the balance factor after insertion

If the nodes are unbalanced, then rebalance the node.
- If `balanceFactor` > 1, it means the height of the left subtree is greater than that of the right subtree. So, do a right rotation or left-right rotation
    - If `newNodeKey` < `leftChildKey` do right rotation.
    - Else, do left-right rotation.

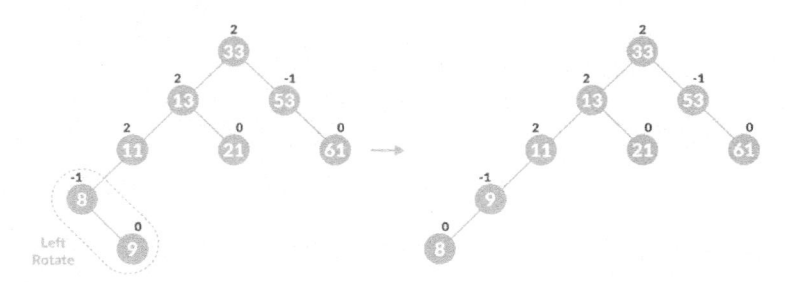

Balancing the tree with rotation

135

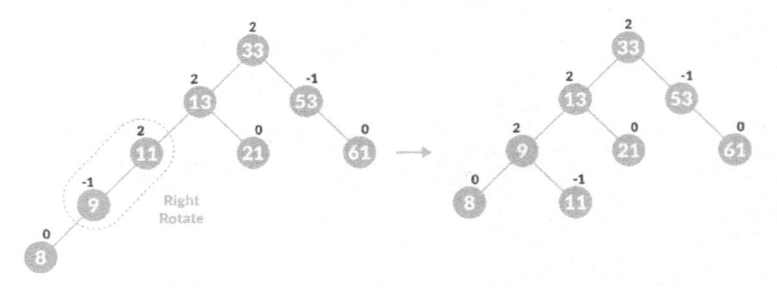

Balancing the tree with rotation

- If balanceFactor < -1, it means the height of the right subtree is greater than that of the left subtree. So, do right rotation or right-left rotation
  - If newNodeKey > rightChildKey do left rotation.
  - Else, do right-left rotation

The final tree is:

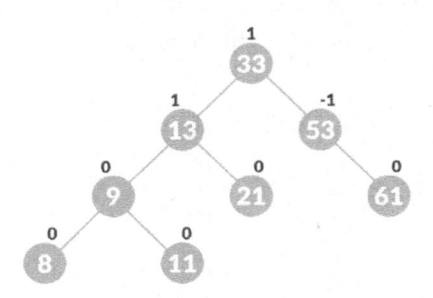

Final balanced tree

Algorithm to Delete a node
A node is always deleted as a leaf node. After deleting a node, the balance factors of the nodes get changed. In order to rebalance the balance factor, suitable rotations are performed.

Locate nodeToBeDeleted (recursion is used to find nodeToBeDeleted in the code used below).

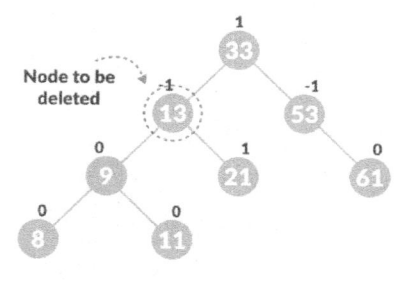

Locating the node to be deleted

There are three cases for deleting a node:
- If nodeToBeDeleted is the leaf node (ie. does not have any child), then remove nodeToBeDeleted.
- If nodeToBeDeleted has one child, then substitute the contents of nodeToBeDeleted with that of the child. Remove the child.
- If nodeToBeDeleted has two children, find the inorder successor w of nodeToBeDeleted (ie. node with a minimum value of key in the right subtree).

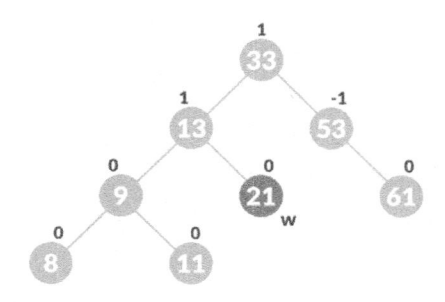

Finding the successor

Substitute the contents of nodeToBeDeleted with that of w.

Substitute the content of nodeToBeDeleted with that of w

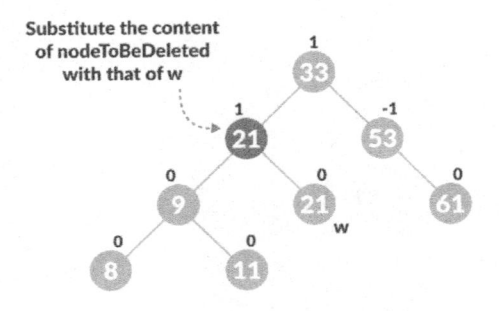

Substitute the node to be deleted

Remove the leaf node w.

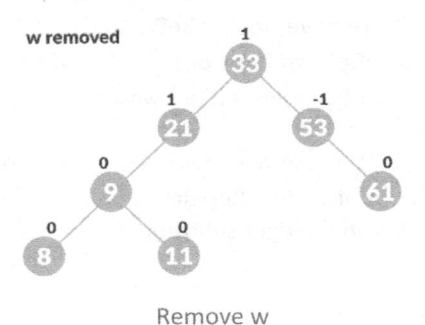

Remove w

Update balanceFactor of the nodes.

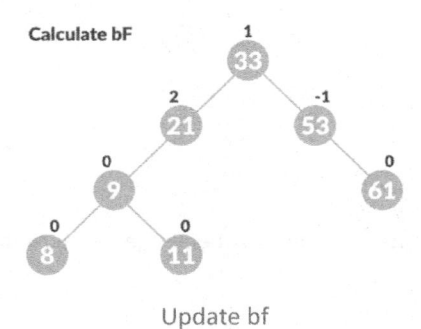

Update bf

Rebalance the tree if the balance factor of any of the nodes is not equal to -1, 0 or 1.

138

- If balanceFactor of currentNode > 1,
    - If balanceFactor of leftChild >= 0, do right rotation.

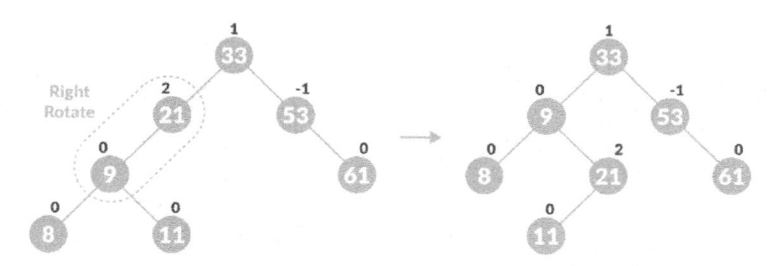

Right-rotate for balancing the tree

Else do left-right rotation.

- If balanceFactor of currentNode < -1,
    - If balanceFactor of rightChild <= 0, do left rotation.
    - Else do right-left rotation.

The final tree is:

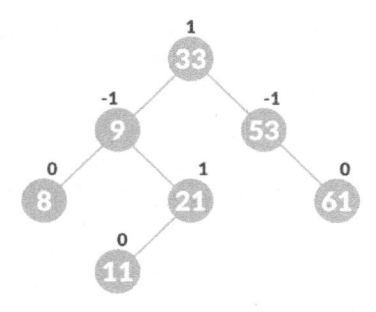

Avl tree final

```
# AVL tree implementation in Python

import sys

# Create a tree node
class TreeNode(object):
    def __init__(self, key):
```

```python
        self.key = key
        self.left = None
        self.right = None
        self.height = 1

class AVLTree(object):

    # Function to insert a node
    def insert_node(self, root, key):

        # Find the correct location and insert the node
        if not root:
            return TreeNode(key)
        elif key < root.key:
            root.left = self.insert_node(root.left, key)
        else:
            root.right = self.insert_node(root.right, key)

        root.height = 1 + max(self.getHeight(root.left),
                              self.getHeight(root.right))

        # Update the balance factor and balance the tree
        balanceFactor = self.getBalance(root)
        if balanceFactor > 1:
            if key < root.left.key:
                return self.rightRotate(root)
            else:
                root.left = self.leftRotate(root.left)
                return self.rightRotate(root)

        if balanceFactor < -1:
            if key > root.right.key:
                return self.leftRotate(root)
            else:
                root.right = self.rightRotate(root.right)
                return self.leftRotate(root)

        return root

    # Function to delete a node
    def delete_node(self, root, key):

        # Find the node to be deleted and remove it
        if not root:
            return root
        elif key < root.key:
            root.left = self.delete_node(root.left, key)
        elif key > root.key:
            root.right = self.delete_node(root.right, key)
        else:
            if root.left is None:
                temp = root.right
                root = None
                return temp
            elif root.right is None:
```

```python
            temp = root.left
            root = None
            return temp
        temp = self.getMinValueNode(root.right)
        root.key = temp.key
        root.right = self.delete_node(root.right,
                                      temp.key)
    if root is None:
        return root

    # Update the balance factor of nodes
    root.height = 1 + max(self.getHeight(root.left),
                          self.getHeight(root.right))

    balanceFactor = self.getBalance(root)

    # Balance the tree
    if balanceFactor > 1:
        if self.getBalance(root.left) >= 0:
            return self.rightRotate(root)
        else:
            root.left = self.leftRotate(root.left)
            return self.rightRotate(root)
    if balanceFactor < -1:
        if self.getBalance(root.right) <= 0:
            return self.leftRotate(root)
        else:
            root.right = self.rightRotate(root.right)
            return self.leftRotate(root)
    return root

# Function to perform left rotation
def leftRotate(self, z):
    y = z.right
    T2 = y.left
    y.left = z
    z.right = T2
    z.height = 1 + max(self.getHeight(z.left),
                       self.getHeight(z.right))
    y.height = 1 + max(self.getHeight(y.left),
                       self.getHeight(y.right))

    return y

# Function to perform right rotation
def rightRotate(self, z):
    y = z.left
    T3 = y.right
    y.right = z
    z.left = T3
    z.height = 1 + max(self.getHeight(z.left),
                       self.getHeight(z.right))
    y.height = 1 + max(self.getHeight(y.left),
                       self.getHeight(y.right))

    return y
```

```python
    # Get the height of the node
    def getHeight(self, root):
        if not root:
            return 0
        return root.height

    # Get balance factore of the node
    def getBalance(self, root):
        if not root:
            return 0
        return self.getHeight(root.left) - self.getHeight(root.right)

    def getMinValueNode(self, root):
        if root is None or root.left is None:
            return root
        return self.getMinValueNode(root.left)

    def preOrder(self, root):
        if not root:
            return
        print("{0} ".format(root.key), end="")
        self.preOrder(root.left)
        self.preOrder(root.right)

    # Print the tree
    def printHelper(self, currPtr, indent, last):
        if currPtr != None:
            sys.stdout.write(indent)
            if last:
                sys.stdout.write("R----")
                indent += "     "
            else:
                sys.stdout.write("L----")
                indent += "|    "
            print(currPtr.key)
            self.printHelper(currPtr.left, indent, False)
            self.printHelper(currPtr.right, indent, True)


myTree = AVLTree()
root = None
nums = [33, 13, 52, 9, 21, 61, 8, 11]
for num in nums:
    root = myTree.insert_node(root, num)
myTree.printHelper(root, "", True)
key = 13
root = myTree.delete_node(root, key)
print("After Deletion: ")
myTree.printHelper(root, "", True)
```

Output
R----33
    L----13

```
       |       L----9
       |       |       L----8
       |       |       R----11
       |       R----21
       R----52
               R----61
After Deletion:
R----33
       L----9
       |       L----8
       |       R----21
       |               L----11
       R----52
               R----61
```

Complexities of Different Operations on an AVL Tree

Insertion	Deletion	Search
O(log n)	O(log n)	O(log n)

AVL Tree Applications
- For indexing large records in databases
- For searching in large databases

B-tree

B-tree is a special type of self-balancing search tree in which each node can contain more than one key and can have more than two children. It is a generalized form of the binary search tree.

It is also known as a height-balanced m-way tree.

```
        20 40
       /  |  \
     10  30 33  50 60
    /  \  / \  / \  / \
   5  15 25 28 31 35 45 55 65
```

B-tree

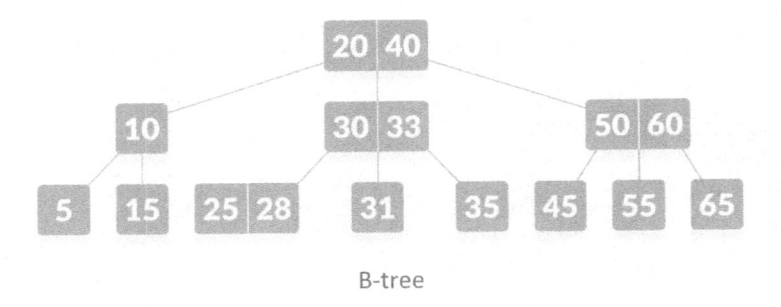

Why B-tree?

The need for B-tree arose with the rise in the need for lesser time in accessing the physical storage media like a hard disk. The secondary storage devices are slower with a larger capacity. There was a need for such types of data structures that minimize the disk accesses.

Other data structures such as a binary search tree, avl tree, red-black tree, etc can store only one key in one node. If you have to store a large number of keys, then the height of such trees becomes very large and the access time increases.

However, B-tree can store many keys in a single node and can have multiple child nodes. This decreases the height significantly allowing faster disk accesses.

B-tree Properties

1. For each node x, the keys are stored in increasing order.
2. In each node, there is a boolean value x.leaf which is true if x is a leaf.
3. If n is the order of the tree, each internal node can contain at most n - 1 keys along with a pointer to each child.
4. Each node except root can have at most n children and at least n/2 children.
5. All leaves have the same depth (i.e. height-h of the tree).
6. The root has at least 2 children and contains a minimum of 1 key.
7. If $n \geq 1$, then for any n-key B-tree of height h and minimum degree $t \geq 2$, $h \geq \log_t (n+1)/2$.

Operations

Searching

Searching for an element in a B-tree is the generalized form of searching an element in a Binary Search Tree. The following steps are followed.
1. Starting from the root node, compare k with the first key of the node.
   If k = the first key of the node, return the node and the index.
2. If k.leaf = true, return NULL (i.e. not found).
3. If k < the first key of the root node, search the left child of this key recursively.
4. If there is more than one key in the current node and k > the first key, compare k with the next key in the node. If k < next key, search the left child of this key (ie. k lies in between the first and the second keys). Else, search the right child of the key.
5. Repeat steps 1 to 4 until the leaf is reached.

Searching Example

Let us search key k = 17 in the tree below of degree 3.

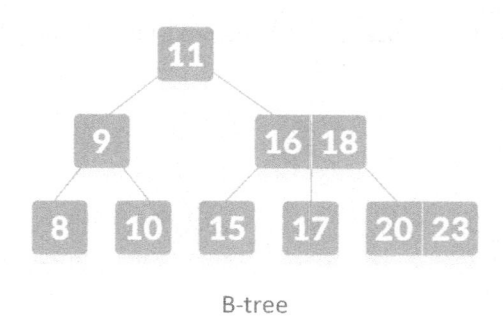

B-tree

k is not found in the root so, compare it with the root key.

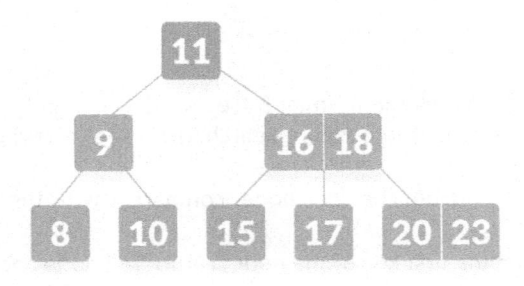

k is not found on the root node

Since k > 11, go to the right child of the root node.

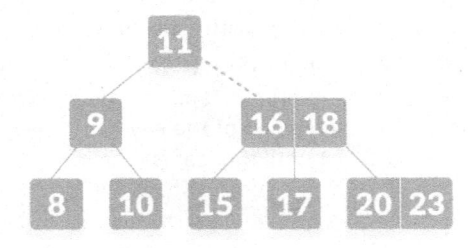

Go to the right subtree

Compare k with 16. Since k > 16, compare k with the next key 18.

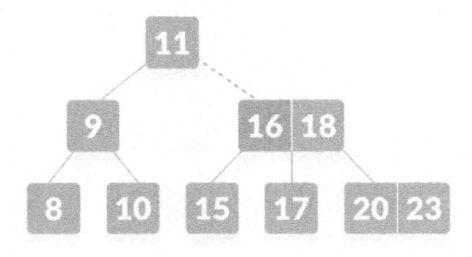

Compare with the keys from left to right

Since k < 18, k lies between 16 and 18. Search in the right child of 16 or the left child of 18.

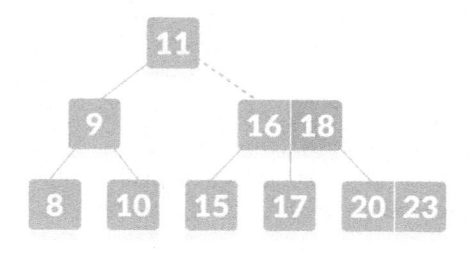

k lies in between 16 and 18

k is found.

k is found

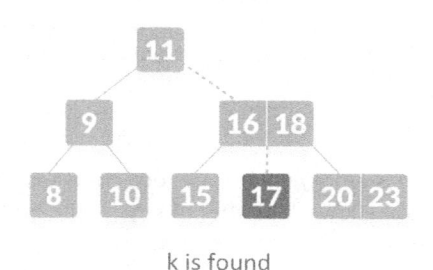

Algorithm for Searching an Element

```
BtreeSearch(x, k)
i = 1
while i ≤ n[x] and k ≥ keyi[x]      // n[x] means number of keys in x node
   do i = i + 1
if i  n[x] and k = keyi[x]
   then return (x, i)
if leaf [x]
   then return NIL
else
   return BtreeSearch(ci[x], k)
```

Searching Complexity on B Tree
- Worst case Time complexity: $\Theta(\log n)$
- Average case Time complexity: $\Theta(\log n)$
- Best case Time complexity: $\Theta(\log n)$

- Average case Space complexity: Θ(n)
- Worst case Space complexity: Θ(n)

B Tree Applications
- databases and file systems
- to store blocks of data (secondary storage media)
- multilevel indexing

Insertion into a B-tree

Inserting an element on a B-tree consists of two events: searching the appropriate node to insert the element and splitting the node if required. Insertion operation always takes place in the bottom-up approach.

Insertion Operation
1. If the tree is empty, allocate a root node and insert the key.
2. Update the allowed number of keys in the node.
3. Search the appropriate node for insertion.
4. If the node is full, follow the steps below.
5. Insert the elements in increasing order.
6. Now, there are elements greater than its limit. So, split at the median.
7. Push the median key upwards and make the left keys as a left child and the right keys as a right child.
8. If the node is not full, follow the steps below.
9. Insert the node in increasing order.

Insertion Example

Let us understand the insertion operation with the illustrations below. The elements to be inserted are 8, 9, 10, 11, 15, 16, 17, 18, 20, 23.

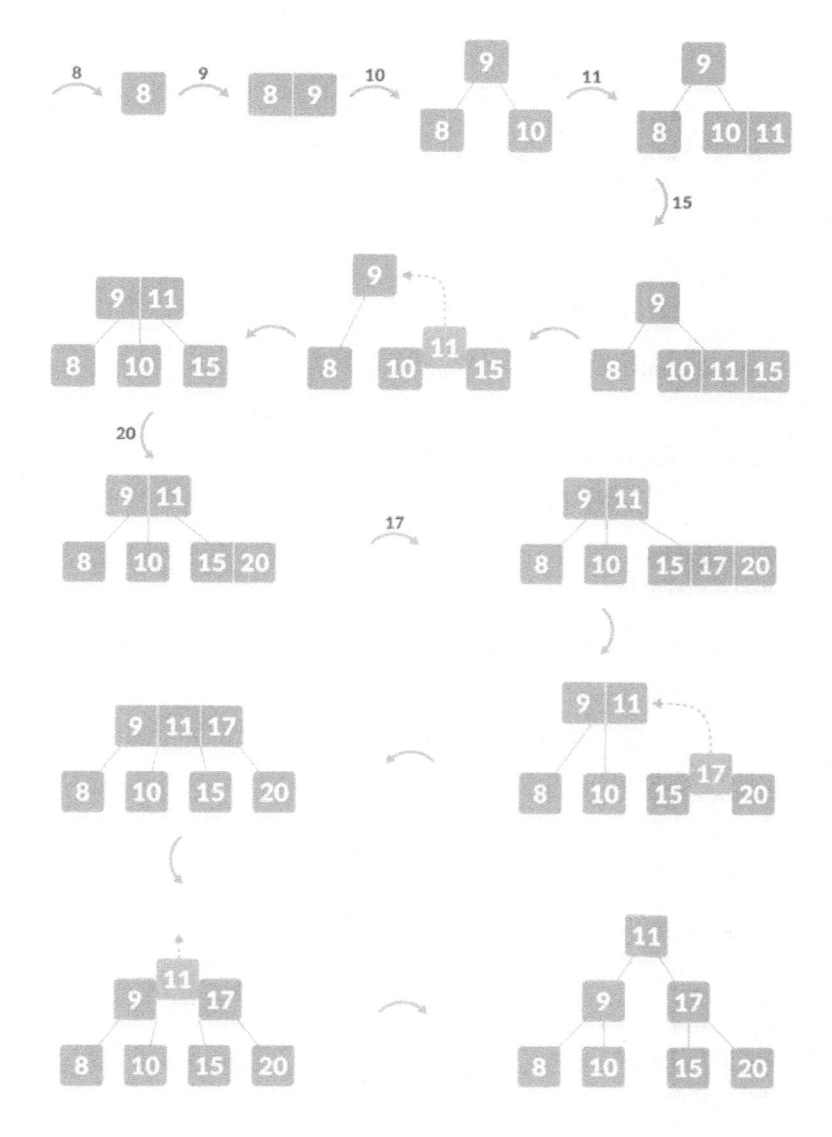

Inserting elements into a B-tree

Algorithm for Inserting an Element

BreeInsertion(T, k)

```
r  root[T]
if n[r] = 2t - 1
   s = AllocateNode()
   root[T] = s
   leaf[s] = FALSE
   n[s] <- 0
   c1[s] <- r
   BtreeSplitChild(s, 1, r)
   BtreeInsertNonFull(s, k)
else BtreeInsertNonFull(r, k)
BtreeInsertNonFull(x, k)
i = n[x]
if leaf[x]
   while i ≥ 1 and k < keyi[x]
      keyi+1 [x] = keyi[x]
      i = i - 1
   keyi+1[x] = k
   n[x] = n[x] + 1
else while i ≥ 1 and k < keyi[x]
      i = i - 1
   i = i + 1
   if n[ci[x]] == 2t - 1
      BtreeSplitChild(x, i, ci[x])
      if k &rt; keyi[x]
         i = i + 1
   BtreeInsertNonFull(ci[x], k)
BtreeSplitChild(x, i)
BtreeSplitChild(x, i, y)
z = AllocateNode()
leaf[z] = leaf[y]
n[z] = t - 1
for j = 1 to t - 1
   keyj[z] = keyj+t[y]
if not leaf [y]
   for j = 1 to t
      cj[z] = cj + t[y]
n[y] = t - 1
for j = n[x] + 1 to i + 1
   cj+1[x] = cj[x]
ci+1[x] = z
for j = n[x] to i
```

```
    keyj+1[x] = keyj[x]
keyi[x] = keyt[y]
n[x] = n[x] + 1
```

```python
# Inserting a key on a B-tree in Python

# Create a node
class BTreeNode:
    def __init__(self, leaf=False):
        self.leaf = leaf
        self.keys = []
        self.child = []

# Tree
class BTree:
    def __init__(self, t):
        self.root = BTreeNode(True)
        self.t = t

    # Insert node
    def insert(self, k):
        root = self.root
        if len(root.keys) == (2 * self.t) - 1:
            temp = BTreeNode()
            self.root = temp
            temp.child.insert(0, root)
            self.split_child(temp, 0)
            self.insert_non_full(temp, k)
        else:
            self.insert_non_full(root, k)

    # Insert nonfull
    def insert_non_full(self, x, k):
        i = len(x.keys) - 1
        if x.leaf:
            x.keys.append((None, None))
            while i >= 0 and k[0] < x.keys[i][0]:
                x.keys[i + 1] = x.keys[i]
                i -= 1
            x.keys[i + 1] = k
        else:
            while i >= 0 and k[0] < x.keys[i][0]:
                i -= 1
            i += 1
            if len(x.child[i].keys) == (2 * self.t) - 1:
                self.split_child(x, i)
                if k[0] > x.keys[i][0]:
                    i += 1
            self.insert_non_full(x.child[i], k)

    # Split the child
    def split_child(self, x, i):
        t = self.t
```

```python
            y = x.child[i]
            z = BTreeNode(y.leaf)
            x.child.insert(i + 1, z)
            x.keys.insert(i, y.keys[t - 1])
            z.keys = y.keys[t: (2 * t) - 1]
            y.keys = y.keys[0: t - 1]
            if not y.leaf:
                z.child = y.child[t: 2 * t]
                y.child = y.child[0: t - 1]

    # Print the tree
    def print_tree(self, x, l=0):
        print("Level ", l, " ", len(x.keys), end=":")
        for i in x.keys:
            print(i, end=" ")
        print()
        l += 1
        if len(x.child) > 0:
            for i in x.child:
                self.print_tree(i, l)


def main():
    B = BTree(3)

    for i in range(10):
        B.insert((i, 2 * i))

    B.print_tree(B.root)


if __name__ == '__main__':
    main()
```

Output
```
Level  0   2:(2, 4) (5, 10)
Level  1   2:(0, 0) (1, 2)
Level  1   2:(3, 6) (4, 8)
Level  1   4:(6, 12) (7, 14) (8, 16) (9, 18)
```

Deletion from a B-tree

Deleting an element on a B-tree consists of three main events: searching the node where the key to be deleted exists, deleting the key and balancing the tree if required.

While deleting a tree, a condition called underflow may occur. Underflow occurs when a node contains less than the minimum number of keys it should hold.

The terms to be understood before studying deletion operation are:

1. Inorder Predecessor

The largest key on the left child of a node is called its inorder predecessor.

2. Inorder Successor

The smallest key on the right child of a node is called its inorder successor.

Deletion Operation

Before going through the steps below, one must know these facts about a B tree of degree m.
1. A node can have a maximum of m children. (i.e. 3)
2. A node can contain a maximum of m - 1 keys. (i.e. 2)
3. A node should have a minimum of ⌈m/2⌉ children. (i.e. 2)
4. A node (except root node) should contain a minimum of ⌈m/2⌉ - 1 keys. (i.e. 1)

There are three main cases for deletion operation in a B tree.

Case I

The key to be deleted lies in the leaf. There are two cases for it.

The deletion of the key does not violate the property of the minimum number of keys a node should hold.

In the tree below, deleting 32 does not violate the above properties.

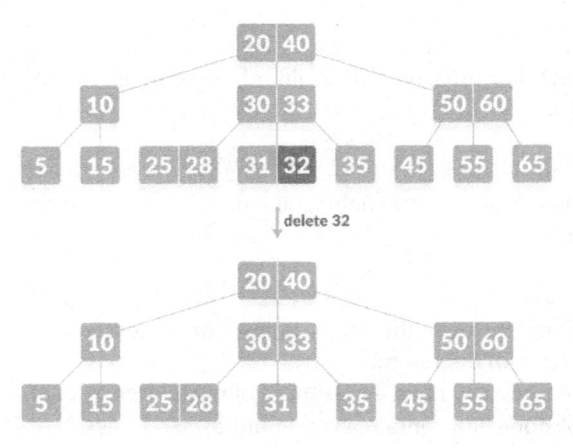

Deleting a leaf key (32) from B-tree

The deletion of the key violates the property of the minimum number of keys a node should hold. In this case, we borrow a key from its immediate neighboring sibling node in the order of left to right.

First, visit the immediate left sibling. If the left sibling node has more than a minimum number of keys, then borrow a key from this node.

Else, check to borrow from the immediate right sibling node.

In the tree below, deleting 31 results in the above condition. Let us borrow a key from the left sibling node.

Deleting a leaf key (31)

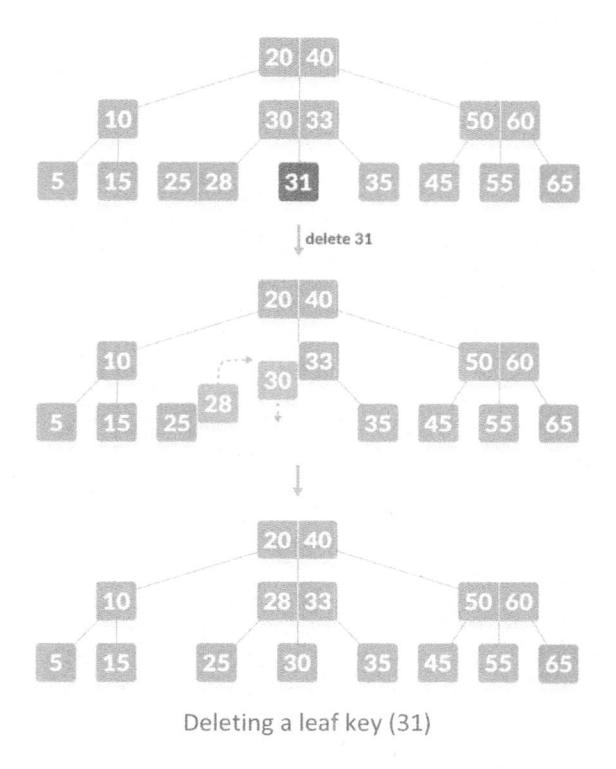

If both the immediate sibling nodes already have a minimum number of keys, then merge the node with either the left sibling node or the right sibling node. This merging is done through the parent node.

Deleting 30 results in the above case.

155

Delete a leaf key (30)

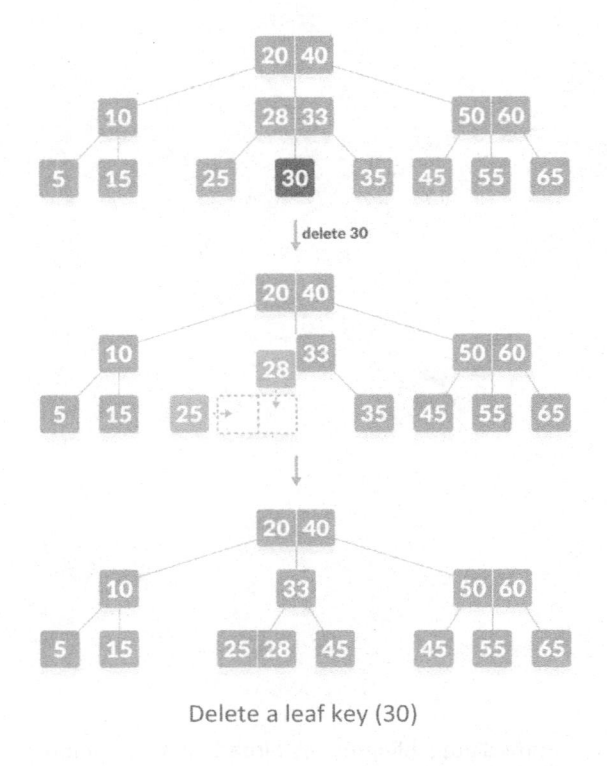

Case II
If the key to be deleted lies in the internal node, the following cases occur.

The internal node, which is deleted, is replaced by an inorder predecessor if the left child has more than the minimum number of keys.

156

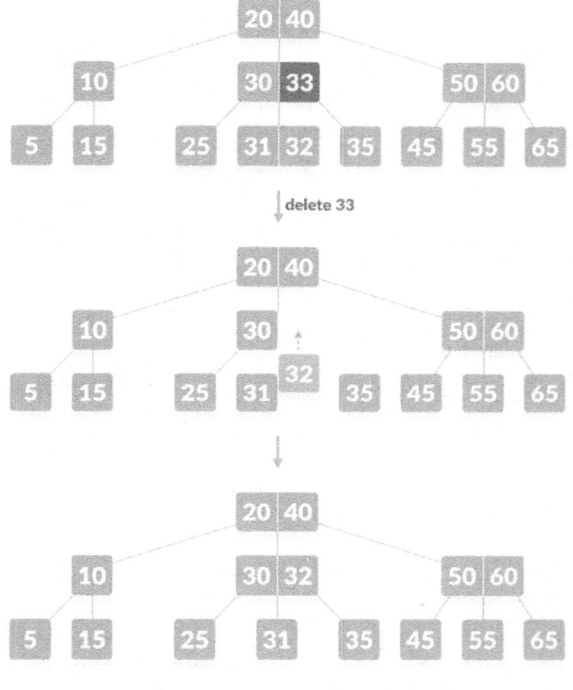

Deleting an internal node (33)

The internal node, which is deleted, is replaced by an inorder successor if the right child has more than the minimum number of keys.

If either child has exactly a minimum number of keys then, merge the left and the right children.

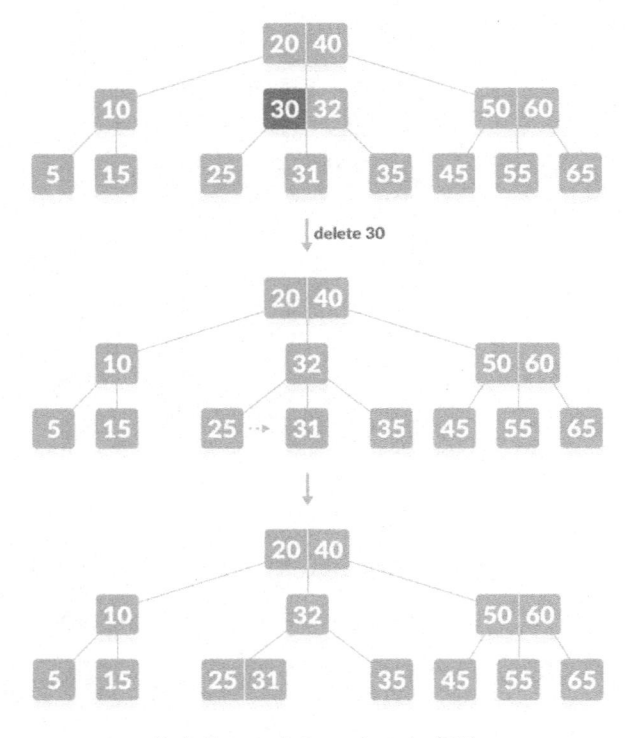

Deleting an internal node (30)

After merging if the parent node has less than the minimum number of keys then, look for the siblings as in Case I.

Case III
In this case, the height of the tree shrinks. If the target key lies in an internal node, and the deletion of the key leads to a fewer number of keys in the node (i.e. less than the minimum required), then look for the inorder predecessor and the inorder successor. If both the children contain a minimum number of keys then, borrowing cannot take place. This leads to Case II(3) i.e. merging the children.

Again, look for the sibling to borrow a key. But, if the sibling also has only a minimum number of keys then, merge the node with the sibling along with the parent. Arrange the children accordingly (increasing order).

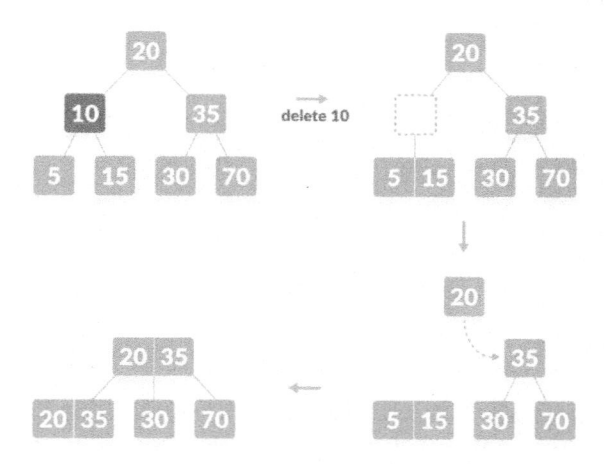

Deleting an internal node (10)

```python
# Deleting a key on a B-tree in Python

# Btree node
class BTreeNode:
    def __init__(self, leaf=False):
        self.leaf = leaf
        self.keys = []
        self.child = []


class BTree:
    def __init__(self, t):
        self.root = BTreeNode(True)
        self.t = t

    # Insert a key
    def insert(self, k):
        root = self.root
        if len(root.keys) == (2 * self.t) - 1:
            temp = BTreeNode()
            self.root = temp
            temp.child.insert(0, root)
            self.split_child(temp, 0)
            self.insert_non_full(temp, k)
        else:
            self.insert_non_full(root, k)

    # Insert non full
    def insert_non_full(self, x, k):
```

```python
        i = len(x.keys) - 1
        if x.leaf:
            x.keys.append((None, None))
            while i >= 0 and k[0] < x.keys[i][0]:
                x.keys[i + 1] = x.keys[i]
                i -= 1
            x.keys[i + 1] = k
        else:
            while i >= 0 and k[0] < x.keys[i][0]:
                i -= 1
            i += 1
            if len(x.child[i].keys) == (2 * self.t) - 1:
                self.split_child(x, i)
                if k[0] > x.keys[i][0]:
                    i += 1
            self.insert_non_full(x.child[i], k)

    # Split the child
    def split_child(self, x, i):
        t = self.t
        y = x.child[i]
        z = BTreeNode(y.leaf)
        x.child.insert(i + 1, z)
        x.keys.insert(i, y.keys[t - 1])
        z.keys = y.keys[t: (2 * t) - 1]
        y.keys = y.keys[0: t - 1]
        if not y.leaf:
            z.child = y.child[t: 2 * t]
            y.child = y.child[0: t - 1]

    # Delete a node
    def delete(self, x, k):
        t = self.t
        i = 0
        while i < len(x.keys) and k[0] > x.keys[i][0]:
            i += 1
        if x.leaf:
            if i < len(x.keys) and x.keys[i][0] == k[0]:
                x.keys.pop(i)
                return
            return

        if i < len(x.keys) and x.keys[i][0] == k[0]:
            return self.delete_internal_node(x, k, i)
        elif len(x.child[i].keys) >= t:
            self.delete(x.child[i], k)
        else:
            if i != 0 and i + 2 < len(x.child):
                if len(x.child[i - 1].keys) >= t:
                    self.delete_sibling(x, i, i - 1)
                elif len(x.child[i + 1].keys) >= t:
                    self.delete_sibling(x, i, i + 1)
                else:
                    self.delete_merge(x, i, i + 1)
            elif i == 0:
```

```python
            if len(x.child[i + 1].keys) >= t:
                self.delete_sibling(x, i, i + 1)
            else:
                self.delete_merge(x, i, i + 1)
        elif i + 1 == len(x.child):
            if len(x.child[i - 1].keys) >= t:
                self.delete_sibling(x, i, i - 1)
            else:
                self.delete_merge(x, i, i - 1)
        self.delete(x.child[i], k)

    # Delete internal node
    def delete_internal_node(self, x, k, i):
        t = self.t
        if x.leaf:
            if x.keys[i][0] == k[0]:
                x.keys.pop(i)
                return
            return

        if len(x.child[i].keys) >= t:
            x.keys[i] = self.delete_predecessor(x.child[i])
            return
        elif len(x.child[i + 1].keys) >= t:
            x.keys[i] = self.delete_successor(x.child[i + 1])
            return
        else:
            self.delete_merge(x, i, i + 1)
            self.delete_internal_node(x.child[i], k, self.t - 1)

    # Delete the predecessor
    def delete_predecessor(self, x):
        if x.leaf:
            return x.pop()
        n = len(x.keys) - 1
        if len(x.child[n].keys) >= self.t:
            self.delete_sibling(x, n + 1, n)
        else:
            self.delete_merge(x, n, n + 1)
        self.delete_predecessor(x.child[n])

    # Delete the successor
    def delete_successor(self, x):
        if x.leaf:
            return x.keys.pop(0)
        if len(x.child[1].keys) >= self.t:
            self.delete_sibling(x, 0, 1)
        else:
            self.delete_merge(x, 0, 1)
        self.delete_successor(x.child[0])

    # Delete resolution
    def delete_merge(self, x, i, j):
```

```python
            cnode = x.child[i]

        if j > i:
            rsnode = x.child[j]
            cnode.keys.append(x.keys[i])
            for k in range(len(rsnode.keys)):
                cnode.keys.append(rsnode.keys[k])
                if len(rsnode.child) > 0:
                    cnode.child.append(rsnode.child[k])
            if len(rsnode.child) > 0:
                cnode.child.append(rsnode.child.pop())
            new = cnode
            x.keys.pop(i)
            x.child.pop(j)
        else:
            lsnode = x.child[j]
            lsnode.keys.append(x.keys[j])
            for i in range(len(cnode.keys)):
                lsnode.keys.append(cnode.keys[i])
                if len(lsnode.child) > 0:
                    lsnode.child.append(cnode.child[i])
            if len(lsnode.child) > 0:
                lsnode.child.append(cnode.child.pop())
            new = lsnode
            x.keys.pop(j)
            x.child.pop(i)

        if x == self.root and len(x.keys) == 0:
            self.root = new

    # Delete the sibling
    def delete_sibling(self, x, i, j):
        cnode = x.child[i]
        if i < j:
            rsnode = x.child[j]
            cnode.keys.append(x.keys[i])
            x.keys[i] = rsnode.keys[0]
            if len(rsnode.child) > 0:
                cnode.child.append(rsnode.child[0])
                rsnode.child.pop(0)
            rsnode.keys.pop(0)
        else:
            lsnode = x.child[j]
            cnode.keys.insert(0, x.keys[i - 1])
            x.keys[i - 1] = lsnode.keys.pop()
            if len(lsnode.child) > 0:
                cnode.child.insert(0, lsnode.child.pop())

    # Print the tree
    def print_tree(self, x, l=0):
        print("Level ", l, " ", len(x.keys), end=":")
        for i in x.keys:
            print(i, end=" ")
        print()
        l += 1
```

```
            if len(x.child) > 0:
                for i in x.child:
                    self.print_tree(i, 1)

B = BTree(3)

for i in range(10):
    B.insert((i, 2 * i))

B.print_tree(B.root)

B.delete(B.root, (8,))
print("\n")
B.print_tree(B.root)
```

Output
```
Level   0       2:(2, 4)  (5, 10)
Level   1       2:(0, 0)  (1, 2)
Level   1       2:(3, 6)  (4, 8)
Level   1       4:(6, 12) (7, 14) (8, 16) (9, 18)

Level   0       2:(2, 4)  (5, 10)
Level   1       2:(0, 0)  (1, 2)
Level   1       2:(3, 6)  (4, 8)
Level   1       3:(6, 12) (7, 14) (9, 18)
```

Deletion Complexity
- Best case Time complexity: $\Theta(\log n)$
- Average case Space complexity: $\Theta(n)$
- Worst case Space complexity: $\Theta(n)$

B+ Tree

A B+ tree is an advanced form of a self-balancing tree in which all the values are present in the leaf level.

An important concept to be understood before learning B+ tree is multilevel indexing. In multilevel indexing, the index of indices is created as in figure below. It makes accessing the data easier and faster.

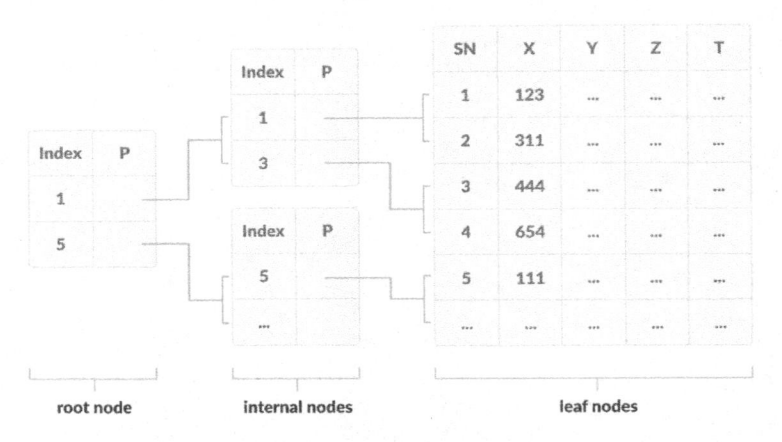

Multilevel Indexing using B+ tree

Properties of a B+ Tree
1. All leaves are at the same level.
2. The root has at least two children.
3. Each node except root can have a maximum of m children and at least m/2 children.
4. Each node can contain a maximum of m - 1 keys and a minimum of ⌈m/2⌉ - 1 keys.

Comparison between a B-tree and a B+ Tree

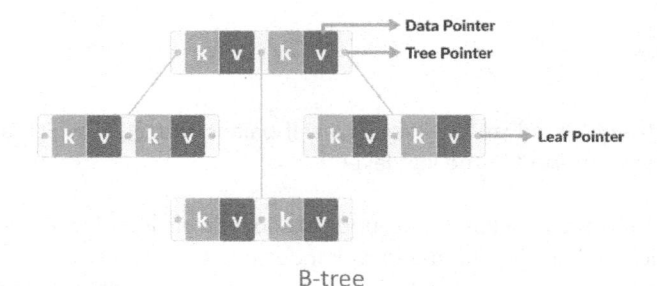

B-tree

164

B+ tree

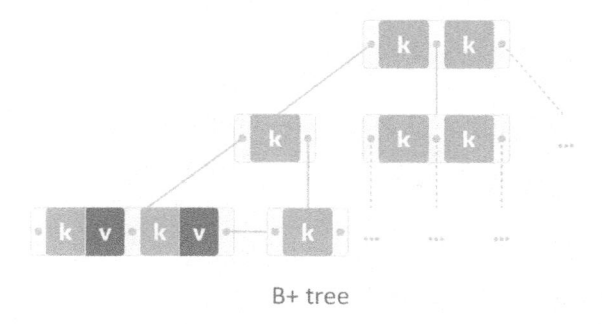

The data pointers are present only at the leaf nodes on a B+ tree whereas the data pointers are present in the internal, leaf or root nodes on a B-tree.

The leaves are not connected with each other on a B-tree whereas they are connected on a B+ tree.

Operations on a B+ tree are faster than on a B-tree.

Searching on a B+ Tree

The following steps are followed to search for data in a B+ Tree of order m. Let the data to be searched be k.
1. Start from the root node. Compare k with the keys at the root node [k1, k2, k3,......km - 1].
2. If k < k1, go to the left child of the root node.
3. Else if k == k1, compare k2. If k < k2, k lies between k1 and k2. So, search in the left child of k2.
4. If k > k2, go for k3, k4,...km-1 as in steps 2 and 3.
5. Repeat the above steps until a leaf node is reached.
6. If k exists in the leaf node, return true else return false.

Searching Example on a B+ Tree

Let us search k = 45 on the following B+ tree.

B+ tree

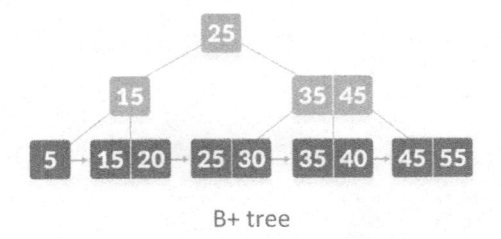

Compare k with the root node.

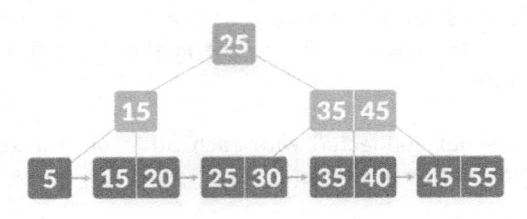

k is not found at the root

Since k > 25, go to the right child.

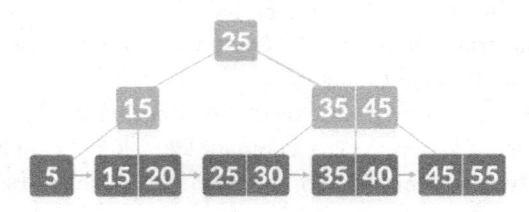

Go to right of the root

Compare k with 35. Since k > 30, compare k with 45.

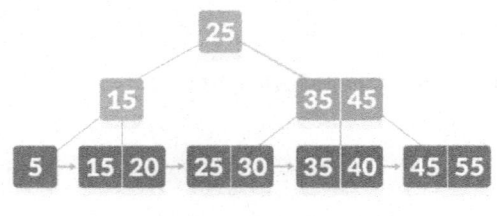

k not found

Since k ≥ 45, so go to the right child.

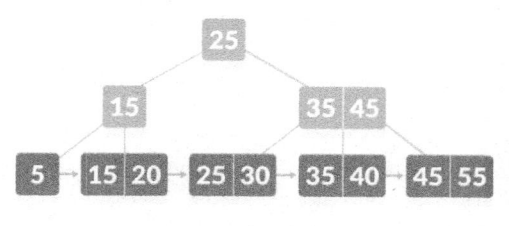

go to the right

k is found.

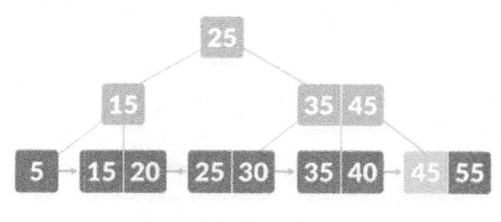

k is found

```python
# B+ tree in python
import math

# Node creation
class Node:
    def __init__(self, order):
        self.order = order
        self.values = []
        self.keys = []
        self.nextKey = None
        self.parent = None
        self.check_leaf = False

    # Insert at the leaf
    def insert_at_leaf(self, leaf, value, key):
        if (self.values):
            temp1 = self.values
            for i in range(len(temp1)):
                if (value == temp1[i]):
                    self.keys[i].append(key)
                    break
                elif (value < temp1[i]):
                    self.values = self.values[:i] + [value] + self.values[i:]
                    self.keys = self.keys[:i] + [[key]] + self.keys[i:]
                    break
                elif (i + 1 == len(temp1)):
                    self.values.append(value)
                    self.keys.append([key])
                    break
        else:
            self.values = [value]
            self.keys = [[key]]
```

```python
# B plus tree
class BplusTree:
    def __init__(self, order):
        self.root = Node(order)
        self.root.check_leaf = True

    # Insert operation
    def insert(self, value, key):
        value = str(value)
        old_node = self.search(value)
        old_node.insert_at_leaf(old_node, value, key)

        if (len(old_node.values) == old_node.order):
            node1 = Node(old_node.order)
            node1.check_leaf = True
            node1.parent = old_node.parent
            mid = int(math.ceil(old_node.order / 2)) - 1
            node1.values = old_node.values[mid + 1:]
            node1.keys = old_node.keys[mid + 1:]
            node1.nextKey = old_node.nextKey
            old_node.values = old_node.values[:mid + 1]
            old_node.keys = old_node.keys[:mid + 1]
            old_node.nextKey = node1
            self.insert_in_parent(old_node, node1.values[0], node1)

    # Search operation for different operations
    def search(self, value):
        current_node = self.root
        while(current_node.check_leaf == False):
            temp2 = current_node.values
            for i in range(len(temp2)):
                if (value == temp2[i]):
                    current_node = current_node.keys[i + 1]
                    break
                elif (value < temp2[i]):
                    current_node = current_node.keys[i]
                    break
                elif (i + 1 == len(current_node.values)):
                    current_node = current_node.keys[i + 1]
                    break
        return current_node

    # Find the node
    def find(self, value, key):
        l = self.search(value)
        for i, item in enumerate(l.values):
            if item == value:
                if key in l.keys[i]:
                    return True
                else:
                    return False
        return False

    # Inserting at the parent
    def insert_in_parent(self, n, value, ndash):
        if (self.root == n):
            rootNode = Node(n.order)
            rootNode.values = [value]
            rootNode.keys = [n, ndash]
            self.root = rootNode
            n.parent = rootNode
            ndash.parent = rootNode
            return

        parentNode = n.parent
        temp3 = parentNode.keys
        for i in range(len(temp3)):
            if (temp3[i] == n):
                parentNode.values = parentNode.values[:i] + \
                    [value] + parentNode.values[i:]
                parentNode.keys = parentNode.keys[:i +
                    1] + [ndash] + parentNode.keys[i + 1:]
```

```python
            if (len(parentNode.keys) > parentNode.order):
                parentdash = Node(parentNode.order)
                parentdash.parent = parentNode.parent
                mid = int(math.ceil(parentNode.order / 2)) - 1
                parentdash.values = parentNode.values[mid + 1:]
                parentdash.keys = parentNode.keys[mid + 1:]
                value_ = parentNode.values[mid]
                if (mid == 0):
                    parentNode.values = parentNode.values[:mid + 1]
                else:
                    parentNode.values = parentNode.values[:mid]
                parentNode.keys = parentNode.keys[:mid + 1]
                for j in parentNode.keys:
                    j.parent = parentNode
                for j in parentdash.keys:
                    j.parent = parentdash
                self.insert_in_parent(parentNode, value_, parentdash)

    # Delete a node
    def delete(self, value, key):
        node_ = self.search(value)

        temp = 0
        for i, item in enumerate(node_.values):
            if item == value:
                temp = 1

                if key in node_.keys[i]:
                    if len(node_.keys[i]) > 1:
                        node_.keys[i].pop(node_.keys[i].index(key))
                    elif node_ == self.root:
                        node_.values.pop(i)
                        node_.keys.pop(i)
                    else:
                        node_.keys[i].pop(node_.keys[i].index(key))
                        del node_.keys[i]
                        node_.values.pop(node_.values.index(value))
                        self.deleteEntry(node_, value, key)
                else:
                    print("Value not in Key")
                    return
        if temp == 0:
            print("Value not in Tree")
            return

    # Delete an entry
    def deleteEntry(self, node_, value, key):

        if not node_.check_leaf:
            for i, item in enumerate(node_.keys):
                if item == key:
                    node_.keys.pop(i)
                    break
            for i, item in enumerate(node_.values):
                if item == value:
                    node_.values.pop(i)
                    break

        if self.root == node_ and len(node_.keys) == 1:
            self.root = node_.keys[0]
            node_.keys[0].parent = None
            del node_
            return
        elif (len(node_.keys) < int(math.ceil(node_.order / 2)) and node_.check
_leaf == False) or (len(node_.values) < int(math.ceil((node_.order - 1) / 2)) a
nd node_.check_leaf == True):

            is_predecessor = 0
            parentNode = node_.parent
            PrevNode = -1
            NextNode = -1
            PrevK = -1
            PostK = -1
            for i, item in enumerate(parentNode.keys):
```

```python
                if item == node_:
                    if i > 0:
                        PrevNode = parentNode.keys[i - 1]
                        PrevK = parentNode.values[i - 1]

                    if i < len(parentNode.keys) - 1:
                        NextNode = parentNode.keys[i + 1]
                        PostK = parentNode.values[i]

        if PrevNode == -1:
            ndash = NextNode
            value_ = PostK
        elif NextNode == -1:
            is_predecessor = 1
            ndash = PrevNode
            value_ = PrevK
        else:
            if len(node_.values) + len(NextNode.values) < node_.order:
                ndash = NextNode
                value_ = PostK
            else:
                is_predecessor = 1
                ndash = PrevNode
                value_ = PrevK

        if len(node_.values) + len(ndash.values) < node_.order:
            if is_predecessor == 0:
                node_, ndash = ndash, node_
            ndash.keys += node_.keys
            if not node_.check_leaf:
                ndash.values.append(value_)
            else:
                ndash.nextKey = node_.nextKey
            ndash.values += node_.values

            if not ndash.check_leaf:
                for j in ndash.keys:
                    j.parent = ndash

            self.deleteEntry(node_.parent, value_, node_)
            del node_
        else:
            if is_predecessor == 1:
                if not node_.check_leaf:
                    ndashpm = ndash.keys.pop(-1)
                    ndashkm_1 = ndash.values.pop(-1)
                    node_.keys = [ndashpm] + node_.keys
                    node_.values = [value_] + node_.values
                    parentNode = node_.parent
                    for i, item in enumerate(parentNode.values):
                        if item == value_:
                            p.values[i] = ndashkm_1
                            break
                else:
                    ndashpm = ndash.keys.pop(-1)
                    ndashkm = ndash.values.pop(-1)
                    node_.keys = [ndashpm] + node_.keys
                    node_.values = [ndashkm] + node_.values
                    parentNode = node_.parent
                    for i, item in enumerate(p.values):
                        if item == value_:
                            parentNode.values[i] = ndashkm
                            break
            else:
                if not node_.check_leaf:
                    ndashp0 = ndash.keys.pop(0)
                    ndashk0 = ndash.values.pop(0)
                    node_.keys = node_.keys + [ndashp0]
                    node_.values = node_.values + [value_]
                    parentNode = node_.parent
                    for i, item in enumerate(parentNode.values):
                        if item == value_:
                            parentNode.values[i] = ndashk0
```

```python
                        break
                    else:
                        ndashp0 = ndash.keys.pop(0)
                        ndashk0 = ndash.values.pop(0)
                        node_.keys = node_.keys + [ndashp0]
                        node_.values = node_.values + [ndashk0]
                        parentNode = node_.parent
                        for i, item in enumerate(parentNode.values):
                            if item == value_:
                                parentNode.values[i] = ndash.values[0]
                                break

                    if not ndash.check_leaf:
                        for j in ndash.keys:
                            j.parent = ndash
                    if not node_.check_leaf:
                        for j in node_.keys:
                            j.parent = node_
                    if not parentNode.check_leaf:
                        for j in parentNode.keys:
                            j.parent = parentNode


# Print the tree
def printTree(tree):
    lst = [tree.root]
    level = [0]
    leaf = None
    flag = 0
    lev_leaf = 0

    node1 = Node(str(level[0]) + str(tree.root.values))

    while (len(lst) != 0):
        x = lst.pop(0)
        lev = level.pop(0)
        if (x.check_leaf == False):
            for i, item in enumerate(x.keys):
                print(item.values)
        else:
            for i, item in enumerate(x.keys):
                print(item.values)
                if (flag == 0):
                    lev_leaf = lev
                    leaf = x
                    flag = 1


record_len = 3
bplustree = BplusTree(record_len)
bplustree.insert('5', '33')
bplustree.insert('15', '21')
bplustree.insert('25', '31')
bplustree.insert('35', '41')
bplustree.insert('45', '10')

printTree(bplustree)

if(bplustree.find('5', '34')):
    print("Found")
else:
    print("Not found")
```

Output
['15', '25']
['35', '45']
['5']
Not found

Search Complexity

Time Complexity
If linear search is implemented inside a node, then total complexity is $\Theta(\log t\ n)$.

If binary search is used, then total complexity is $\Theta(\log_2 t \cdot \log t\ n)$.

B+ Tree Applications
- Multilevel Indexing
- Faster operations on the tree (insertion, deletion, search)
- Database indexing

Insertion on a B+ Tree
Inserting an element into a B+ tree consists of three main events: searching the appropriate leaf, inserting the element and balancing/splitting the tree.

Insertion Operation
Before inserting an element into a B+ tree, these properties must be kept in mind.
- The root has at least two children.
- Each node except root can have a maximum of m children and at least $m/2$ children.
- Each node can contain a maximum of $m - 1$ keys and a minimum of $\lceil m/2 \rceil - 1$ keys.

The following steps are followed for inserting an element.
1. Since every element is inserted into the leaf node, go to the appropriate leaf node.
2. Insert the key into the leaf node.

Case I
1. If the leaf is not full, insert the key into the leaf node in increasing order.

Case II
1. If the leaf is full, insert the key into the leaf node in increasing order and balance the tree in the following way.

2. Break the node at m/2th position.
3. Add m/2th key to the parent node as well.
4. If the parent node is already full, follow steps 2 to 3.

Insertion Example

Let us understand the insertion operation with the illustrations below. The elements to be inserted are 5,15, 25, 35, 45.

Insert 5.

5

Insert 5

Insert 15.

5 15

Insert 15

Insert 25.

5 15 25 → 5 15 25 (with 15 above) → 15 / 5, 15 25 → 15 / 5 → 15 25

Insert 25

Insert 35.

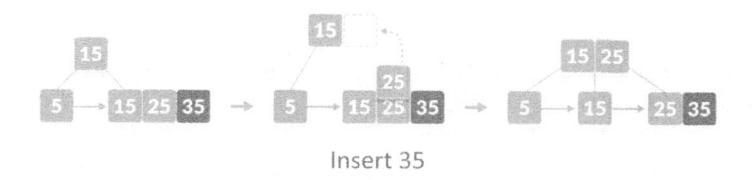

15 / 5 → 15 25 35 → 15 / 5 → 15 25 35 (with 25 promoted) → 15 25 / 5 → 15 → 25 35

Insert 35

Insert 45.

173

Insert 45

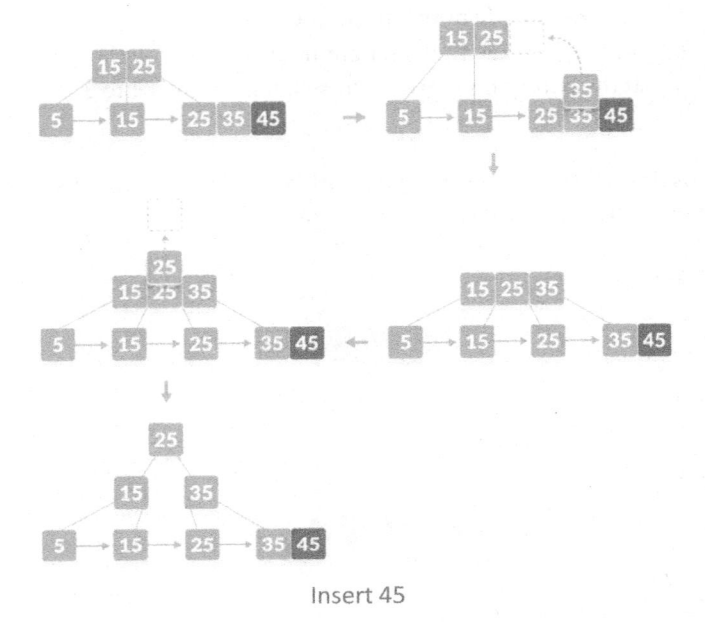

Insertion Complexity
- Time complexity: $\Theta(t.\log_t n)$
- The complexity is dominated by $\Theta(\log_t n)$.

Deletion from a B+ Tree

Deleting an element on a B+ tree consists of three main events: searching the node where the key to be deleted exists, deleting the key and balancing the tree if required. Underflow is a situation when there is less number of keys in a node than the minimum number of keys it should hold.

Deletion Operation
Before going through the steps below, one must know these facts about a B+ tree of degree m.
1. A node can have a maximum of m children. (i.e. 3)
2. A node can contain a maximum of m - 1 keys. (i.e. 2)
3. A node should have a minimum of ⌈m/2⌉ children. (i.e. 2)
4. A node (except root node) should contain a minimum of ⌈m/2⌉ - 1 keys. (i.e. 1)

While deleting a key, we have to take care of the keys present in the internal nodes (i.e. indexes) as well because the values are redundant in a B+ tree. Search the key to be deleted then follow the following steps.

Case I

The key to be deleted is present only at the leaf node not in the indexes (or internal nodes). There are two cases for it:

There is more than the minimum number of keys in the node. Simply delete the key.

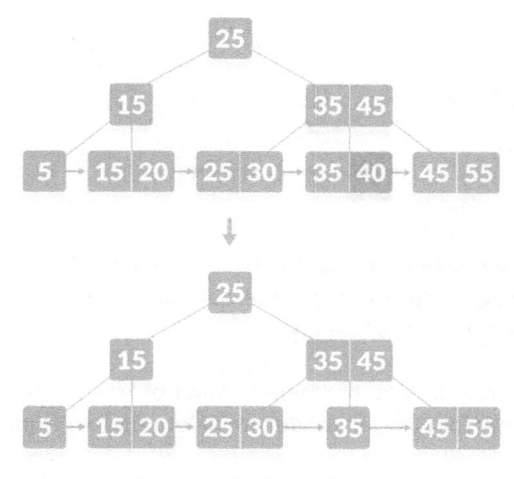

Deleting 40 from B-tree

There is an exact minimum number of keys in the node. Delete the key and borrow a key from the immediate sibling. Add the median key of the sibling node to the parent.

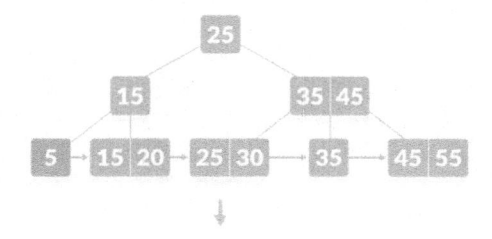

Deleting 5 from B-tree

Case II

The key to be deleted is present in the internal nodes as well. Then we have to remove them from the internal nodes as well. There are the following cases for this situation.

If there is more than the minimum number of keys in the node, simply delete the key from the leaf node and delete the key from the internal node as well.

Fill the empty space in the internal node with the inorder successor.

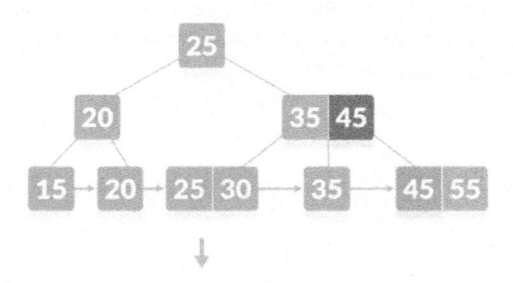

Deleting 45 from B-tree

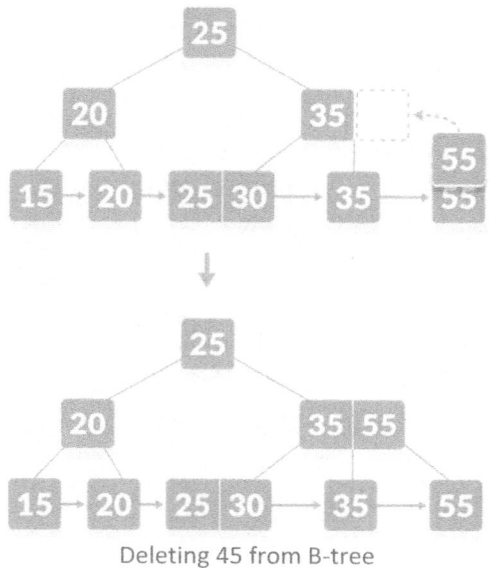

If there is an exact minimum number of keys in the node, then delete the key and borrow a key from its immediate sibling (through the parent).

Fill the empty space created in the index (internal node) with the borrowed key.

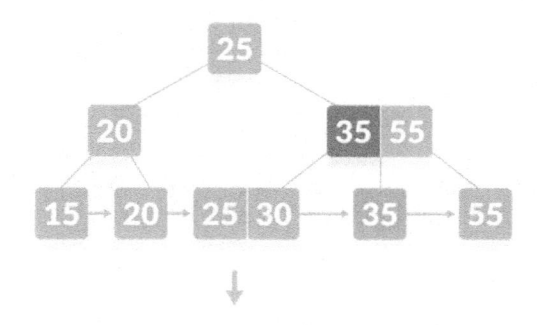

Deleting 35 from B-tree

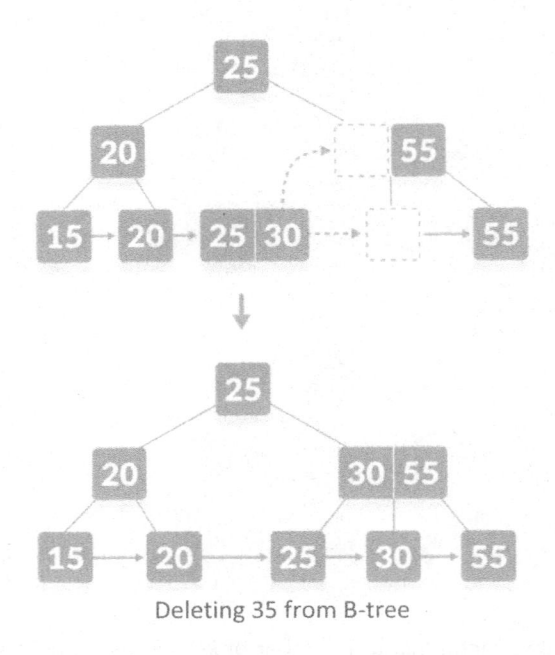

This case is similar to Case II(1) but here, empty space is generated above the immediate parent node.

After deleting the key, merge the empty space with its sibling. Fill the empty space in the grandparent node with the inorder successor.

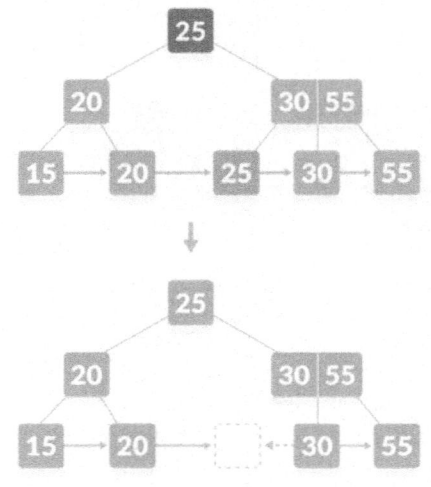

178

Deleting 25 from B-tree

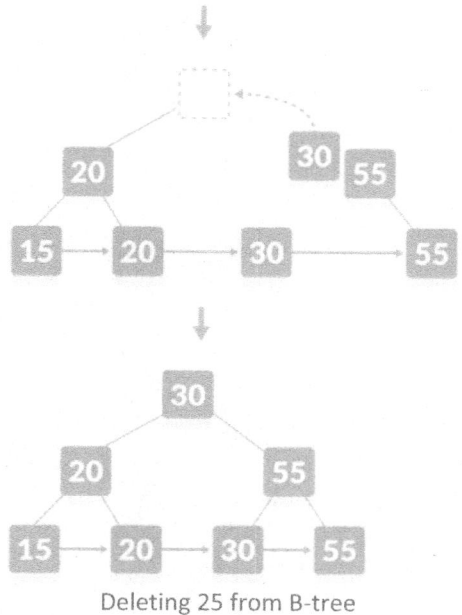

Case III

In this case, the height of the tree gets shrinked. It is a little complicated. Deleting 55 from the tree below leads to this condition. It can be understood in the illustrations below.

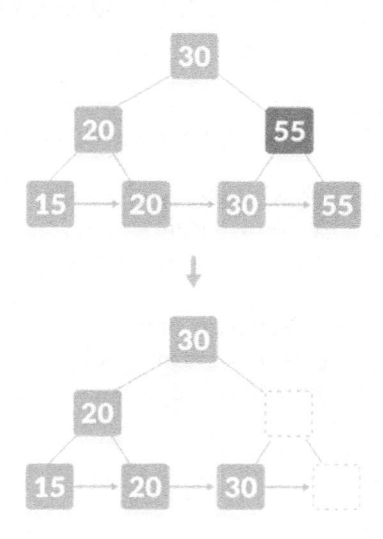

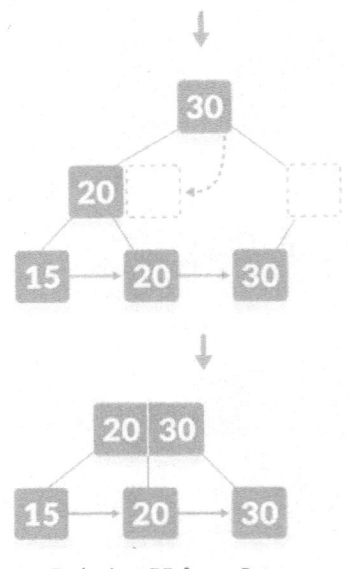

Deleting 55 from B-tree

Red-Black Tree

Red-Black tree is a self-balancing binary search tree in which each node contains an extra bit for denoting the color of the node, either red or black.

A red-black tree satisfies the following properties:
1. Red/Black Property: Every node is colored, either red or black.
2. Root Property: The root is black.
3. Leaf Property: Every leaf (NIL) is black.
4. Red Property: If a red node has children then, the children are always black.
5. Depth Property: For each node, any simple path from this node to any of its descendant leaf has the same black-depth (the number of black nodes).

An example of a red-black tree is:

180

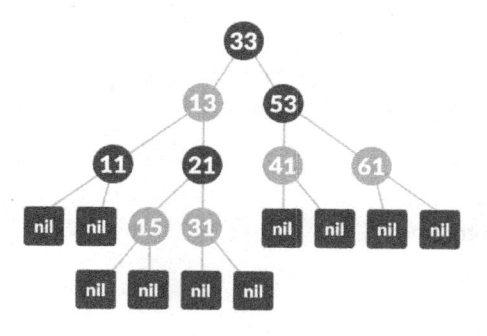

Red Black Tree

Each node has the following attributes:
- color
- key
- leftChild
- rightChild
- parent (except root node)

How the red-black tree maintains the property of self-balancing?
The red-black color is meant for balancing the tree.

The limitations put on the node colors ensure that any simple path from the root to a leaf is not more than twice as long as any other such path. It helps in maintaining the self-balancing property of the red-black tree.

Operations on a Red-Black Tree
Various operations that can be performed on a red-black tree are:

Rotating the subtrees in a Red-Black Tree
In rotation operation, the positions of the nodes of a subtree are interchanged.

Rotation operation is used for maintaining the properties of a red-black tree when they are violated by other operations such as insertion and deletion.

There are two types of rotations:

Left Rotate

In left-rotation, the arrangement of the nodes on the right is transformed into the arrangements on the left node.

Algorithm

Let the initial tree be:

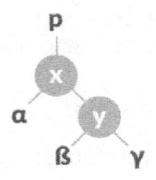

Initial tree

If y has a left subtree, assign x as the parent of the left subtree of y.

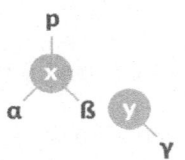

Assign x as the parent of the left subtree of y

If the parent of x is NULL, make y as the root of the tree.

Else if x is the left child of p, make y as the left child of p.
Else assign y as the right child of p.

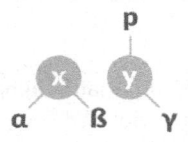

Change the parent of x to that of y

Make y as the parent of x.

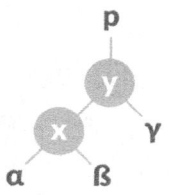

Assign y as the parent of x.

Right Rotate

In right-rotation, the arrangement of the nodes on the left is transformed into the arrangements on the right node.

Let the initial tree be:

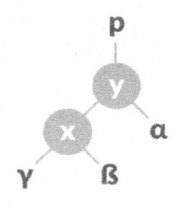

Initial Tree

If x has a right subtree, assign y as the parent of the right subtree of x.

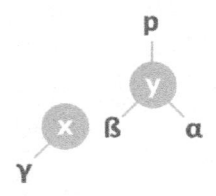

Assign y as the parent of the right subtree of x

If the parent of y is NULL, make x as the root of the tree.

Else if y is the right child of its parent p, make x as the right child of p.

Else assign x as the left child of p.

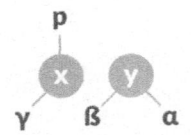

Assign the parent of y as the parent of x

Make x as the parent of y.

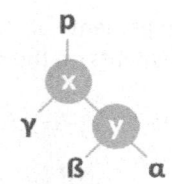

Assign x as the parent of y

Left-Right and Right-Left Rotate
In left-right rotation, the arrangements are first shifted to the left and then to the right.

Do left rotation on x-y.

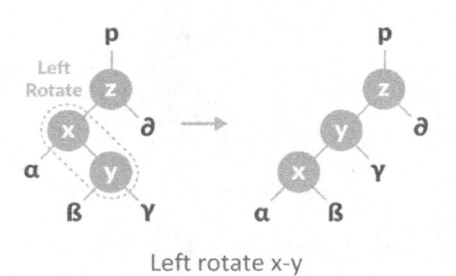

Left rotate x-y

Do right rotation on y-z.

184

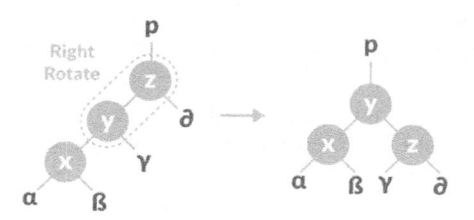

Right rotate z-y

In right-left rotation, the arrangements are first shifted to the right and then to the left.

Do right rotation on x-y.

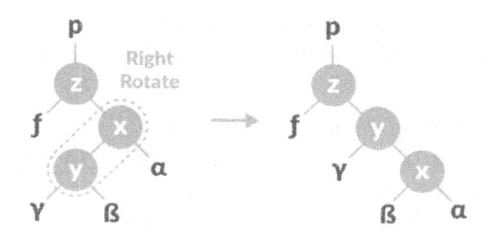

Right rotate x-y

Do left rotation on z-y.

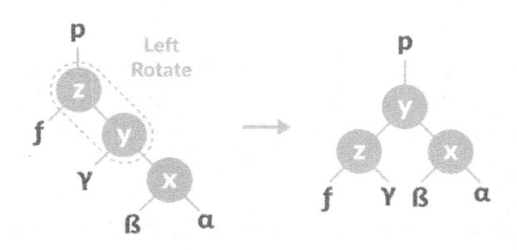

Left rotate z-y

Inserting an element into a Red-Black Tree
While inserting a new node, the new node is always inserted as a RED node. After insertion of a new node, if the tree is violating the properties of the red-black tree then, we do the following operations.

1. Recolor
2. Rotation

Algorithm to insert a node

Following steps are followed for inserting a new element into a red-black tree:
1. Let y be the leaf (ie. NIL) and x be the root of the tree.
2. Check if the tree is empty (ie. whether x is NIL). If yes, insert newNode as a root node and color it black.
3. Else, repeat steps following steps until leaf (NIL) is reached.
   i) Compare newKey with rootKey.
   ii) If newKey is greater than rootKey, traverse through the right subtree.
   iii) Else traverse through the left subtree.
4. Assign the parent of the leaf as a parent of newNode.
5. If leafKey is greater than newKey, make newNode as rightChild.
6. Else, make newNode as leftChild.
7. Assign NULL to the left and rightChild of newNode.
8. Assign RED color to newNode.
9. Call InsertFix-algorithm to maintain the property of red-black tree if violated.

Why newly inserted nodes are always red in a red-black tree?

This is because inserting a red node does not violate the depth property of a red-black tree.

If you attach a red node to a red node, then the rule is violated but it is easier to fix this problem than the problem introduced by violating the depth property.

Algorithm to maintain red-black property after insertion

This algorithm is used for maintaining the property of a red-black tree if the insertion of a newNode violates this property.
1. Do the following until the parent of newNode p is RED.
2. If p is the left child of grandParent gP of z, do the following.

   Case-I:

- If the color of the right child of gP of z is RED, set the color of both the children of gP as BLACK and the color of gP as RED.
- Assign gP to newNode.

Case-II:
- Else if newNode is the right child of p then, assign p to newNode.
- Left-Rotate newNode.

Case-III:
- Set color of p as BLACK and color of gP as RED.
- Right-Rotate gP.

3. Else, do the following.
   - If the color of the left child of gP of z is RED, set the color of both the children of gP as BLACK and the color of gP as RED.
   - Assign gP to newNode.
   - Else if newNode is the left child of p then, assign p to newNode and Right-Rotate newNode.
   - Set color of p as BLACK and color of gP as RED.
   - Left-Rotate gP.

4. Set the root of the tree as BLACK.

Deleting an element from a Red-Black Tree
This operation removes a node from the tree. After deleting a node, the red-black property is maintained again.

Algorithm to delete a node
1. Save the color of nodeToBeDeleted in origrinalColor.
2. If the left child of nodeToBeDeleted is NULL
   - Assign the right child of nodeToBeDeleted to x.
   - Transplant nodeToBeDeleted with x.
3. Else if the right child of nodeToBeDeleted is NULL
   - Assign the left child of nodeToBeDeleted into x.
   - Transplant nodeToBeDeleted with x.
4. Else

- Assign the minimum of right subtree of noteToBeDeleted into y.
- Save the color of y in originalColor.
- Assign the rightChild of y into x.
- If y is a child of nodeToBeDeleted, then set the parent of x as y.
- Else, transplant y with rightChild of y.
- Transplant nodeToBeDeleted with y.
- Set the color of y with originalColor.
5. If the originalColor is BLACK, call DeleteFix(x).

Algorithm to maintain Red-Black property after deletion

This algorithm is implemented when a black node is deleted because it violates the black depth property of the red-black tree.

This violation is corrected by assuming that node x (which is occupying y's original position) has an extra black. This makes node x neither red nor black. It is either doubly black or black-and-red. This violates the red-black properties.

However, the color attribute of x is not changed rather the extra black is represented in x's pointing to the node.

The extra black can be removed if
1. It reaches the root node.
2. If x points to a red-black node. In this case, x is colored black.
3. Suitable rotations and recoloring are performed.

The following algorithm retains the properties of a red-black tree.
1. Do the following until the x is not the root of the tree and the color of x is BLACK
2. If x is the left child of its parent then,
    - Assign w to the sibling of x.
    - If the right child of parent of x is RED,

    Case-I:
    - Set the color of the right child of the parent of x as BLACK.
    - Set the color of the parent of x as RED.

- Left-Rotate the parent of x.
- Assign the rightChild of the parent of x to w.
- If the color of both the right and the leftChild of w is BLACK,

Case-II:
- Set the color of w as RED
- Assign the parent of x to x.
- Else if the color of the rightChild of w is BLACK

Case-III:
- Set the color of the leftChild of w as BLACK
- Set the color of w as RED
- Right-Rotate w.
- Assign the rightChild of the parent of x to w.
- If any of the above cases do not occur, then do the following.

Case-IV:
- Set the color of w as the color of the parent of x.
- Set the color of the parent of x as BLACK.
- Set the color of the right child of w as BLACK.
- Left-Rotate the parent of x.
- Set x as the root of the tree.

3. Else the same as above with right changed to left and vice versa.

4. Set the color of x as BLACK.

```
# Implementing Red-Black Tree in Python

import sys

# Node creation
class Node():
    def __init__(self, item):
        self.item = item
        self.parent = None
        self.left = None
        self.right = None
        self.color = 1

class RedBlackTree():
    def __init__(self):
        self.TNULL = Node(0)
```

```python
        self.TNULL.color = 0
        self.TNULL.left = None
        self.TNULL.right = None
        self.root = self.TNULL

    # Preorder
    def pre_order_helper(self, node):
        if node != TNULL:
            sys.stdout.write(node.item + " ")
            self.pre_order_helper(node.left)
            self.pre_order_helper(node.right)

    # Inorder
    def in_order_helper(self, node):
        if node != TNULL:
            self.in_order_helper(node.left)
            sys.stdout.write(node.item + " ")
            self.in_order_helper(node.right)

    # Postorder
    def post_order_helper(self, node):
        if node != TNULL:
            self.post_order_helper(node.left)
            self.post_order_helper(node.right)
            sys.stdout.write(node.item + " ")

    # Search the tree
    def search_tree_helper(self, node, key):
        if node == TNULL or key == node.item:
            return node

        if key < node.item:
            return self.search_tree_helper(node.left, key)
        return self.search_tree_helper(node.right, key)

    # Balancing the tree after deletion
    def delete_fix(self, x):
        while x != self.root and x.color == 0:
            if x == x.parent.left:
                s = x.parent.right
                if s.color == 1:
                    s.color = 0
                    x.parent.color = 1
                    self.left_rotate(x.parent)
                    s = x.parent.right

                if s.left.color == 0 and s.right.color == 0:
                    s.color = 1
                    x = x.parent
                else:
                    if s.right.color == 0:
                        s.left.color = 0
                        s.color = 1
                        self.right_rotate(s)
```

```python
                    s = x.parent.right

                s.color = x.parent.color
                x.parent.color = 0
                s.right.color = 0
                self.left_rotate(x.parent)
                x = self.root
        else:
            s = x.parent.left
            if s.color == 1:
                s.color = 0
                x.parent.color = 1
                self.right_rotate(x.parent)
                s = x.parent.left

            if s.right.color == 0 and s.right.color ==
0:
                s.color = 1
                x = x.parent
            else:
                if s.left.color == 0:
                    s.right.color = 0
                    s.color = 1
                    self.left_rotate(s)
                    s = x.parent.left

                s.color = x.parent.color
                x.parent.color = 0
                s.left.color = 0
                self.right_rotate(x.parent)
                x = self.root
    x.color = 0

def __rb_transplant(self, u, v):
    if u.parent == None:
        self.root = v
    elif u == u.parent.left:
        u.parent.left = v
    else:
        u.parent.right = v
    v.parent = u.parent

# Node deletion
def delete_node_helper(self, node, key):
    z = self.TNULL
    while node != self.TNULL:
        if node.item == key:
            z = node

        if node.item <= key:
            node = node.right
        else:
            node = node.left

    if z == self.TNULL:
```

```python
            print("Cannot find key in the tree")
            return

    y = z
    y_original_color = y.color
    if z.left == self.TNULL:
        x = z.right
        self.__rb_transplant(z, z.right)
    elif (z.right == self.TNULL):
        x = z.left
        self.__rb_transplant(z, z.left)
    else:
        y = self.minimum(z.right)
        y_original_color = y.color
        x = y.right
        if y.parent == z:
            x.parent = y
        else:
            self.__rb_transplant(y, y.right)
            y.right = z.right
            y.right.parent = y

        self.__rb_transplant(z, y)
        y.left = z.left
        y.left.parent = y
        y.color = z.color
    if y_original_color == 0:
        self.delete_fix(x)

# Balance the tree after insertion
def fix_insert(self, k):
    while k.parent.color == 1:
        if k.parent == k.parent.parent.right:
            u = k.parent.parent.left
            if u.color == 1:
                u.color = 0
                k.parent.color = 0
                k.parent.parent.color = 1
                k = k.parent.parent
            else:
                if k == k.parent.left:
                    k = k.parent
                    self.right_rotate(k)
                k.parent.color = 0
                k.parent.parent.color = 1
                self.left_rotate(k.parent.parent)
        else:
            u = k.parent.parent.right

            if u.color == 1:
                u.color = 0
                k.parent.color = 0
                k.parent.parent.color = 1
                k = k.parent.parent
            else:
```

```python
                    if k == k.parent.right:
                        k = k.parent
                        self.left_rotate(k)
                    k.parent.color = 0
                    k.parent.parent.color = 1
                    self.right_rotate(k.parent.parent)
            if k == self.root:
                break
        self.root.color = 0

    # Printing the tree
    def __print_helper(self, node, indent, last):
        if node != self.TNULL:
            sys.stdout.write(indent)
            if last:
                sys.stdout.write("R----")
                indent += "     "
            else:
                sys.stdout.write("L----")
                indent += "|    "

            s_color = "RED" if node.color == 1 else "BLACK"
            print(str(node.item) + "(" + s_color + ")")
            self.__print_helper(node.left, indent, False)
            self.__print_helper(node.right, indent, True)

    def preorder(self):
        self.pre_order_helper(self.root)

    def inorder(self):
        self.in_order_helper(self.root)

    def postorder(self):
        self.post_order_helper(self.root)

    def searchTree(self, k):
        return self.search_tree_helper(self.root, k)

    def minimum(self, node):
        while node.left != self.TNULL:
            node = node.left
        return node

    def maximum(self, node):
        while node.right != self.TNULL:
            node = node.right
        return node

    def successor(self, x):
        if x.right != self.TNULL:
            return self.minimum(x.right)

        y = x.parent
        while y != self.TNULL and x == y.right:
            x = y
```

```python
            y = y.parent
        return y

    def predecessor(self, x):
        if (x.left != self.TNULL):
            return self.maximum(x.left)

        y = x.parent
        while y != self.TNULL and x == y.left:
            x = y
            y = y.parent

        return y

    def left_rotate(self, x):
        y = x.right
        x.right = y.left
        if y.left != self.TNULL:
            y.left.parent = x

        y.parent = x.parent
        if x.parent == None:
            self.root = y
        elif x == x.parent.left:
            x.parent.left = y
        else:
            x.parent.right = y
        y.left = x
        x.parent = y

    def right_rotate(self, x):
        y = x.left
        x.left = y.right
        if y.right != self.TNULL:
            y.right.parent = x

        y.parent = x.parent
        if x.parent == None:
            self.root = y
        elif x == x.parent.right:
            x.parent.right = y
        else:
            x.parent.left = y
        y.right = x
        x.parent = y

    def insert(self, key):
        node = Node(key)
        node.parent = None
        node.item = key
        node.left = self.TNULL
        node.right = self.TNULL
        node.color = 1

        y = None
```

```python
            x = self.root

        while x != self.TNULL:
            y = x
            if node.item < x.item:
                x = x.left
            else:
                x = x.right

        node.parent = y
        if y == None:
            self.root = node
        elif node.item < y.item:
            y.left = node
        else:
            y.right = node

        if node.parent == None:
            node.color = 0
            return

        if node.parent.parent == None:
            return

        self.fix_insert(node)

    def get_root(self):
        return self.root

    def delete_node(self, item):
        self.delete_node_helper(self.root, item)

    def print_tree(self):
        self.__print_helper(self.root, "", True)


if __name__ == "__main__":
    bst = RedBlackTree()

    bst.insert(55)
    bst.insert(40)
    bst.insert(65)
    bst.insert(60)
    bst.insert(75)
    bst.insert(57)

    bst.print_tree()

    print("\nAfter deleting an element")
    bst.delete_node(40)
    bst.print_tree()
```

Output
R----55(BLACK)

```
        L----40(BLACK)
        R----65(RED)
              L----60(BLACK)
              |     L----57(RED)
              R----75(BLACK)

After deleting an element
R----65(BLACK)
      L----57(RED)
      |     L----55(BLACK)
      |     R----60(BLACK)
      R----75(BLACK)
```

Red-Black Tree Applications
1. To implement finite maps
2. To implement Java packages: java.util.TreeMap and java.util.TreeSet
3. To implement Standard Template Libraries (STL) in C++: multiset, map, multimap
4. In Linux Kernel

Insertion in a Red-Black Tree
Red-Black tree is a self-balancing binary search tree in which each node contains an extra bit for denoting the color of the node, either red or black.

While inserting a new node, the new node is always inserted as a RED node. After insertion of a new node, if the tree is violating the properties of the red-black tree then, we do the following operations.
1. Recolor
2. Rotation

Algorithm to Insert a New Node
Following steps are followed for inserting a new element into a red-black tree:

The newNode be:

New node

196

Let y be the leaf (ie. NIL) and x be the root of the tree. The new node is inserted in the following tree.

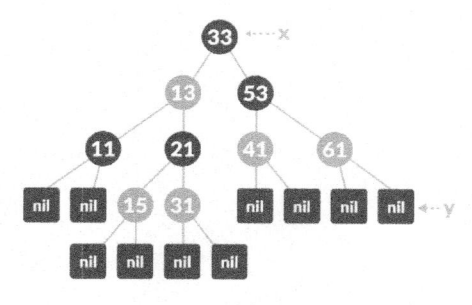

Initial tree

Check if the tree is empty (ie. whether x is NIL). If yes, insert newNode as a root node and color it black.

Else, repeat steps following steps until leaf (NIL) is reached.

- Compare newKey with rootKey.
- If newKey is greater than rootKey, traverse through the right subtree.
- Else traverse through the left subtree.

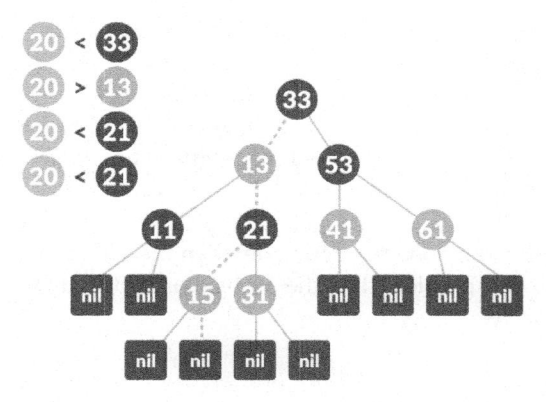

Path leading to the node where newNode is to be inserted

Assign the parent of the leaf as parent of newNode.

If leafKey is greater than newKey, make newNode as rightChild.

Else, make newNode as leftChild.

```
    15
     \
      20
```

New node inserted

Assign NULL to the left and rightChild of newNode.

Assign RED color to newNode.

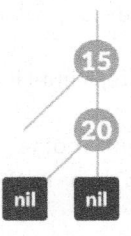

```
    15
     \
      20
     /  \
   nil  nil
```

Set the color of the newNode red and assign null to the children

Call InsertFix-algorithm to maintain the property of red-black tree if violated.

Why newly inserted nodes are always red in a red-black tree?
This is because inserting a red node does not violate the depth property of a red-black tree.

If you attach a red node to a red node, then the rule is violated but it is easier to fix this problem than the problem introduced by violating the depth property.

Algorithm to Maintain Red-Black Property After Insertion
This algorithm is used for maintaining the property of a red-black tree if insertion of a newNode violates this property.

1. Do the following until the parent of newNode p is RED.
2. If p is the left child of grandParent gP of newNode, do the following.

   Case-I:
   - If the color of the right child of gP of newNode is RED, set the color of both the children of gP as BLACK and the color of gP as RED.

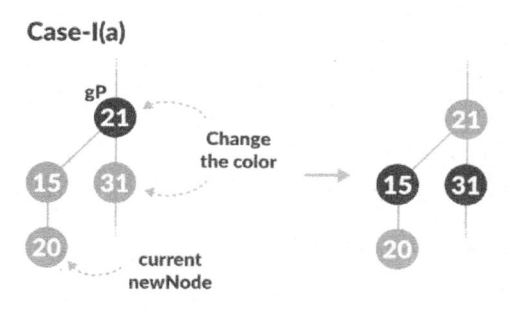

   Case-I(a)

   Color change

   - Assign gP to newNode.

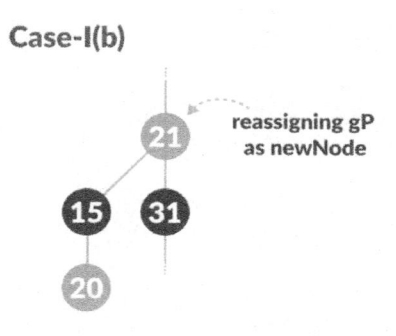

   Case-I(b)

   Reassigning newNode

   Case-II:
   - (Before moving on to this step, while loop is checked. If conditions are not satisfied, it the loop is broken.)

Else if newNode is the right child of p then, assign p to newNode.

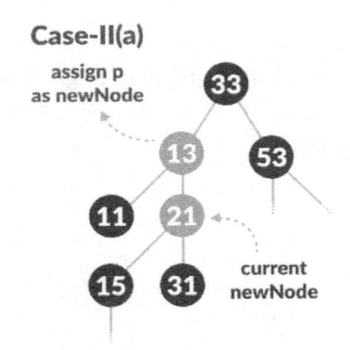

Case-II(a)

Assigning parent of newNode as newNode

Left-Rotate newNode.

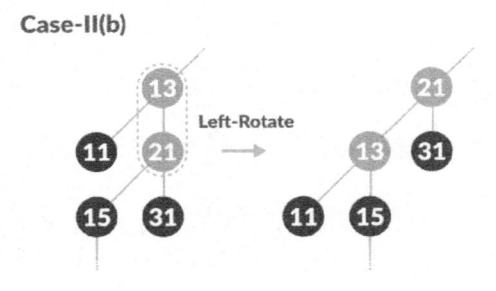

Case-II(b)

Left Rotate

Case-III:
- (Before moving on to this step, while loop is checked. If conditions are not satisfied, it the loop is broken.)

    Set color of p as BLACK and color of gP as RED.

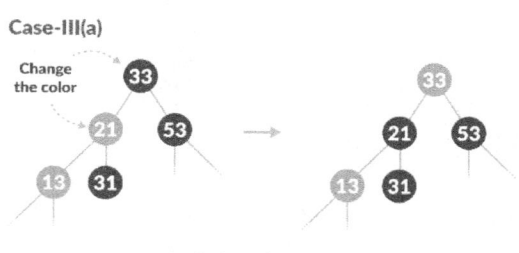

Case-III(a)

Color change

Right-Rotate gP.

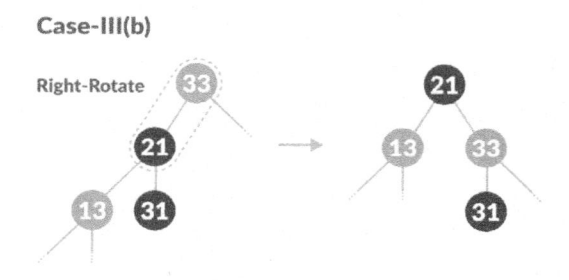

Case-III(b)

Right Rotate

3. Else, do the following.
    - If the color of the left child of gP of z is RED, set the color of both the children of gP as BLACK and the color of gP as RED.
    - Assign gP to newNode.
    - Else if newNode is the left child of p then, assign p to newNode and Right-Rotate newNode.
    - Set color of p as BLACK and color of gP as RED.
    - Left-Rotate gP.

4. (This step is performed after coming out of the while loop.)

    Set the root of the tree as BLACK.

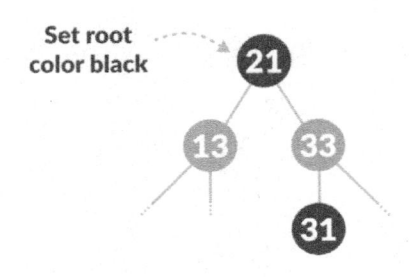

Set root's color black

The final tree look like this:

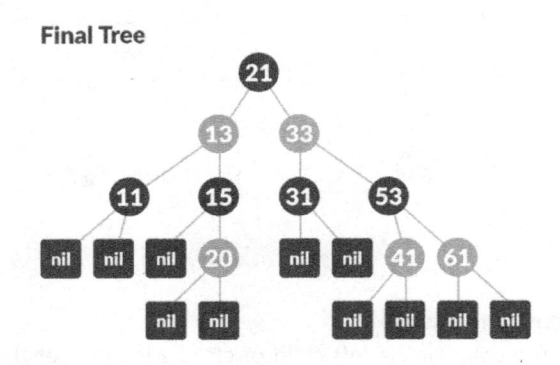

Final Tree

Final tree

Deletion From a Red-Black Tree

Red-Black tree is a self-balancing binary search tree in which each node contains an extra bit for denoting the color of the node, either red or black.

Deleting a node may or may not disrupt the red-black properties of a red-black tree. If this action violates the red-black properties, then a fixing algorithm is used to regain the red-black properties.

Deleting an element from a Red-Black Tree

This operation removes a node from the tree. After deleting a node, the red-black property is maintained again.

1. Let the nodeToBeDeleted be:

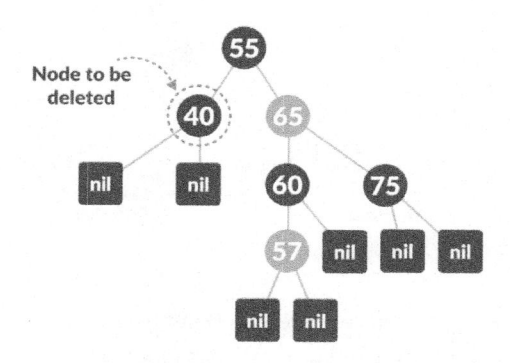

Node to be deleted

2. Save the color of nodeToBeDeleted in origrinalColor.

originalColor = Black

Saving original color

3. If the left child of nodeToBeDeleted is NULL

- Assign the right child of nodeToBeDeleted to x.

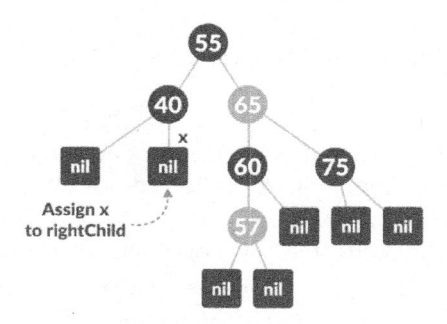

Assign x to the rightChild

- Transplant nodeToBeDeleted with x.

203

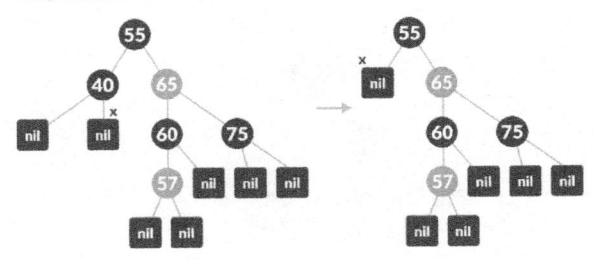

Transplant nodeToBeDeleted with x

4. Else if the right child of nodeToBeDeleted is NULL
   - Assign the left child of nodeToBeDeleted into x.
   - Transplant nodeToBeDeleted with x.

5. Else
   - Assign the minimum of right subtree of noteToBeDeleted into y.
   - Save the color of y in originalColor.
   - Assign the rightChild of y into x.
   - If y is a child of nodeToBeDeleted, then set the parent of x as y.
   - Else, transplant y with rightChild of y.
   - Transplant nodeToBeDeleted with y.
   - Set the color of y with originalColor.

6. If the originalColor is BLACK, call DeleteFix(x).

Algorithm to maintain Red-Black property after deletion
This algorithm is implemented when a black node is deleted because it violates the black depth property of the red-black tree.

This violation is corrected by assuming that node x (which is occupying y's original position) has an extra black. This makes node x neither red nor black. It is either doubly black or black-and-red. This violates the red-black properties.

However, the color attribute of x is not changed rather the extra black is represented in x's pointing to the node.

The extra black can be removed if
1. It reaches the root node.
2. If x points to a red-black node. In this case, x is colored black.
3. Suitable rotations and recolorings are performed.

Following algorithm retains the properties of a red-black tree.
1. Do the following until the x is not the root of the tree and the color of x is BLACK
2. If x is the left child of its parent then,

    - Assign w to the sibling of x.

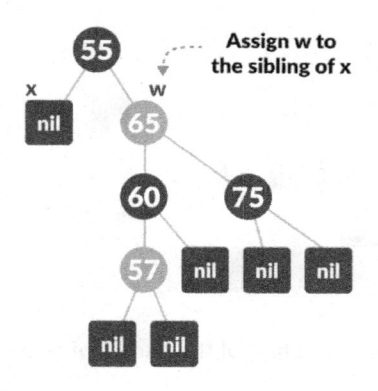

Assigning w

- If the sibling of x is RED,

Case-I:
- Set the color of the right child of the parent of x as BLACK.
- Set the color of the parent of x as RED.

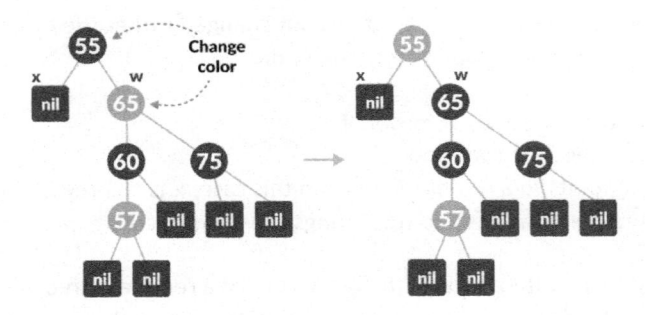

Color change

- Left-Rotate the parent of x.

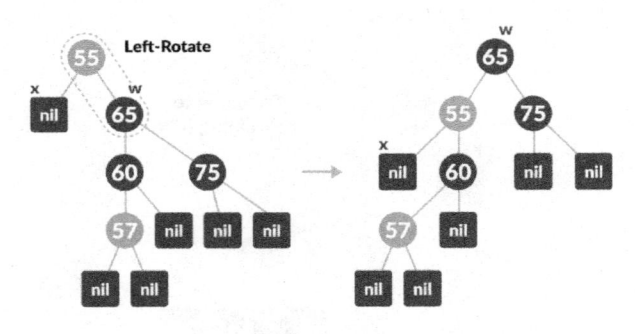

Left-rotate

- Assign the rightChild of the parent of x to w.

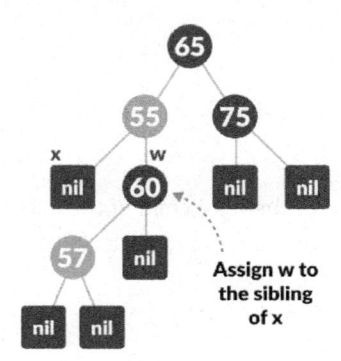

Reassign w

206

- If the color of both the right and the leftChild of w is BLACK,

Case-II:
  - Set the color of w as RED
  - Assign the parent of x to x.

- Else if the color of the rightChild of w is BLACK

Case-III:
  - Set the color of the leftChild of w as BLACK
  - Set the color of w as RED

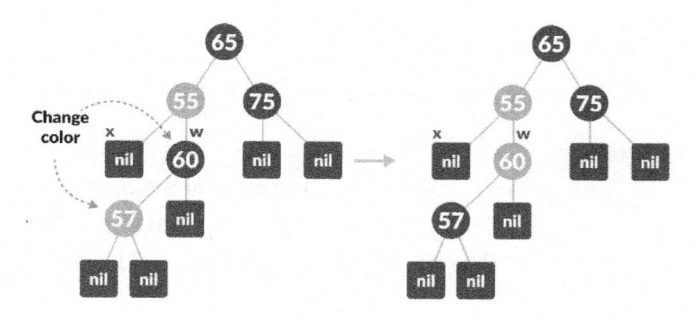

Color change

Right-Rotate w.

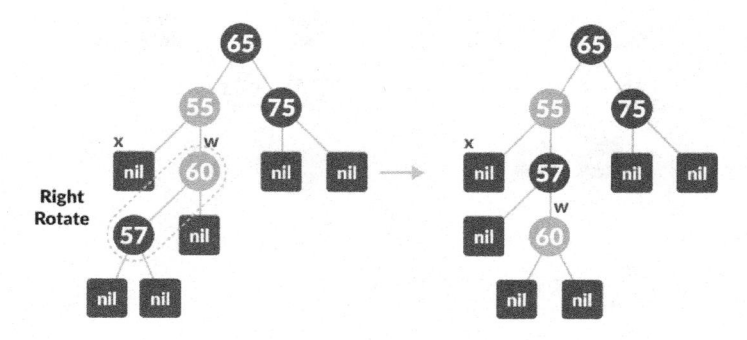

Right rotate

- Assign the rightChild of the parent of x to w.

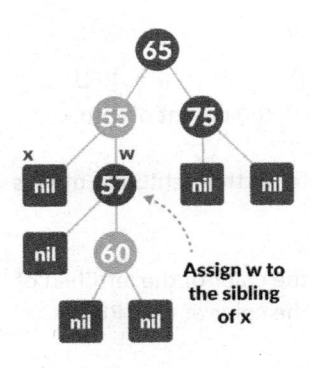

Reassign w

- If any of the above cases do not occur, then do the following.

Case-IV:
- Set the color of w as the color of the parent of x.
- Set the color of the parent of parent of x as BLACK.
- Set the color of the right child of w as BLACK.

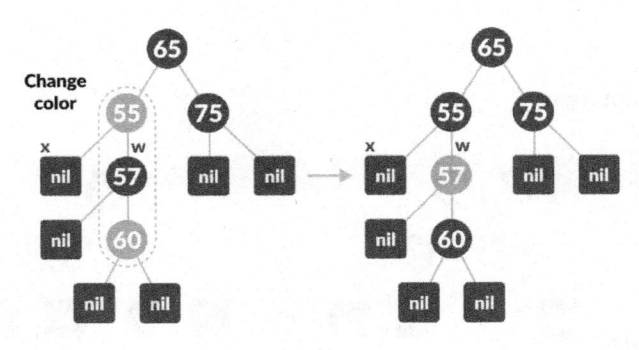

Color change

- Left-Rotate the parent of x.

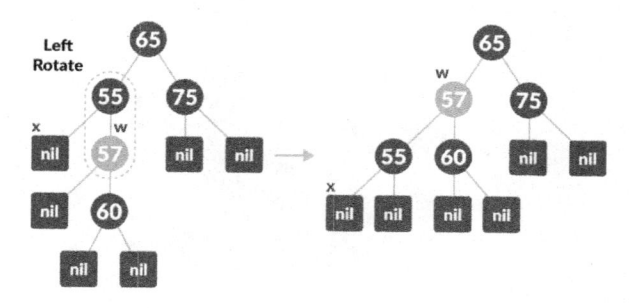

Left-rotate

- Set x as the root of the tree.

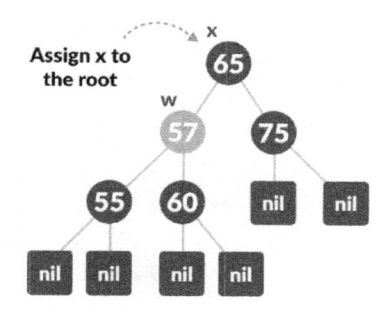

Set x as root

3. Else same as above with right changed to left and vice versa.

4. Set the color of x as BLACK.

The workflow of the above cases can be understood with the help of the flowchart below.

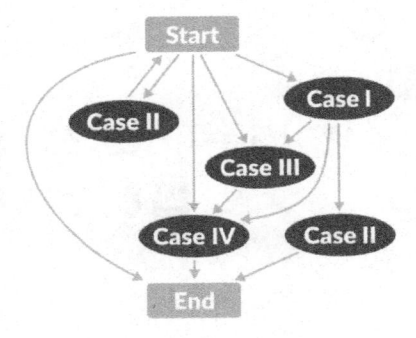

Flowchart for deletion operation

Graph

A graph data structure is a collection of nodes that have data and are connected to other nodes.

Let's try to understand this through an example. On facebook, everything is a node. That includes User, Photo, Album, Event, Group, Page, Comment, Story, Video, Link, Note...anything that has data is a node.

Every relationship is an edge from one node to another. Whether you post a photo, join a group, like a page, etc., a new edge is created for that relationship.

Example of graph data structure

All of facebook is then a collection of these nodes and edges. This is because facebook uses a graph data structure to store its data.

More precisely, a graph is a data structure (V, E) that consists of
- A collection of vertices V
- A collection of edges E, represented as ordered pairs of vertices (u,v)

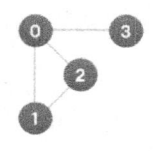

Vertices and edges

In the graph,
V = {0, 1, 2, 3}
E = {(0,1), (0,2), (0,3), (1,2)}
G = {V, E}

Graph Terminology
- Adjacency: A vertex is said to be adjacent to another vertex if there is an edge connecting them. Vertices 2 and 3 are not adjacent because there is no edge between them.
- Path: A sequence of edges that allows you to go from vertex A to vertex B is called a path. 0-1, 1-2 and 0-2 are paths from vertex 0 to vertex 2.
- Directed Graph: A graph in which an edge (u,v) doesn't necessarily mean that there is an edge (v, u) as well. The edges in such a graph are represented by arrows to show the direction of the edge.

Graph Representation
Graphs are commonly represented in two ways:

1. Adjacency Matrix
An adjacency matrix is a 2D array of V x V vertices. Each row and column represent a vertex.

If the value of any element a[i][j] is 1, it represents that there is an edge connecting vertex i and vertex j.

The adjacency matrix for the graph we created above is

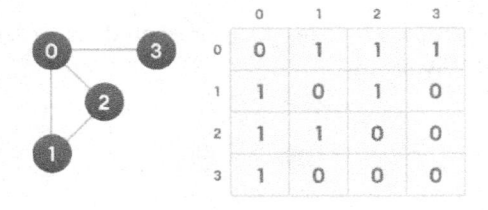

	0	1	2	3
0	0	1	1	1
1	1	0	1	0
2	1	1	0	0
3	1	0	0	0

Graph adjacency matrix

Since it is an undirected graph, for edge (0,2), we also need to mark edge (2,0); making the adjacency matrix symmetric about the diagonal.

Edge lookup(checking if an edge exists between vertex A and vertex B) is extremely fast in adjacency matrix representation but we have to reserve space for every possible link between all vertices(V x V), so it requires more space.

2. Adjacency List
An adjacency list represents a graph as an array of linked lists.

The index of the array represents a vertex and each element in its linked list represents the other vertices that form an edge with the vertex.

The adjacency list for the graph we made in the first example is as follows:

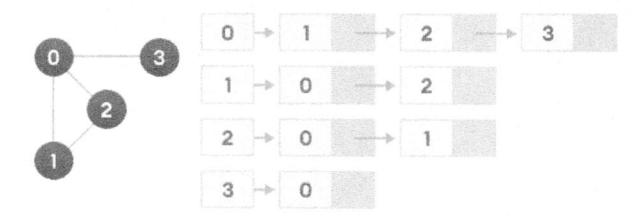

Adjacency list representation

An adjacency list is efficient in terms of storage because we only need to store the values for the edges. For a graph with millions of vertices, this can mean a lot of saved space.

Graph Operations
The most common graph operations are:
- Check if the element is present in the graph
- Graph Traversal
- Add elements(vertex, edges) to graph
- Finding the path from one vertex to another

Spanning Tree

An undirected graph is a graph in which the edges do not point in any direction (ie. the edges are bidirectional).

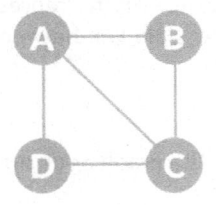

Undirected Graph

A connected graph is a graph in which there is always a path from a vertex to any other vertex.

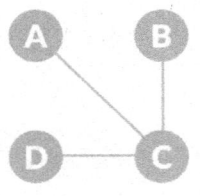

Connected Graph

Spanning tree
A spanning tree is a sub-graph of an undirected connected graph, which includes all the vertices of the graph with a minimum possible number of edges. If a vertex is missed, then it is not a spanning tree.

The edges may or may not have weights assigned to them.

The total number of spanning trees with n vertices that can be created from a complete graph is equal to $n^{(n-2)}$.

If we have $n = 4$, the maximum number of possible spanning trees is equal to $4^{4-2} = 16$. Thus, 16 spanning trees can be formed from a complete graph with 4 vertices.

Example of a Spanning Tree

Let's understand the spanning tree with examples below:

Let the original graph be:

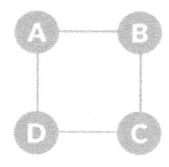

Normal graph

Some of the possible spanning trees that can be created from the above graph are:

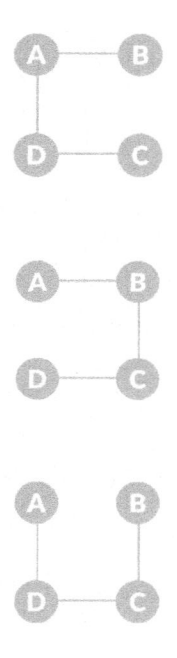

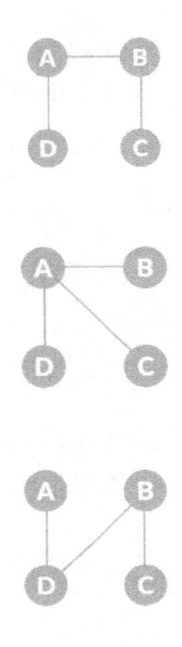

Minimum Spanning Tree
A minimum spanning tree is a spanning tree in which the sum of the weight of the edges is as minimum as possible.

Example of a Spanning Tree
Let's understand the above definition with the help of the example below.

The initial graph is:

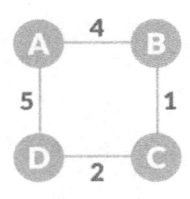

Weighted graph

The possible spanning trees from the above graph are:

216

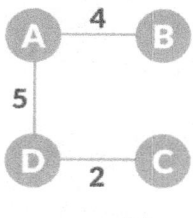

sum = 11

Minimum spanning tree – 1

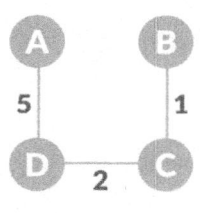

sum = 8

Minimum spanning tree – 2

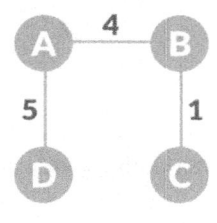

sum = 10

Minimum spanning tree – 3

```
    A —4— B
           |
           1
    D —2— C
      sum = 7
```

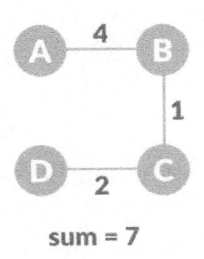

Minimum spanning tree – 4

The minimum spanning tree from the above spanning trees is:

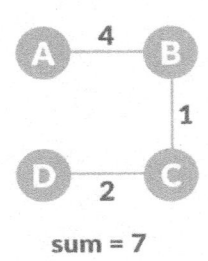

```
    A —4— B
           |
           1
    D —2— C
      sum = 7
```

Minimum spanning tree

The minimum spanning tree from a graph is found using the following algorithms:
1. Prim's Algorithm
2. Kruskal's Algorithm

Spanning Tree Applications
- Computer Network Routing Protocol
- Cluster Analysis
- Civil Network Planning

Minimum Spanning tree Applications
- To find paths in the map
- To design networks like telecommunication networks, water supply networks, and electrical grids.

Strongly Connected Components

A strongly connected component is the portion of a directed graph in which there is a path from each vertex to another vertex. It is applicable only on a directed graph.

For example:
Let us take the graph below.

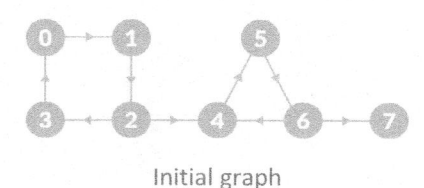

Initial graph

The strongly connected components of the above graph are:

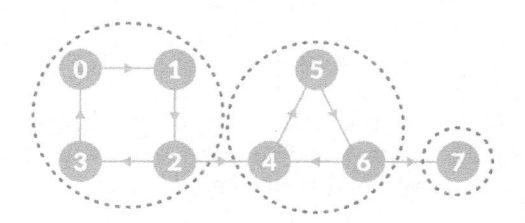

Strongly connected components

You can observe that in the first strongly connected component, every vertex can reach the other vertex through the directed path.

These components can be found using Kosaraju's Algorithm.

Kosaraju's Algorithm
Kosaraju's Algorithm is based on the depth-first search algorithm implemented twice.

Three steps are involved.

1. Perform a depth first search on the whole graph.

Let us start from vertex-0, visit all of its child vertices, and mark the visited vertices as done. If a vertex leads to an already visited vertex, then push this vertex to the stack.

For example: Starting from vertex-0, go to vertex-1, vertex-2, and then to vertex-3. Vertex-3 leads to already visited vertex-0, so push the source vertex (ie. vertex-3) into the stack.

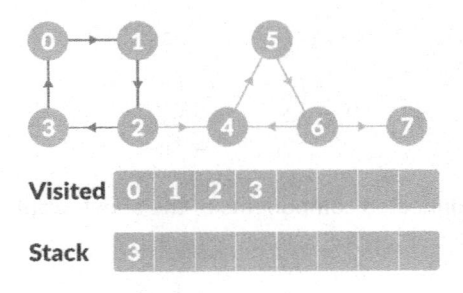

DFS on the graph

Go to the previous vertex (vertex-2) and visit its child vertices i.e. vertex-4, vertex-5, vertex-6 and vertex-7 sequentially. Since there is nowhere to go from vertex-7, push it into the stack.

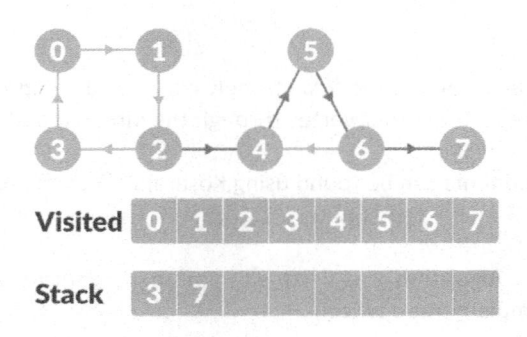

DFS on the graph

Go to the previous vertex (vertex-6) and visit its child vertices. But, all of its child vertices are visited, so push it into the stack.

Visited	0	1	2	3	4	5	6	7
Stack	3	7	6					

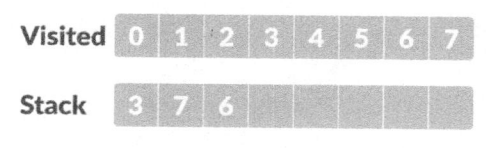

Stacking

Similarly, a final stack is created.

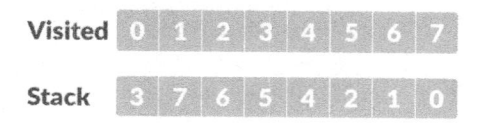

Visited	0	1	2	3	4	5	6	7
Stack	3	7	6	5	4	2	1	0

Final Stack

2. Reverse the original graph.

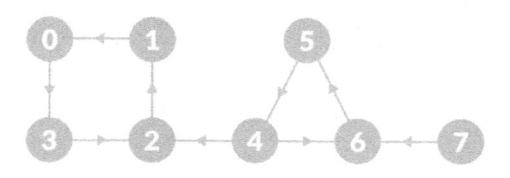

DFS on reversed graph

3. Perform depth-first search on the reversed graph.

Start from the top vertex of the stack. Traverse through all of its child vertices. Once the already visited vertex is reached, one strongly connected component is formed.

For example: Pop vertex-0 from the stack. Starting from vertex-0, traverse through its child vertices (vertex-0, vertex-1, vertex-2, vertex-3 in sequence) and mark them as visited. The child of vertex-3 is already visited, so these visited vertices form one strongly connected component.

221

Visited	0	1	2	3				
Stack	3	7	6	5	4	2	1	
SCC	0	1	2	3				

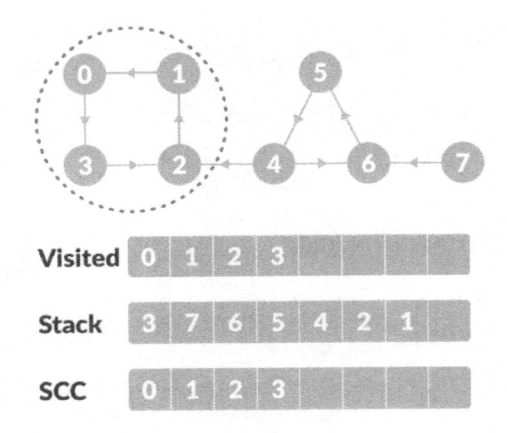

Start from the top and traverse through all the vertices

Go to the stack and pop the top vertex if already visited. Otherwise, choose the top vertex from the stack and traverse through its child vertices as presented above.

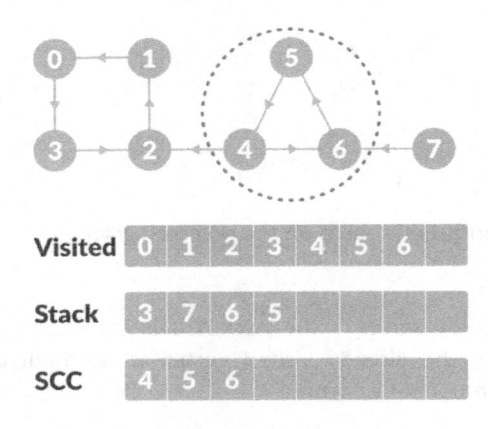

Visited	0	1	2	3	4	5	6	
Stack	3	7	6	5				
SCC	4	5	6					

Pop the top vertex if already visited

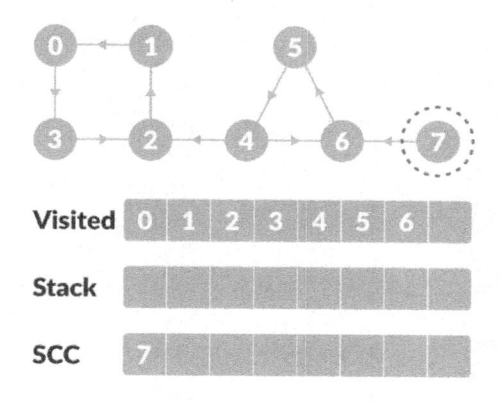

Strongly connected component

Thus, the strongly connected components are:

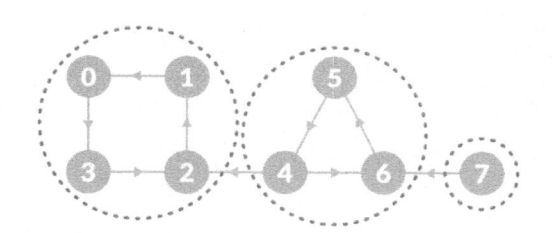

All strongly connected components

```
# Kosaraju's algorithm to find strongly connected component
s in Python

from collections import defaultdict

class Graph:

    def __init__(self, vertex):
        self.V = vertex
        self.graph = defaultdict(list)

    # Add edge into the graph
    def add_edge(self, s, d):
        self.graph[s].append(d)

    # dfs
    def dfs(self, d, visited_vertex):
        visited_vertex[d] = True
        print(d, end='')
```

223

```python
            for i in self.graph[d]:
                if not visited_vertex[i]:
                    self.dfs(i, visited_vertex)

    def fill_order(self, d, visited_vertex, stack):
        visited_vertex[d] = True
        for i in self.graph[d]:
            if not visited_vertex[i]:
                self.fill_order(i, visited_vertex, stack)
        stack = stack.append(d)

    # transpose the matrix
    def transpose(self):
        g = Graph(self.V)

        for i in self.graph:
            for j in self.graph[i]:
                g.add_edge(j, i)
        return g

    # Print stongly connected components
    def print_scc(self):
        stack = []
        visited_vertex = [False] * (self.V)

        for i in range(self.V):
            if not visited_vertex[i]:
                self.fill_order(i, visited_vertex, stack)

        gr = self.transpose()

        visited_vertex = [False] * (self.V)

        while stack:
            i = stack.pop()
            if not visited_vertex[i]:
                gr.dfs(i, visited_vertex)
                print("")

g = Graph(8)
g.add_edge(0, 1)
g.add_edge(1, 2)
g.add_edge(2, 3)
g.add_edge(2, 4)
g.add_edge(3, 0)
g.add_edge(4, 5)
g.add_edge(5, 6)
g.add_edge(6, 4)
g.add_edge(6, 7)

print("Strongly Connected Components:")
g.print_scc()
```

Output
```
Strongly Connected Components:
0 3 2 1
4 6 5
7
```

Kosaraju's Algorithm Complexity
Kosaraju's algorithm runs in linear time i.e. O(V+E).

Strongly Connected Components Applications
- Vehicle routing applications
- Maps
- Model-checking in formal verification

Adjacency Matrix

An adjacency matrix is a way of representing a graph G = {V, E} as a matrix of booleans.

Adjacency matrix representation
The size of the matrix is VxV where V is the number of vertices in the graph and the value of an entry A_{ij} is either 1 or 0 depending on whether there is an edge from vertex i to vertex j.

Adjacency Matrix Example
The image below shows a graph and its equivalent adjacency matrix.

	0	1	2	3
0	0	1	1	1
1	1	0	1	0
2	1	1	0	0
3	1	0	0	0

Adjacency matrix from a graph

In case of undirected graphs, the matrix is symmetric about the diagonal because of every edge (i,j), there is also an edge (j,i).

Pros of adjacency matrix

The basic operations like adding an edge, removing an edge and checking whether there is an edge from vertex i to vertex j are extremely time efficient, constant time operations.

If the graph is dense and the number of edges is large, adjacency matrix should be the first choice. Even if the graph and the adjacency matrix is sparse, we can represent it using data structures for sparse matrices.

The biggest advantage however, comes from the use of matrices. The recent advances in hardware enable us to perform even expensive matrix operations on the GPU.

By performing operations on the adjacent matrix, we can get important insights into the nature of the graph and the relationship between its vertices.

Cons of adjacency matrix

The VxV space requirement of the adjacency matrix makes it a memory hog. Graphs out in the wild usually don't have too many connections and this is the major reason why adjacency lists are the better choice for most tasks.

While basic operations are easy, operations like inEdges and outEdges are expensive when using the adjacency matrix representation.

```python
# Adjacency Matrix representation in Python

class Graph(object):

    # Initialize the matrix
    def __init__(self, size):
        self.adjMatrix = []
        for i in range(size):
            self.adjMatrix.append([0 for i in range(size)])
        self.size = size

    # Add edges
    def add_edge(self, v1, v2):
        if v1 == v2:
```

```python
            print("Same vertex %d and %d" % (v1, v2))
        self.adjMatrix[v1][v2] = 1
        self.adjMatrix[v2][v1] = 1

    # Remove edges
    def remove_edge(self, v1, v2):
        if self.adjMatrix[v1][v2] == 0:
            print("No edge between %d and %d" % (v1, v2))
            return
        self.adjMatrix[v1][v2] = 0
        self.adjMatrix[v2][v1] = 0

    def __len__(self):
        return self.size

    # Print the matrix
    def print_matrix(self):
        for row in self.adjMatrix:
            for val in row:
                print('{:4}'.format(val)),
            print

def main():
    g = Graph(5)
    g.add_edge(0, 1)
    g.add_edge(0, 2)
    g.add_edge(1, 2)
    g.add_edge(2, 0)
    g.add_edge(2, 3)

    g.print_matrix()


if __name__ == '__main__':
    main()
```

Output
```
   0
   1
   1
   0
   0
   1
   0
   1
   0
   0
   1
   1
   0
   1
   0
   0
   0
```

1
0
0
0
0
0
0
0

Adjacency Matrix Applications
1. Creating routing table in networks
2. Navigation tasks

Adjacency List

An adjacency list represents a graph as an array of linked lists. The index of the array represents a vertex and each element in its linked list represents the other vertices that form an edge with the vertex.

Adjacency List representation
A graph and its equivalent adjacency list representation are shown below.

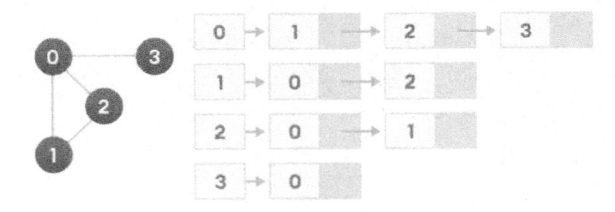

Adjacency List representation

An adjacency list is efficient in terms of storage because we only need to store the values for the edges. For a sparse graph with millions of vertices and edges, this can mean a lot of saved space.

Adjacency List Structure
The simplest adjacency list needs a node data structure to store a vertex and a graph data structure to organize the nodes.

We stay close to the basic definition of a graph - a collection of vertices and edges {V, E}. For simplicity, we use an unlabeled graph as opposed to a labeled one i.e. the vertices are identified by their indices 0,1,2,3.

Let's dig into the data structures at play here.

```
struct node
{
    int vertex;
    struct node* next;
};

struct Graph
{
    int numVertices;
    struct node** adjLists;
};
```

Don't let the struct node** adjLists overwhelm you.

All we are saying is we want to store a pointer to struct node*. This is because we don't know how many vertices the graph will have and so we cannot create an array of Linked Lists at compile time.

Adjacency List Python

There is a reason Python gets so much love. A simple dictionary of vertices and its edges is a sufficient representation of a graph. You can make the vertex itself as complex as you want.

```
graph = {'A': set(['B', 'C']),
        'B': set(['A', 'D', 'E']),
        'C': set(['A', 'F']),
        'D': set(['B']),
        'E': set(['B', 'F']),
        'F': set(['C', 'E'])}
```

```python
# Adjacency List representation in Python
class AdjNode:
    def __init__(self, value):
```

```python
            self.vertex = value
            self.next = None

class Graph:
    def __init__(self, num):
        self.V = num
        self.graph = [None] * self.V

    # Add edges
    def add_edge(self, s, d):
        node = AdjNode(d)
        node.next = self.graph[s]
        self.graph[s] = node

        node = AdjNode(s)
        node.next = self.graph[d]
        self.graph[d] = node

    # Print the graph
    def print_agraph(self):
        for i in range(self.V):
            print("Vertex " + str(i) + ":", end="")
            temp = self.graph[i]
            while temp:
                print(" -> {}".format(temp.vertex), end="")
                temp = temp.next
            print(" \n")

if __name__ == "__main__":
    V = 5

    # Create graph and edges
    graph = Graph(V)
    graph.add_edge(0, 1)
    graph.add_edge(0, 2)
    graph.add_edge(0, 3)
    graph.add_edge(1, 2)

    graph.print_agraph()
```

Output
Vertex 0: -> 3 -> 2 -> 1

Vertex 1: -> 2 -> 0

Vertex 2: -> 1 -> 0

Vertex 3: -> 0

Vertex 4:

Depth First Search

Traversal means visiting all the nodes of a graph. Depth first traversal or Depth first Search is a recursive algorithm for searching all the vertices of a graph or tree data structure.

DFS algorithm
A standard DFS implementation puts each vertex of the graph into one of two categories:
1. Visited
2. Not Visited

The purpose of the algorithm is to mark each vertex as visited while avoiding cycles.

The DFS algorithm works as follows:
1. Start by putting any one of the graph's vertices on top of a stack.
2. Take the top item of the stack and add it to the visited list.
3. Create a list of that vertex's adjacent nodes. Add the ones which aren't in the visited list to the top of the stack.
4. Keep repeating steps 2 and 3 until the stack is empty.

DFS example
Let's see how the Depth First Search algorithm works with an example. We use an undirected graph with 5 vertices.

Undirected graph with 5 vertices

We start from vertex 0, the DFS algorithm starts by putting it in the Visited list and putting all its adjacent vertices in the stack.

Visit the element and put it in the visited list

Next, we visit the element at the top of stack i.e. 1 and go to its adjacent nodes. Since 0 has already been visited, we visit 2 instead.

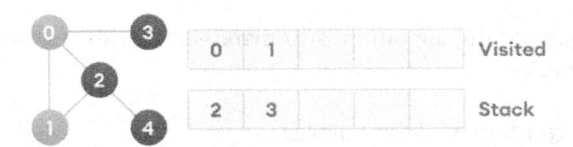

Visit the element at the top of stack

Vertex 2 has an unvisited adjacent vertex in 4, so we add that to the top of the stack and visit it.

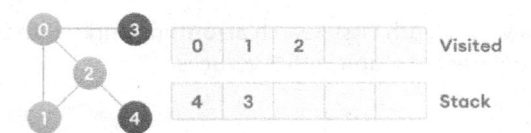

Vertex 2 has an unvisited adjacent vertex in 4, so we add that to the top of the stack and visit it.

Vertex 2 has an unvisited adjacent vertex in 4, so we add that to the top of the stack and visit it.

After we visit the last element 3, it doesn't have any unvisited adjacent nodes, so we have completed the Depth First Traversal of the graph.

| 0 | 1 | 2 | 4 | 3 | Visited |

| | | | | | Stack |

After we visit the last element 3, it doesn't have any unvisited adjacent nodes, so we have completed the Depth First Traversal of the graph.

DFS pseudocode (recursive implementation)
The pseudocode for DFS is shown below. In the init() function, notice that we run the DFS function on every node. This is because the graph might have two different disconnected parts so to make sure that we cover every vertex, we can also run the DFS algorithm on every node.

```
DFS(G, u)
    u.visited = true
    for each v ∈ G.Adj[u]
        if v.visited == false
            DFS(G,v)

init() {
    For each u ∈ G
        u.visited = false
    For each u ∈ G
        DFS(G, u)
}
```

```python
# DFS algorithm in Python

def dfs(graph, start, visited=None):
    if visited is None:
        visited = set()
    visited.add(start)

    print(start)

    for next in graph[start] - visited:
        dfs(graph, next, visited)
    return visited
```

```
graph = {'0': set(['1', '2']),
         '1': set(['0', '3', '4']),
         '2': set(['0']),
         '3': set(['1']),
         '4': set(['2', '3'])}

dfs(graph, '0')
```

Output

0
1
4
2
3
3
2
{'0', '1', '2', '3', '4'}

DFS Algorithm Complexity
The time complexity of the DFS algorithm is represented in the form of $O(V + E)$, where V is the number of nodes and E is the number of edges.

The space complexity of the algorithm is $O(V)$.

DFS Algorithm Applications
1. For finding the path
2. To test if the graph is bipartite
3. For finding the strongly connected components of a graph
4. For detecting cycles in a graph

Breadth First Search

Traversal means visiting all the nodes of a graph. Breadth First Traversal or Breadth First Search is a recursive algorithm for searching all the vertices of a graph or tree data structure.

BFS algorithm

A standard BFS implementation puts each vertex of the graph into one of two categories:
1. Visited
2. Not Visited

The purpose of the algorithm is to mark each vertex as visited while avoiding cycles.

The algorithm works as follows:
1. Start by putting any one of the graph's vertices at the back of a queue.
2. Take the front item of the queue and add it to the visited list.
3. Create a list of that vertex's adjacent nodes. Add the ones which aren't in the visited list to the back of the queue.
4. Keep repeating steps 2 and 3 until the queue is empty.

The graph might have two different disconnected parts so to make sure that we cover every vertex, we can also run the BFS algorithm on every node

BFS example

Let's see how the Breadth First Search algorithm works with an example. We use an undirected graph with 5 vertices.

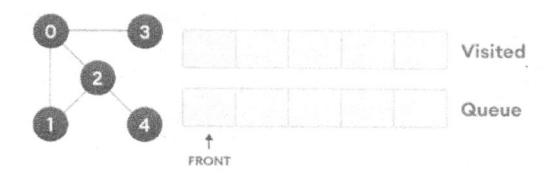

Undirected graph with 5 vertices

We start from vertex 0, the BFS algorithm starts by putting it in the Visited list and putting all its adjacent vertices in the stack.

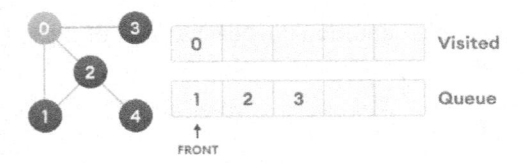

Visit start vertex and add its adjacent vertices to queue

Next, we visit the element at the front of queue i.e. 1 and go to its adjacent nodes. Since 0 has already been visited, we visit 2 instead.

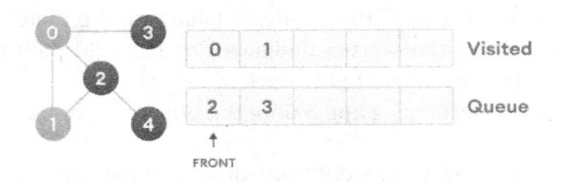

Visit the first neighbour of start node 0, which is 1

Vertex 2 has an unvisited adjacent vertex in 4, so we add that to the back of the queue and visit 3, which is at the front of the queue.

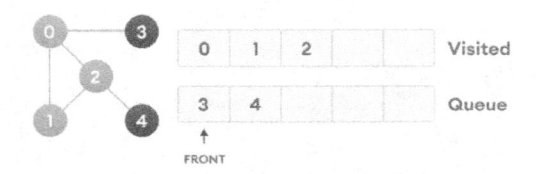

Visit 2 which was added to queue earlier to add its neighbours

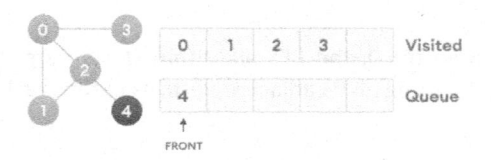

4 remains in the queue

236

Only 4 remains in the queue since the only adjacent node of 3 i.e. 0 is already visited. We visit it.

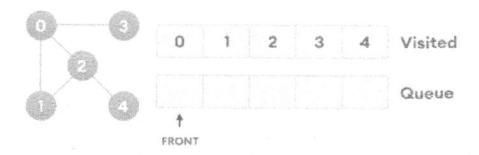

Visit last remaining item in the stack to check if it has unvisited neighbors

Since the queue is empty, we have completed the Breadth First Traversal of the graph.

BFS pseudocode

```
create a queue Q
mark v as visited and put v into Q
while Q is non-empty
    remove the head u of Q
    mark and enqueue all (unvisited) neighbours of u
```

```python
# BFS algorithm in Python

import collections

# BFS algorithm
def bfs(graph, root):

    visited, queue = set(), collections.deque([root])
    visited.add(root)

    while queue:

        # Dequeue a vertex from queue
        vertex = queue.popleft()
        print(str(vertex) + " ", end="")

        # If not visited, mark it as visited, and
        # enqueue it
        for neighbour in graph[vertex]:
            if neighbour not in visited:
                visited.add(neighbour)
                queue.append(neighbour)
```

```
if __name__ == '__main__':
    graph = {0: [1, 2], 1: [2], 2: [3], 3: [1, 2]}
    print("Following is Breadth First Traversal: ")
    bfs(graph, 0)
```

Output
```
Following is Breadth First Traversal:
0 1 2 3
```

BFS Algorithm Complexity
The time complexity of the BFS algorithm is represented in the form of O(V + E), where V is the number of nodes and E is the number of edges.

The space complexity of the algorithm is O(V).

BFS Algorithm Applications
1. To build index by search index
2. For GPS navigation
3. Path finding algorithms
4. In Ford-Fulkerson algorithm to find maximum flow in a network
5. Cycle detection in an undirected graph
6. In minimum spanning tree

Bellman Ford's Algorithm

Bellman Ford algorithm helps us find the shortest path from a vertex to all other vertices of a weighted graph.

It is similar to Dijkstra's algorithm but it can work with graphs in which edges can have negative weights.

Why would one ever have edges with negative weights in real life?
Negative weight edges might seem useless at first but they can explain a lot of phenomena like cashflow, the heat released/absorbed in a chemical reaction, etc.

For instance, if there are different ways to reach from one chemical A to another chemical B, each method will have sub-reactions involving both heat dissipation and absorption.

If we want to find the set of reactions where minimum energy is required, then we will need to be able to factor in the heat absorption as negative weights and heat dissipation as positive weights.

Why do we need to be careful with negative weights?
Negative weight edges can create negative weight cycles i.e. a cycle that will reduce the total path distance by coming back to the same point.

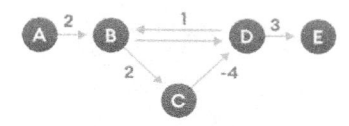

Negative weight cycles can give an incorrect result when trying to find out the shortest path

Shortest path algorithms like Dijkstra's Algorithm that aren't able to detect such a cycle can give an incorrect result because they can go through a negative weight cycle and reduce the path length.

How Bellman Ford's algorithm works
Bellman Ford algorithm works by overestimating the length of the path from the starting vertex to all other vertices. Then it iteratively relaxes those estimates by finding new paths that are shorter than the previously overestimated paths.

By doing this repeatedly for all vertices, we can guarantee that the result is optimized.

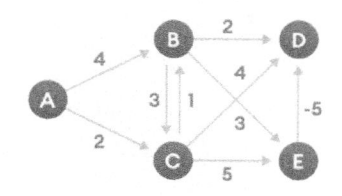

Step-1 for Bellman Ford's algorithm

Step 2: Choose a starting vertex and assign infinity path values to all other vertices

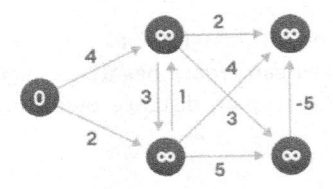

Step-2 for Bellman Ford's algorithm

Step 3: Visit each edge and relax the path distances if they are inaccurate

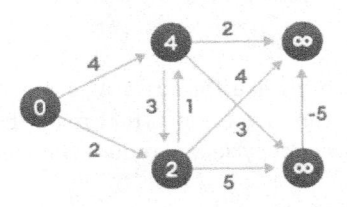

Step-3 for Bellman Ford's algorithm

Step 4: We need to do this V times because in the worst case, a vertex's path length might need to be readjusted V times

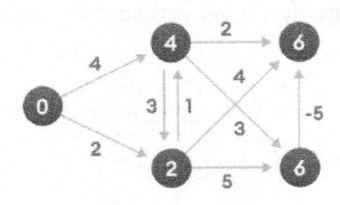

Step-4 for Bellman Ford's algorithm

Step 5: Notice how the vertex at the top right corner had its path length adjusted

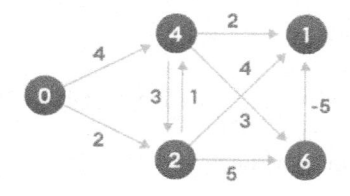

Step-5 for Bellman Ford's algorithm

Step 6: After all the vertices have their path lengths, we check if a negative cycle is present

	B	C	D	E
0	∞	∞	∞	∞
0	4	2	∞	∞
0	3	2	6	6
0	3	2	1	6
0	3	2	1	6

Step-6 for Bellman Ford's algorithm

Bellman Ford Pseudocode
We need to maintain the path distance of every vertex. We can store that in an array of size v, where v is the number of vertices.

We also want to be able to get the shortest path, not only know the length of the shortest path. For this, we map each vertex to the vertex that last updated its path length.

Once the algorithm is over, we can backtrack from the destination vertex to the source vertex to find the path.

```
function bellmanFord(G, S)
    for each vertex V in G
```

```
    distance[V] <- infinite
    previous[V] <- NULL
distance[S] <- 0

for each vertex V in G
  for each edge (U,V) in G
    tempDistance <- distance[U] + edge_weight(U, V)
    if tempDistance < distance[V]
      distance[V] <- tempDistance
      previous[V] <- U

for each edge (U,V) in G
  If distance[U] + edge_weight(U, V) < distance[V}
    Error: Negative Cycle Exists

return distance[], previous[]
```

Bellman Ford vs Dijkstra

Bellman Ford's algorithm and Dijkstra's algorithm are very similar in structure. While Dijkstra looks only to the immediate neighbors of a vertex, Bellman goes through each edge in every iteration.

```
function bellmanFord(G, S)                        function dijkstra(G, S)
  for each vertex V in G                            for each vertex V in G
    distance[V] <- infinite                           distance[V] <- infinite
    previous[V] <- NULL                               previous[V] <- NULL
                                                      If V != S, add V to Priority Queue Q
  distance[S] <- 0                                  distance[S] <- 0

  for each vertex V in G                            while Q IS NOT EMPTY
                                                      U <- Extract MIN from Q
    for each edge (U,V) in G                          for each unvisited neighbour V of U
      tempDistance <- distance[U] + edge_weight(U, V)   tempDistance <- distance[U] + edge_weight(U, V)
      if tempDistance < distance[V]                     if tempDistance < distance[V]
        distance[V] <- tempDistance                       distance[V] <- tempDistance
        previous[V] <- U                                  previous[V] <- U

  for each edge (U,V) in G
    If distance[U] + edge_weight(U, V) < distance[V}
      Error: Negative Cycle Exists

  return distance[], previous[]                     return distance[], previous[]
```

Dijkstra's vs Bellman Ford's Algorithm

```python
# Bellman Ford Algorithm in Python

class Graph:

    def __init__(self, vertices):
        self.V = vertices    # Total number of vertices in the graph
        self.graph = []      # Array of edges

    # Add edges
    def add_edge(self, s, d, w):
```

```python
            self.graph.append([s, d, w])

    # Print the solution
    def print_solution(self, dist):
        print("Vertex Distance from Source")
        for i in range(self.V):
            print("{0}\t\t{1}".format(i, dist[i]))

    def bellman_ford(self, src):

        # Step 1: fill the distance array and predecessor array
        dist = [float("Inf")] * self.V
        # Mark the source vertex
        dist[src] = 0

        # Step 2: relax edges |V| - 1 times
        for _ in range(self.V - 1):
            for s, d, w in self.graph:
                if dist[s] != float("Inf") and dist[s] + w < dist[d]:
                    dist[d] = dist[s] + w

        # Step 3: detect negative cycle
        # if value changes then we have a negative cycle in the graph
        # and we cannot find the shortest distances
        for s, d, w in self.graph:
            if dist[s] != float("Inf") and dist[s] + w < dist[d]:
                print("Graph contains negative weight cycle")
                return

        # No negative weight cycle found!
        # Print the distance and predecessor array
        self.print_solution(dist)


g = Graph(5)
g.add_edge(0, 1, 5)
g.add_edge(0, 2, 4)
g.add_edge(1, 3, 3)
g.add_edge(2, 1, 6)
g.add_edge(3, 2, 2)

g.bellman_ford(0)
```

Output
```
Vertex Distance from Source
0                0
1                5
2                4
3                8
```

Bellman Ford's Complexity

Time Complexity

Best Case Complexity	O(E)
Average Case Complexity	O(VE)
Worst Case Complexity	O(VE)

Space Complexity
And, the space complexity is O(V).

Bellman Ford's Algorithm Applications
1. For calculating shortest paths in routing algorithms
2. For finding the shortest path

Sorting

Bubble Sort

Bubble sort is an algorithm that compares the adjacent elements and swaps their positions if they are not in the intended order. The order can be ascending or descending.

How Bubble Sort Works?
1. Starting from the first index, compare the first and the second elements. If the first element is greater than the second element, they are swapped.
Now, compare the second and the third elements. Swap them if they are not in order.
The above process goes on until the last element.

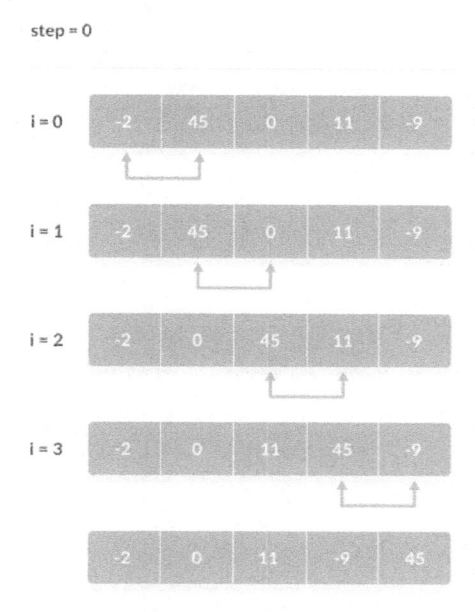

step = 0

i = 0 | -2 | 45 | 0 | 11 | -9 |

i = 1 | -2 | 45 | 0 | 11 | -9 |

i = 2 | -2 | 0 | 45 | 11 | -9 |

i = 3 | -2 | 0 | 11 | 45 | -9 |

         | -2 | 0 | 11 | -9 | 45 |

Compare the adjacent elements

245

2. The same process goes on for the remaining iterations. After each iteration, the largest element among the unsorted elements is placed at the end.

In each iteration, the comparison takes place up to the last unsorted element.

The array is sorted when all the unsorted elements are placed at their correct positions.

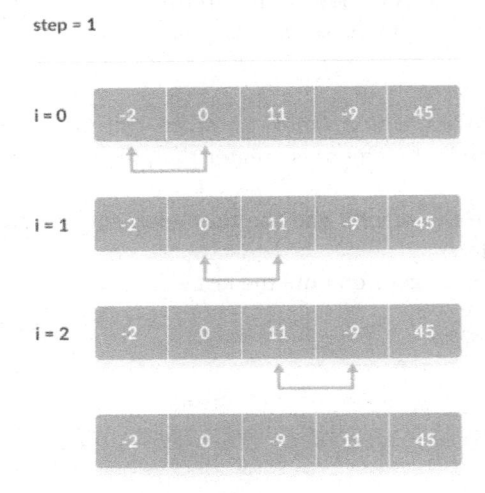

step = 1

i = 0 | -2 | 0 | 11 | -9 | 45 |

i = 1 | -2 | 0 | 11 | -9 | 45 |

i = 2 | -2 | 0 | 11 | -9 | 45 |

| -2 | 0 | -9 | 11 | 45 |

Compare the adjacent elements

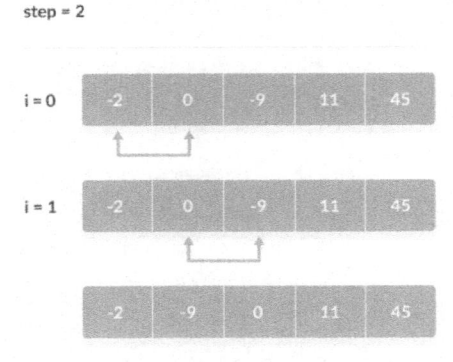

step = 2

i = 0 | -2 | 0 | -9 | 11 | 45 |

i = 1 | -2 | 0 | -9 | 11 | 45 |

| -2 | -9 | 0 | 11 | 45 |

Compare the adjacent elements

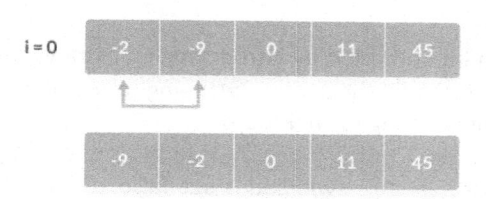

step = 3

i = 0 | -2 | -9 | 0 | 11 | 45 |

| -9 | -2 | 0 | 11 | 45 |

Compare the adjacent elements

Bubble Sort Algorithm

bubbleSort(array)
  for i <- 1 to indexOfLastUnsortedElement-1
   if leftElement > rightElement
    swap leftElement and rightElement
end bubbleSort

```python
# Bubble sort in Python

def bubbleSort(array):

    # run loops two times: one for walking throught the array
    # and the other for comparison
    for i in range(len(array)):
        for j in range(0, len(array) - i - 1):

            # To sort in descending order, change > to < in this line.
            if array[j] > array[j + 1]:

                # swap if greater is at the rear position
                (array[j], array[j + 1]) = (array[j + 1], array[j])


data = [-2, 45, 0, 11, -9]
bubbleSort(data)
print('Sorted Array in Asc ending Order:')
print(data)
```

Output
```
Sorted Array in Ascending Order:
[-9, -2, 0, 11, 45]
```

Optimized Bubble Sort

In the above code, all possible comparisons are made even if the array is already sorted. It increases the execution time.

The code can be optimized by introducing an extra variable swapped. After each iteration, if there is no swapping taking place then, there is no need for performing further loops.

In such a case, variable swapped is set false. Thus, we can prevent further iterations.

Algorithm for optimized bubble sort is

```
bubbleSort(array)
  swapped <- false
  for i <- 1 to indexOfLastUnsortedElement-1
    if leftElement > rightElement
      swap leftElement and rightElement
      swapped <- true
end bubbleSort
```

```python
# Optimized bubble sort in python

def bubbleSort(array):

    # Run loops two times: one for walking throught the array
    # and the other for comparison
    for i in range(len(array)):

        # swapped keeps track of swapping
        swapped = True
        for j in range(0, len(array) - i - 1):

            # To sort in descending order, change > to < in this line.
            if array[j] > array[j + 1]:

                # Swap if greater is at the rear position
                (array[j], array[j + 1]) = (array[j + 1], array[j])

                swapped = False

        # If there is not swapping in the last swap, then the array is already sorted.
        if swapped:
            break
```

248

```
data = [-2, 45, 0, 11, -9]
bubbleSort(data)
print('Sorted Array in Ascending Order:')
print(data)
```

Output
```
Sorted Array in Ascending Order:
[-9, -2, 0, 11, 45]
```

Complexity
Bubble Sort is one of the simplest sorting algorithms. Two loops are implemented in the algorithm.

Cycle	Number of Comparisons
1st	(n-1)
2nd	(n-2)
3rd	(n-3)
......	......
last	1

Number of comparisons:
$(n - 1) + (n - 2) + (n - 3) + ... + 1 = n(n - 1) / 2$ nearly equals to n^2

Complexity: $O(n^2)$
Also, we can analyze the complexity by simply observing the number of loops. There are 2 loops so the complexity is $n*n = n^2$

Time Complexities:
- Worst Case Complexity: $O(n^2)$

If we want to sort in ascending order and the array is in descending order then, the worst case occurs.

- Best Case Complexity: $O(n)$

If the array is already sorted, then there is no need for sorting.

- Average Case Complexity: $O(n^2)$

It occurs when the elements of the array are in jumbled order (neither ascending nor descending).

Space Complexity:
Space complexity is O(1) because an extra variable temp is used for swapping.

In the optimized algorithm, the variable swapped adds to the space complexity thus, making it O(2).

Bubble Sort Applications
Bubble sort is used in the following cases where
1. the complexity of the code does not matter.
2. a short code is preferred.

Selection Sort

Selection sort is an algorithm that selects the smallest element from an unsorted list in each iteration and places that element at the beginning of the unsorted list.

How Selection Sort Works?

1. Set the first element as minimum.

| 20 | 12 | 10 | 15 | 2 |

Select first element as minimum

Compare minimum with the second element. If the second element is smaller than minimum, assign the second element as minimum.

Compare minimum with the third element. Again, if the third element is smaller, then assign minimum to the third element otherwise do nothing. The process goes on until the last element.

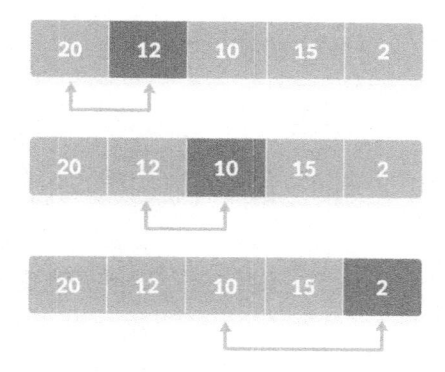

Compare minimum with the remaining elements

After each iteration, minimum is placed in the front of the unsorted list.

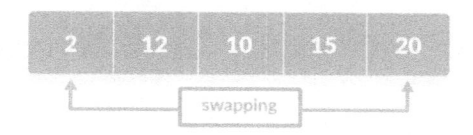

Swap the first with minimum

For each iteration, indexing starts from the first unsorted element. Step 1 to 3 are repeated until all the elements are placed at their correct positions.

step = 0

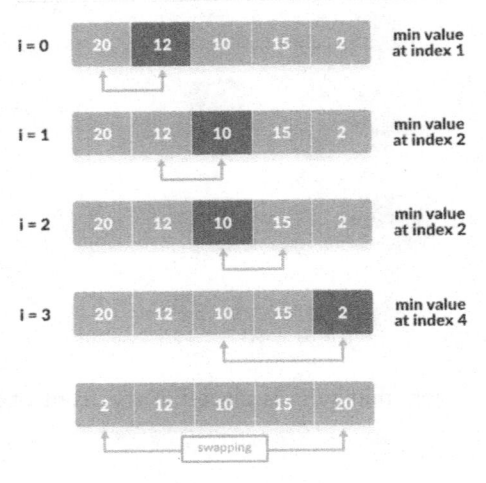

i = 0	20	12	10	15	2	min value at index 1
i = 1	20	12	10	15	2	min value at index 2
i = 2	20	12	10	15	2	min value at index 2
i = 3	20	12	10	15	2	min value at index 4

| | 2 | 12 | 10 | 15 | 20 |

swapping

The first iteration

step = 1

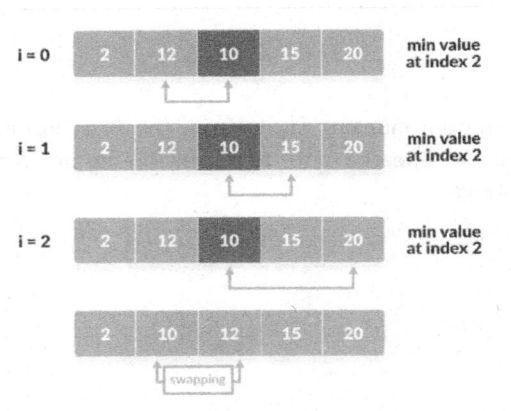

i = 0	2	12	10	15	20	min value at index 2
i = 1	2	12	10	15	20	min value at index 2
i = 2	2	12	10	15	20	min value at index 2

| | 2 | 10 | 12 | 15 | 20 |

swapping

The second iteration

step = 2

i = 0 | 2 | 10 | **12** | 15 | 20 | min value at index 2

i = 2 | 2 | 10 | **12** | 15 | 20 | min value at index 2

2 | 10 | 12 | 15 | 20
already in place

The third iteration

step = 3

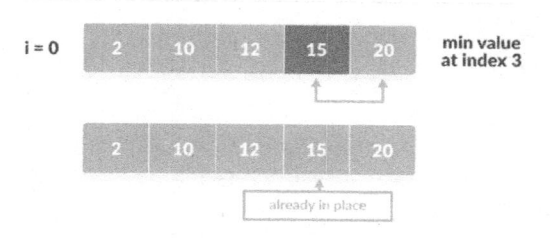

i = 0 | 2 | 10 | 12 | **15** | 20 | min value at index 3

2 | 10 | 12 | 15 | 20
already in place

The fourth iteration

Selection Sort Algorithm

```
selectionSort(array, size)
  repeat (size - 1) times
  set the first unsorted element as the minimum
  for each of the unsorted elements
    if element < currentMinimum
      set element as new minimum
  swap minimum with first unsorted position
end selectionSort
```

```
# Selection sort in Python

def selectionSort(array, size):
```

```python
    for step in range(size):
        min_idx = step

        for i in range(step + 1, size):

            # to sort in descending order, change > to < in this line
            # select the minimum element in each loop
            if array[i] < array[min_idx]:
                min_idx = i

        # put min at the correct position
        (array[step], array[min_idx]) = (array[min_idx], array[step])


data = [-2, 45, 0, 11, -9]
size = len(data)
selectionSort(data, size)
print('Sorted Array in Ascending Order:')
print(data)
```

Output
Sorted Array in Ascending Order:
[-9, -2, 0, 11, 45]

Complexity

Cycle	Number of Comparison
1st	(n-1)
2nd	(n-2)
3rd	(n-3)
...	...
last	1

Number of comparisons: (n - 1) + (n - 2) + (n - 3) + ... + 1 = n(n - 1) / 2 nearly equals to n^2.

Complexity = $O(n^2)$

Also, we can analyze the complexity by simply observing the number of loops. There are 2 loops so the complexity is $n*n = n^2$.

Time Complexities:

- **Worst Case Complexity:** $O(n^2)$

If we want to sort in ascending order and the array is in descending order then, the worst case occurs.

- Best Case Complexity: $O(n^2)$

It occurs when the array is already sorted

- Average Case Complexity: $O(n^2)$

It occurs when the elements of the array are in jumbled order (neither ascending nor descending).

The time complexity of the selection sort is the same in all cases. At every step, you have to find the minimum element and put it in the right place. The minimum element is not known until the end of the array is not reached.

Space Complexity:
Space complexity is $O(1)$ because an extra variable temp is used.

Selection Sort Applications
The selection sort is used when:
- a small list is to be sorted
- cost of swapping does not matter
- checking of all the elements is compulsory
- cost of writing to a memory matters like in flash memory (number of writes/swaps is $O(n)$ as compared to $O(n^2)$ of bubble sort)

Insertion Sort

Insertion sort works similarly as we sort cards in our hand in a card game.

We assume that the first card is already sorted then, we select an unsorted card. If the unsorted card is greater than the card in hand, it is placed on the right otherwise, to the left. In the same way, other unsorted cards are taken and put at their right place.

A similar approach is used by insertion sort.

Insertion sort is a sorting algorithm that places an unsorted element at its suitable place in each iteration.

How Insertion Sort Works?
Suppose we need to sort the following array.

| 9 | 5 | 1 | 4 | 3 |

Initial array

1. The first element in the array is assumed to be sorted. Take the second element and store it separately in key.

Compare key with the first element. If the first element is greater than key, then key is placed in front of the first element.

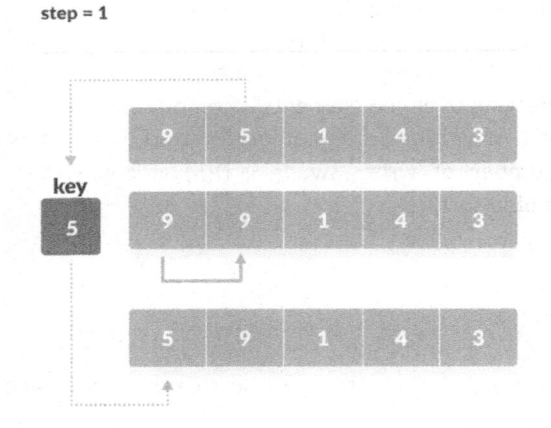

step = 1

If the first element is greater than key, then key is placed in front of the first element.

2. Now, the first two elements are sorted.

Take the third element and compare it with the elements on the left of it. Placed it just behind the element smaller than it. If there is no element smaller than it, then place it at the beginning of the array.

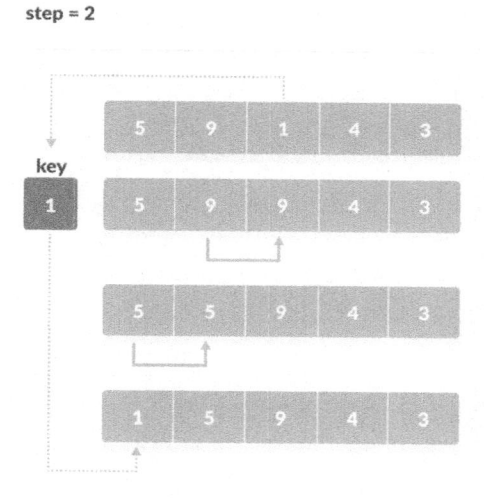

step = 2

Place 1 at the beginning

Similarly, place every unsorted element at its correct position.

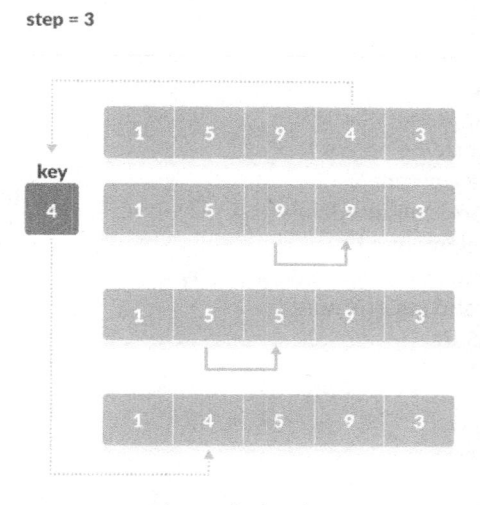

step = 3

Place 4 behind 1

step = 4

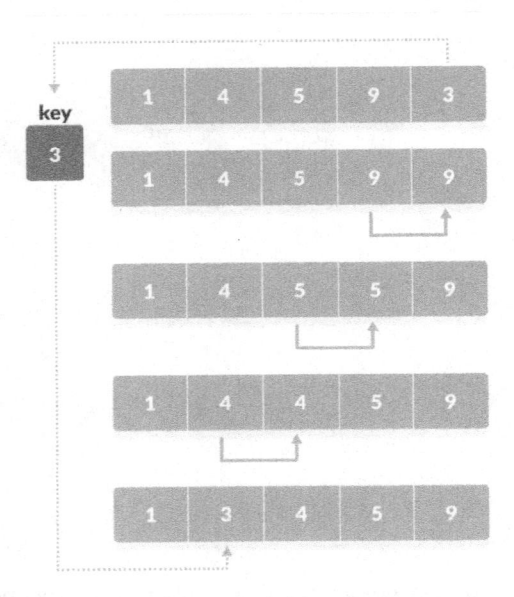

Place 3 behind 1 and the array is sorted

Insertion Sort Algorithm

insertionSort(array)
  mark first element as sorted
  for each unsorted element X
    'extract' the element X
    for j <- lastSortedIndex down to 0
      if current element j > X
        move sorted element to the right by 1
      break loop and insert X here
end insertionSort

```python
# Insertion sort in Python

def insertionSort(array):

    for step in range(1, len(array)):
        key = array[step]
        j = step - 1
```

```
        # Compare key with each element on the left of it u
ntil an element smaller than it is found
        # For descending order, change key<array[j] to key>
array[j].
        while j >= 0 and key < array[j]:
            array[j + 1] = array[j]
            j = j - 1

        # Place key at after the element just smaller than
it.
        array[j + 1] = key
data = [9, 5, 1, 4, 3]
insertionSort(data)
print('Sorted Array in Ascending Order:')
print(data)
```

Output
Sorted Array in Ascending Order:
[1, 3, 4, 5, 9]

Complexity

Time Complexities

- Worst Case Complexity: O(n²)

Suppose, an array is in ascending order, and you want to sort it in descending order. In this case, worst case complexity occurs.

Each element has to be compared with each of the other elements so, for every nth element, (n-1) number of comparisons are made.

Thus, the total number of comparisons = n*(n-1) ~ n²

- Best Case Complexity: O(n)

When the array is already sorted, the outer loop runs for n number of times whereas the inner loop does not run at all. So, there are only n number of comparisons. Thus, complexity is linear.

- Average Case Complexity: O(n²)

It occurs when the elements of an array are in jumbled order (neither ascending nor descending).

Space Complexity
Space complexity is O(1) because an extra variable key is used.

Insertion Sort Applications
The insertion sort is used when:
- the array is has a small number of elements
- there are only a few elements left to be sorted

Merge Sort

Merge Sort is a kind of Divide and Conquer algorithm in computer programming. It is one of the most popular sorting algorithms and a great way to develop confidence in building recursive algorithms.

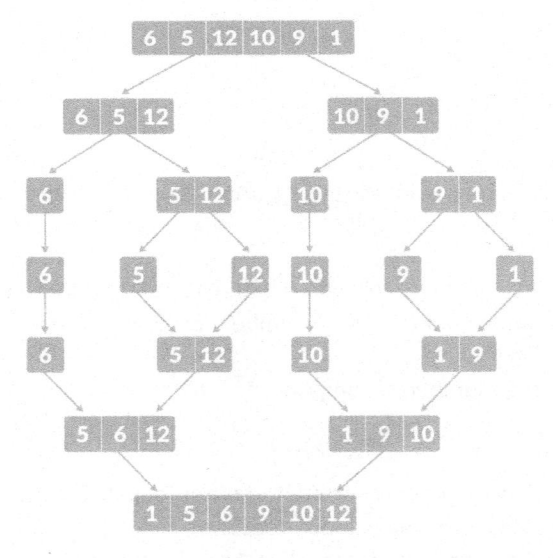

Merge Sort example

Divide and Conquer Strategy
Using the Divide and Conquer technique, we divide a problem into subproblems. When the solution to each subproblem is ready, we 'combine' the results from the subproblems to solve the main problem.

260

Suppose we had to sort an array A. A subproblem would be to sort a sub-section of this array starting at index p and ending at index r, denoted as A[p..r].

Divide
If q is the half-way point between p and r, then we can split the subarray A[p..r] into two arrays A[p..q] and A[q+1, r].

Conquer
In the conquer step, we try to sort both the subarrays A[p..q] and A[q+1, r]. If we haven't yet reached the base case, we again divide both these subarrays and try to sort them.

Combine
When the conquer step reaches the base step and we get two sorted subarrays A[p..q] and A[q+1, r] for array A[p..r], we combine the results by creating a sorted array A[p..r] from two sorted subarrays A[p..q] and A[q+1, r].

The MergeSort Algorithm
The MergeSort function repeatedly divides the array into two halves until we reach a stage where we try to perform MergeSort on a subarray of size 1 i.e. p == r.

After that, the merge function comes into play and combines the sorted arrays into larger arrays until the whole array is merged.

```
MergeSort(A, p, r):
  if p > r
    return
  q = (p+r)/2
  mergeSort(A, p, q)
  mergeSort(A, q+1, r)
  merge(A, p, q, r)
```

To sort an entire array, we need to call MergeSort(A, 0, length(A)-1).

As shown in the image below, the merge sort algorithm recursively divides the array into halves until we reach the base case of array with 1 element. After that, the merge function picks up the sorted sub-arrays and merges them to gradually sort the entire array.

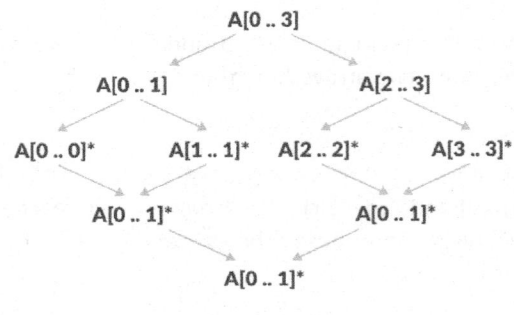

```
                        A[0 .. 3]
                       /        \
                  A[0 .. 1]      A[2 .. 3]
                  /      \       /       \
            A[0 .. 0]*  A[1 .. 1]*  A[2 .. 2]*  A[3 .. 3]*
                  \      /              \      /
                  A[0 .. 1]*             A[0 .. 1]*
                          \             /
                           A[0 .. 1]*
```

Merge sort in action

The merge Step of Merge Sort

Every recursive algorithm is dependent on a base case and the ability to combine the results from base cases. Merge sort is no different. The most important part of the merge sort algorithm is, you guessed it, merge step.

The merge step is the solution to the simple problem of merging two sorted lists(arrays) to build one large sorted list(array).

The algorithm maintains three pointers, one for each of the two arrays and one for maintaining the current index of the final sorted array.

Have we reached the end of any of the arrays?
  No:
    Compare current elements of both arrays
    Copy smaller element into sorted array
    Move pointer of element containing smaller element
  Yes:
    Copy all remaining elements of non-empty array

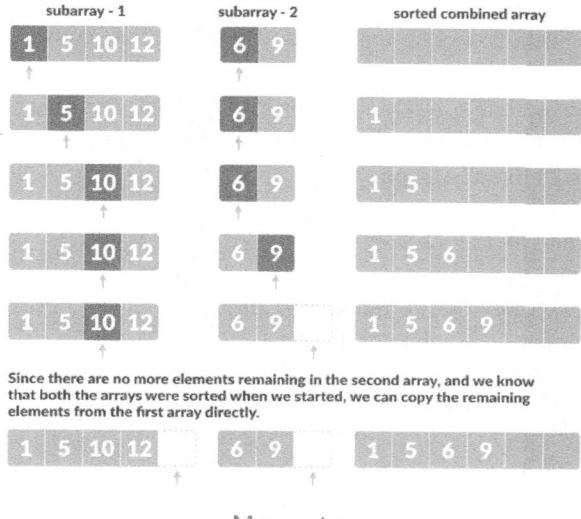

Merge step

Writing the Code for Merge Algorithm

A noticeable difference between the merging step we described above and the one we use for merge sort is that we only perform the merge function on consecutive sub-arrays.

This is why we only need the array, the first position, the last index of the first subarray(we can calculate the first index of the second subarray) and the last index of the second subarray.

Our task is to merge two subarrays A[p..q] and A[q+1..r] to create a sorted array A[p..r]. So the inputs to the function are A, p, q and r

The merge function works as follows:
1. Create copies of the subarrays L ← A[p..q] and M ← A[q+1..r].

2. Create three pointers i, j and k
- i maintains current index of L, starting at 1
- j maintains current index of M, starting at 1
- k maintains the current index of A[p..q], starting at p.

3. Until we reach the end of either L or M, pick the larger among the elements from L and M and place them in the correct position at A[p..q]

4. When we run out of elements in either L or M, pick up the remaining elements and put in A[p..q]

In code, this would look like:

```
// Merge two subarrays L and M into arr
void merge(int arr[], int p, int q, int r) {

    // Create L ← A[p..q] and M ← A[q+1..r]
    int n1 = q - p + 1;
    int n2 = r - q;

    int L[n1], M[n2];

    for (int i = 0; i < n1; i++)
        L[i] = arr[p + i];
    for (int j = 0; j < n2; j++)
        M[j] = arr[q + 1 + j];

    // Maintain current index of sub-arrays and main array
    int i, j, k;
    i = 0;
    j = 0;
    k = p;

    // Until we reach either end of either L or M, pick larger among
    // elements L and M and place them in the correct position at A[p..r]
    while (i < n1 && j < n2) {
        if (L[i] <= M[j]) {
            arr[k] = L[i];
            i++;
        } else {
            arr[k] = M[j];
            j++;
        }
        k++;
```

```
    }

    // When we run out of elements in either L or M,
    // pick up the remaining elements and put in A[p..r]
    while (i < n1) {
        arr[k] = L[i];
        i++;
        k++;
    }

    while (j < n2) {
        arr[k] = M[j];
        j++;
        k++;
    }
}
```

Merge( ) Function Explained Step-By-Step
A lot is happening in this function, so let's take an example to see how this would work.

As usual, a picture speaks a thousand words.

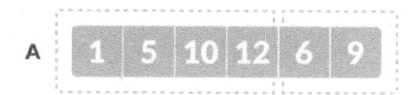

A | 1 | 5 | 10 | 12 | 6 | 9 |

Merging two consecutive subarrays of array

The array A[0..5] contains two sorted subarrays A[0..3] and A[4..5]. Let us see how the merge function will merge the two arrays.

```
void merge(int arr[], int p, int q, int r) {
// Here, p = 0, q = 4, r = 6 (size of array)
```

Step 1: Create duplicate copies of sub-arrays to be sorted

```
// Create L ← A[p..q] and M ← A[q+1..r]
int n1 = q - p + 1 = 3 - 0 + 1 = 4;
int n2 = r - q = 5 - 3 = 2;
```

```
int L[4], M[2];

for (int i = 0; i < 4; i++)
    L[i] = arr[p + i];
    // L[0,1,2,3] = A[0,1,2,3] = [1,5,10,12]

for (int j = 0; j < 2; j++)
    M[j] = arr[q + 1 + j];
    // M[0,1,2,3] = A[4,5] = [6,9]
```

Create copies of subarrays for merging

Step 2: Maintain current index of sub-arrays and main array

```
int i, j, k;
i = 0;
j = 0;
k = p;
```

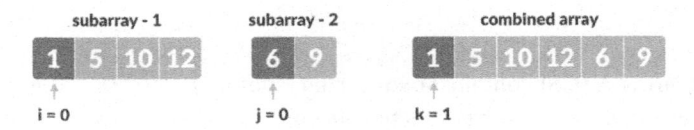

Maintain indices of copies of sub array and main array

Step 3: Until we reach the end of either L or M, pick larger among elements L and M and place them in the correct position at A[p..r]

```
while (i < n1 && j < n2) {
    if (L[i] <= M[j]) {
        arr[k] = L[i]; i++;
```

```
      }
      else {
         arr[k] = M[j];
         j++;
      }
      k++;
   }
```

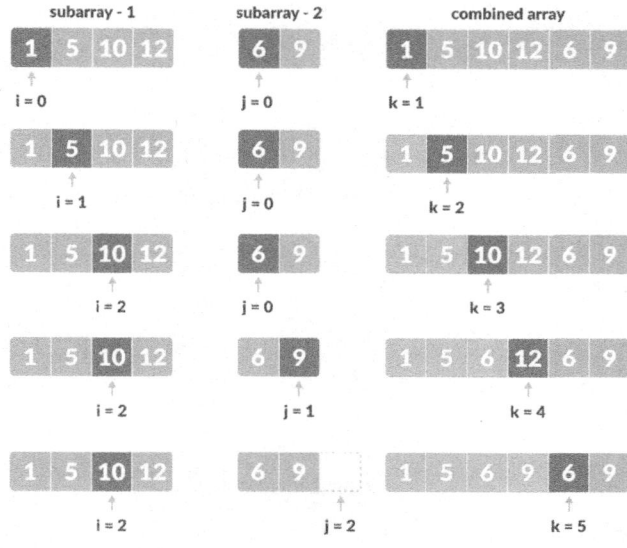

Comparing individual elements of sorted subarrays until we reach end of one

Step 4: When we run out of elements in either L or M, pick up the remaining elements and put in A[p..r]

```
   // We exited the earlier loop because j < n2 doesn't hold
   while (i < n1)
   {
      arr[k] = L[i];
      i++;
      k++;
   }
```

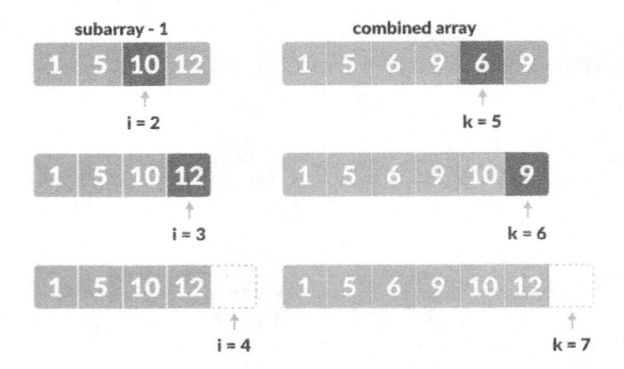

subarray - 1   **combined array**

| 1 | 5 | 10 | 12 | | 1 | 5 | 6 | 9 | 6 | 9 |
              ↑   ↑
            i = 2   k = 5

| 1 | 5 | 10 | 12 | | 1 | 5 | 6 | 9 | 10 | 9 |
                   ↑   ↑
                 i = 3   k = 6

| 1 | 5 | 10 | 12 | | 1 | 5 | 6 | 9 | 10 | 12 |
                       ↑   ↑
                     i = 4   k = 7

Copy the remaining elements from the first array to main subarray

```
// We exited the earlier loop because i < n1 doesn't hold
while (j < n2)
{
    arr[k] = M[j];
    j++;
    k++;
}
}
```

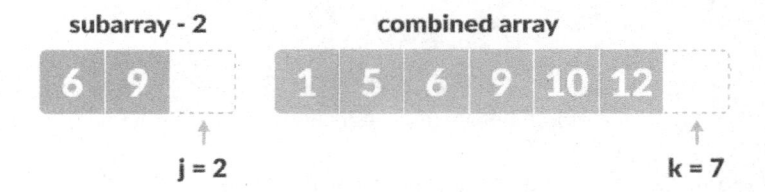

subarray - 2   **combined array**

| 6 | 9 | | 1 | 5 | 6 | 9 | 10 | 12 |
       ↑   ↑
     j = 2   k = 7

Copy remaining elements of second array to main subarray

This step would have been needed if the size of M was greater than L. At the end of the merge function, the subarray A[p..r] is sorted.

```
# MergeSort in Python

def mergeSort(array):
    if len(array) > 1:

        # r is the point where the array is divided into two subarrays
        r = len(array)//2
```

```python
        L = array[:r]
        M = array[r:]

        # Sort the two halves
        mergeSort(L)
        mergeSort(M)

        i = j = k = 0

        # Until we reach either end of either L or M, pick larger among
        # elements L and M and place them in the correct position at A[p..r]
        while i < len(L) and j < len(M):
            if L[i] < M[j]:
                array[k] = L[i]
                i += 1
            else:
                array[k] = M[j]
                j += 1
            k += 1

        # When we run out of elements in either L or M,
        # pick up the remaining elements and put in A[p..r]
        while i < len(L):
            array[k] = L[i]
            i += 1
            k += 1

        while j < len(M):
            array[k] = M[j]
            j += 1
            k += 1

# Print the array
def printList(array):
    for i in range(len(array)):
        print(array[i], end=" ")
    print()

# Driver program
if __name__ == '__main__':
    array = [6, 5, 12, 10, 9, 1]

    mergeSort(array)

    print("Sorted array is: ")
    printList(array)
```

Output
Sorted array is:
1 5 6 9 10 12

Merge Sort Complexity

Time Complexity
Best Case Complexity: O(n*log n)
Worst Case Complexity: O(n*log n)
Average Case Complexity: O(n*log n)

Space Complexity
The space complexity of merge sort is O(n).

Merge Sort Applications
- Inversion count problem
- External sorting
- E-commerce applications

Quicksort

Quicksort is an algorithm based on divide and conquer approach in which the array is split into subarrays and these sub-arrays are recursively called to sort the elements.

How QuickSort Works?
1. A pivot element is chosen from the array. You can choose any element from the array as the pivot element.

Here, we have taken the rightmost (ie. the last element) of the array as the pivot element.

| 8 | 7 | 6 | 1 | 0 | 9 | 2 |

Select a pivot element

2. The elements smaller than the pivot element are put on the left and the elements greater than the pivot element are put on the right.

| 1 | 0 | 2 | 8 | 7 | 9 | 6 |

Put all the smaller elements on the left and greater on the right of pivot element

The above arrangement is achieved by the following steps.

- A pointer is fixed at the pivot element. The pivot element is compared with the elements beginning from the first index. If the element greater than the pivot element is reached, a second pointer is set for that element.
- Now, the pivot element is compared with the other elements (a third pointer). If an element smaller than the pivot element is reached, the smaller element is swapped with the greater element found earlier.

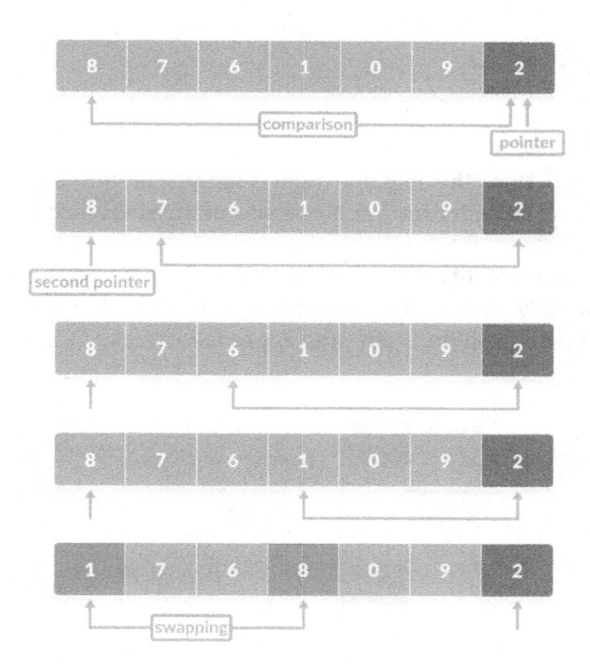

Comparison of pivot element with other elements

- The process goes on until the second last element is reached.

Finally, the pivot element is swapped with the second pointer.

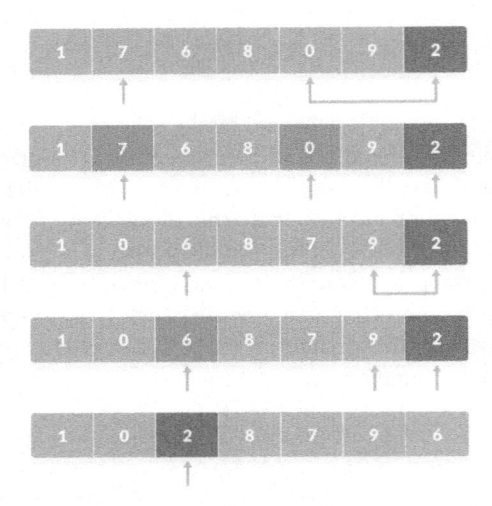

Swap pivot element with the second pointer

- Now the left and right subparts of this pivot element are taken for further processing in the steps below.

3. Pivot elements are again chosen for the left and the right sub-parts separately. Within these sub-parts, the pivot elements are placed at their right position. Then, step 2 is repeated.

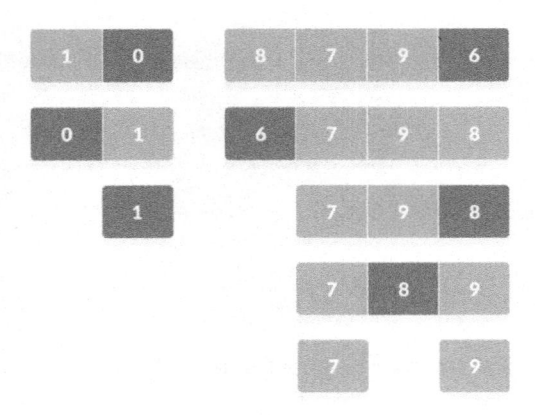

272

Select pivot element of in each half and put at correct place using recursion

4. The sub-parts are again divided into smaller sub-parts until each subpart is formed of a single element.

5. At this point, the array is already sorted.

Quicksort uses recursion for sorting the sub-parts.
On the basis of Divide and conquer approach, quicksort algorithm can be explained as:

- Divide
  The array is divided into subparts taking pivot as the partitioning point. The elements smaller than the pivot are placed to the left of the pivot and the elements greater than the pivot are placed to the right.

- Conquer
  The left and the right subparts are again partitioned using the by selecting pivot elements for them. This can be achieved by recursively passing the subparts into the algorithm.

- Combine
  This step does not play a significant role in quicksort. The array is already sorted at the end of the conquer step.

You can understand the working of quicksort with the help of the illustrations below.

quicksort(arr, low, pi-1)

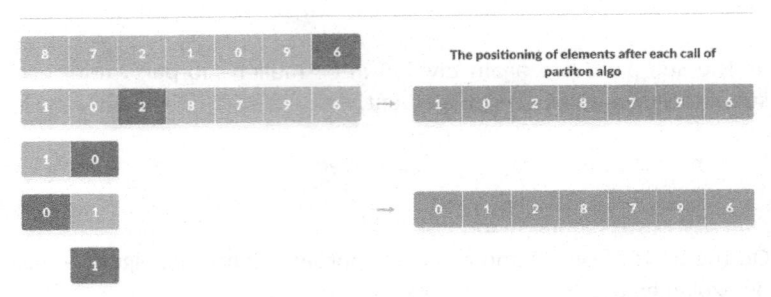

Sorting the elements on the left of pivot using recursion

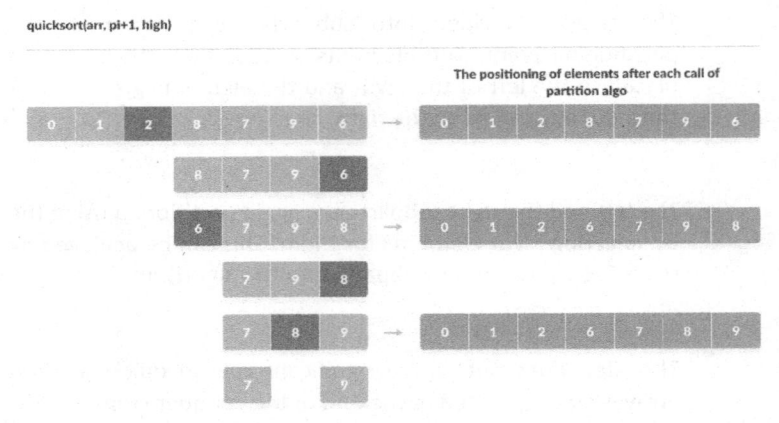

quicksort(arr, pi+1, high)

Sorting the elements on the right of pivot using recursion

Quick Sort Algorithm

```
quickSort(array, leftmostIndex, rightmostIndex)
  if (leftmostIndex < rightmostIndex)
    pivotIndex <- partition(array,leftmostIndex, rightmostIndex)
    quickSort(array, leftmostIndex, pivotIndex)
    quickSort(array, pivotIndex + 1, rightmostIndex)

partition(array, leftmostIndex, rightmostIndex)
  set rightmostIndex as pivotIndex
  storeIndex <- leftmostIndex - 1
```

```
for i <- leftmostIndex + 1 to rightmostIndex
  if element[i] < pivotElement
    swap element[i] and element[storeIndex]
    storeIndex++
  swap pivotElement and element[storeIndex+1]
return storeIndex + 1
```

```python
# Quick sort in Python

# Function to partition the array on the basis of pivot element
def partition(array, low, high):

    # Select the pivot element
    pivot = array[high]
    i = low - 1

    # Put the elements smaller than pivot on the left and greater
    #than pivot on the right of pivot
    for j in range(low, high):
        if array[j] <= pivot:
            i = i + 1
            (array[i], array[j]) = (array[j], array[i])

    (array[i + 1], array[high]) = (array[high], array[i + 1])

    return i + 1

def quickSort(array, low, high):
    if low < high:

        # Select pivot position and put all the elements smaller
        # than pivot on left and greater than pivot on right
        pi = partition(array, low, high)

        # Sort the elements on the left of pivot
        quickSort(array, low, pi - 1)

        # Sort the elements on the right of pivot
        quickSort(array, pi + 1, high)

data = [8, 7, 2, 1, 0, 9, 6]
size = len(data)
quickSort(data, 0, size - 1)
print('Sorted Array in Ascending Order:')
print(data)
```

Output
Sorted Array in Ascending Order:
[0, 1, 2, 6, 7, 8, 9]

Quicksort Complexity

Time Complexities

Worst Case Complexity [Big-O]: $O(n^2)$
It occurs when the pivot element picked is either the greatest or the smallest element.

This condition leads to the case in which the pivot element lies in an extreme end of the sorted array. One sub-array is always empty and another sub-array contains $n - 1$ elements. Thus, quicksort is called only on this sub-array.

However, the quick sort algorithm has better performance for scattered pivots.

- Best Case Complexity [Big-omega]: $O(n*\log n)$

It occurs when the pivot element is always the middle element or near to the middle element.

- Average Case Complexity [Big-theta]: $O(n*\log n)$

It occurs when the above conditions do not occur.

Space Complexity
The space complexity for quicksort is $O(\log n)$.

Quicksort Applications
Quicksort is implemented when
- the programming language is good for recursion
- time complexity matters
- space complexity matters

Counting Sort

Counting sort is a sorting algorithm that sorts the elements of an array by counting the number of occurrences of each unique element in the array. The count is stored in an auxiliary array and the sorting is done by mapping the count as an index of the auxiliary array.

How Counting Sort Works?
1. Find out the maximum element (let it be max) from the given array.

max							
8	4	2	2	8	3	3	1

Given array

2. Initialize an array of length max+1 with all elements 0. This array is used for storing the count of the elements in the array.

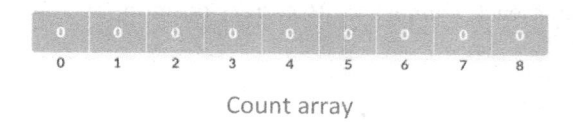

0	0	0	0	0	0	0	0	0
0	1	2	3	4	5	6	7	8

Count array

3. Store the count of each element at their respective index in count array

For example: if the count of element 3 is 2 then, 2 is stored in the 3rd position of count array. If element "5" is not present in the array, then 0 is stored in 5th position.

0	1	2	2	1	0	0	0	1
0	1	2	3	4	5	6	7	8

Count of each element stored

4. Store cumulative sum of the elements of the count array. It helps in placing the elements into the correct index of the sorted array.

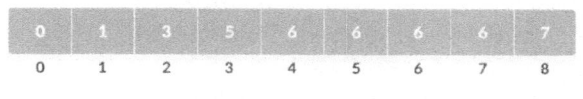

0	1	3	5	6	6	6	6	7
0	1	2	3	4	5	6	7	8

Cumulative count

5. Find the index of each element of the original array in the count array. This gives the cumulative count. Place the element at the index calculated as shown in figure below.

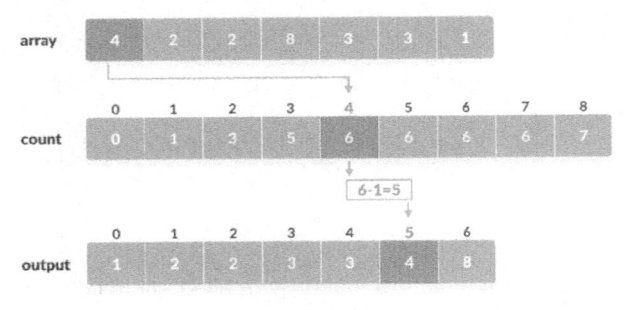

Counting sort

After placing each element at its correct position, decrease its count by one.

Counting Sort Algorithm

countingSort(array, size)
  max <- find largest element in array
  initialize count array with all zeros
  for j <- 0 to size
    find the total count of each unique element and
    store the count at jth index in count array
  for i <- 1 to max
    find the cumulative sum and store it in count array itself
  for j <- size down to 1
    restore the elements to array
    decrease count of each element restored by 1

```python
# Counting sort in Python programming

def countingSort(array):
    size = len(array)
    output = [0] * size

    # Initialize count array
    count = [0] * 10

    # Store the count of each elements in count array
    for i in range(0, size):
```

```
        count[array[i]] += 1

    # Store the cummulative count
    for i in range(1, 10):
        count[i] += count[i - 1]

    # Find the index of each element of the original array
in count array
    # place the elements in output array
    i = size - 1
    while i >= 0:
        output[count[array[i]] - 1] = array[i]
        count[array[i]] -= 1
        i -= 1

    # Copy the sorted elements into original array
    for i in range(0, size):
        array[i] = output[i]
data = [4, 2, 2, 8, 3, 3, 1]
countingSort(data)
print("Sorted Array in Ascending Order: ")
print(data)
```

Output
```
Sorted Array in Ascending Order:
[1, 2, 2, 3, 3, 4, 8]
```

Complexity

Time Complexities:
There are mainly four main loops. (Finding the greatest value can be done outside the function.)

for-loop	time of counting
1st	O(max)
2nd	O(size)
3rd	O(max)
4th	O(size)

Overall complexity = O(max)+O(size)+O(max)+O(size) = O(max+size)
- Worst Case Complexity: O(n+k)
- Best Case Complexity: O(n+k)
- Average Case Complexity: O(n+k)

In all the above cases, the complexity is the same because no matter how the elements are placed in the array, the algorithm goes through n+k times.

There is no comparison between any elements, so it is better than comparison based sorting techniques. But, it is bad if the integers are very large because the array of that size should be made.

Space Complexity:
The space complexity of Counting Sort is O(max). Larger the range of elements, larger is the space complexity.

Counting Sort Applications
Counting sort is used when:
- there are smaller integers with multiple counts.
- linear complexity is the need.

Radix Sort

Radix sort is a sorting technique that sorts the elements by first grouping the individual digits of the same place value. Then, sort the elements according to their increasing/decreasing order.

Suppose, we have an array of 8 elements. First, we will sort elements based on the value of the unit place. Then, we will sort elements based on the value of the tenth place. This process goes on until the last significant place.

Let the initial array be [121, 432, 564, 23, 1, 45, 788]. It is sorted according to radix sort as shown in the figure below.

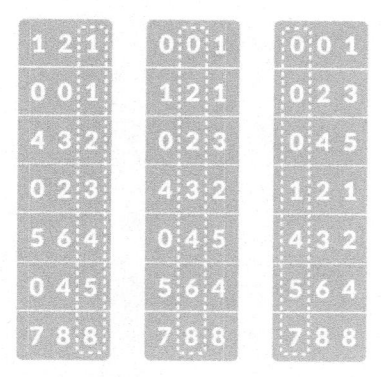

1 2 1	0 0 1	0 0 1
0 0 1	1 2 1	0 2 3
4 3 2	0 2 3	0 4 5
0 2 3	4 3 2	1 2 1
5 6 4	0 4 5	4 3 2
0 4 5	5 6 4	5 6 4
7 8 8	7 8 8	7 8 8

sorting the integers according to units, tens and hundreds place digits

Working of Radix Sort

Please go through the counting sort before reading this article because counting sort is used as an intermediate sort in radix sort.

How Radix Sort Works?

1. Find the largest element in the array, i.e. max. Let X be the number of digits in max. X is calculated because we have to go through all the significant places of all elements.

In this array [121, 432, 564, 23, 1, 45, 788], we have the largest number 788. It has 3 digits. Therefore, the loop should go up to hundreds place (3 times).

2. Now, go through each significant place one by one.

Use any stable sorting technique to sort the digits at each significant place. We have used counting sort for this.

Sort the elements based on the unit place digits (X=0).

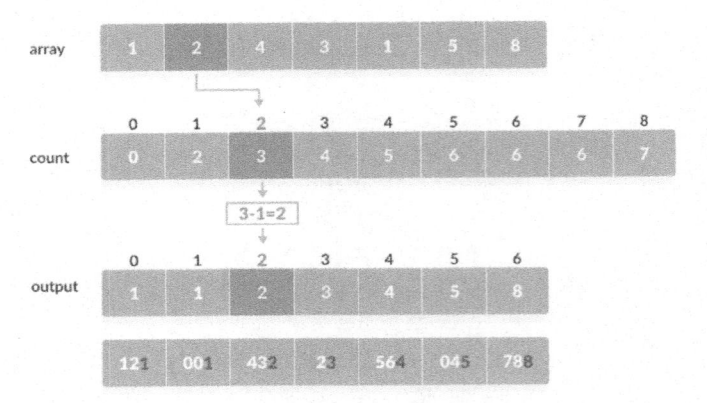

Using counting sort to sort elements based on unit place

3. Now, sort the elements based on digits at tens place.

Sort elements based on tens place

4. Finally, sort the elements based on the digits at hundreds place.

Sort elements based on hundreds place

Radix Sort Algorithm

```
radixSort(array)
  d <- maximum number of digits in the largest element
  create d buckets of size 0-9
  for i <- 0 to d
    sort the elements according to ith place digits using countingSort

countingSort(array, d)
  max <- find largest element among dth place elements
  initialize count array with all zeros
```

for j <- 0 to size
   find the total count of each unique digit in dth place of elements and
   store the count at jth index in count array
for i <- 1 to max
   find the cumulative sum and store it in count array itself
for j <- size down to 1
   restore the elements to array
   decrease count of each element restored by 1

```python
# Radix sort in Python

# Using counting sort to sort the elements in the basis of
significant places
def countingSort(array, place):
    size = len(array)
    output = [0] * size
    count = [0] * 10

    # Calculate count of elements
    for i in range(0, size):
        index = array[i] // place
        count[index % 10] += 1

    # Calculate cummulative count
    for i in range(1, 10):
        count[i] += count[i - 1]

    # Place the elements in sorted order
    i = size - 1
    while i >= 0:
        index = array[i] // place
        output[count[index % 10] - 1] = array[i]
        count[index % 10] -= 1
        i -= 1

    for i in range(0, size):
        array[i] = output[i]

# Main function to implement radix sort
def radixSort(array):
    # Get maximum element
    max_element = max(array)

    # Apply counting sort to sort elements based on place value.
    place = 1
    while max_element // place > 0:
        countingSort(array, place)
        place *= 10
```

```
data = [121, 432, 564, 23, 1, 45, 788]
radixSort(data)
print(data)
```

Output
[1, 23, 45, 121, 432, 564, 788]

Complexity
Since radix sort is a non-comparative algorithm, it has advantages over comparative sorting algorithms.

For the radix sort that uses counting sort as an intermediate stable sort, the time complexity is $O(d(n+k))$.

Here, d is the number cycle and $O(n+k)$ is the time complexity of counting sort.

Thus, radix sort has linear time complexity which is better than $O(n\log n)$ of comparative sorting algorithms.

If we take very large digit numbers or the number of other bases like 32-bit and 64-bit numbers then it can perform in linear time however the intermediate sort takes large space.

This makes radix sort space inefficient. This is the reason why this sort is not used in software libraries.

Radix Sort Applications
Radix sort is implemented in
- DC3 algorithm (Kärkkäinen-Sanders-Burkhardt) while making a suffix array.
- places where there are numbers in large ranges.

Bucket Sort

Bucket Sort is a sorting technique that sorts the elements by first dividing the elements into several groups called buckets. The elements inside each bucket are sorted using any of the suitable sorting algorithms or recursively calling the same algorithm.

Several buckets are created. Each bucket is filled with a specific range of elements. The elements inside the bucket are sorted using any other algorithm. Finally, the elements of the bucket are gathered to get the sorted array.

The process of bucket sort can be understood as a scatter-gather approach. The elements are first scattered into buckets then the elements of buckets are sorted. Finally, the elements are gathered in order.

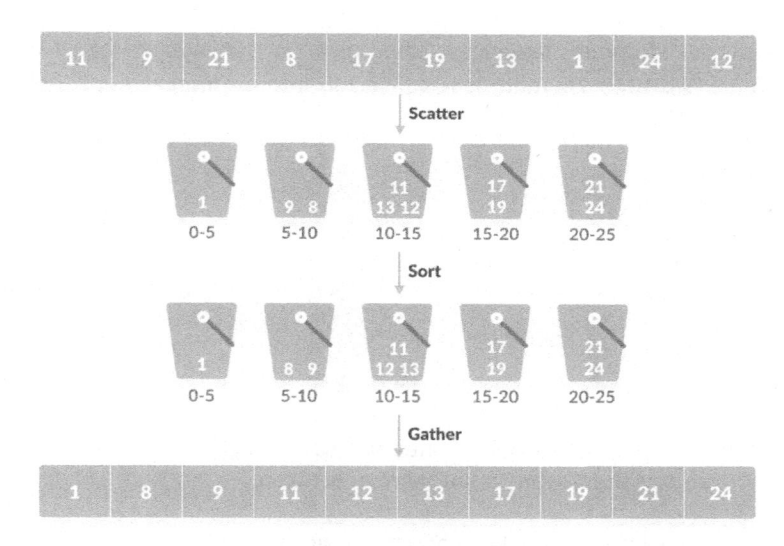

Working of Bucket Sort

How Bucket Sort Works?

1. Suppose, the input array is:

Input array

Create an array of size 10. Each slot of this array is used as a bucket for storing elements.

Array in which each position is a bucket

2. Insert elements into the buckets from the array. The elements are inserted according to the range of the bucket.

In our example code, we have buckets each of ranges from 0 to 1, 1 to 2, 2 to 3,...... (n-1) to n.

Suppose, an input element is .23 is taken. It is multiplied by size = 10 (ie. .23*10=2.3). Then, it is converted into an integer (ie. 2.3≈2). Finally, .23 is inserted into bucket-2.

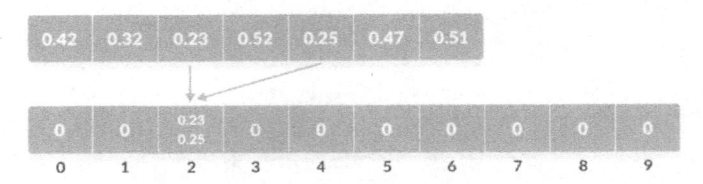

Insert elements into the buckets from the array

Similarly, .25 is also inserted into the same bucket. Everytime, the floor value of the floating point number is taken.

If we take integer numbers as input, we have to divide it by the interval (10 here) to get the floor value.

Similarly, other elements are inserted into their respective buckets.

Insert all the elements into the buckets from the array

3. The elements of each bucket are sorted using any of the stable sorting algorithms. Here, we have used quicksort (inbuilt function).

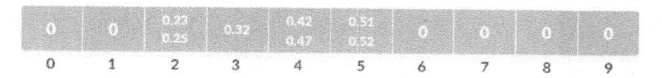

Sort the elements in each bucket

4. The elements from each bucket are gathered.

It is done by iterating through the bucket and inserting an individual element into the original array in each cycle. The element from the bucket is erased once it is copied into the original array.

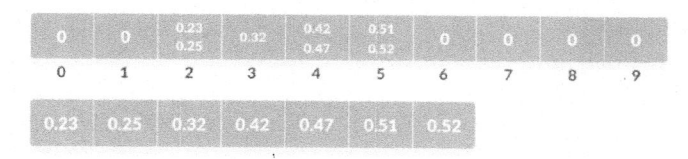

Gather elements from each bucket

Bucket Sort Algorithm

bucketSort()
  create N buckets each of which can hold a range of values
  for all the buckets
    initialize each bucket with 0 values
  for all the buckets
    put elements into buckets matching the range
  for all the buckets
    sort elements in each bucket
  gather elements from each bucket
end bucketSort

```python
# Bucket Sort in Python

def bucketSort(array):
    bucket = []

    # Create empty buckets
    for i in range(len(array)):
        bucket.append([])

    # Insert elements into their respective buckets
    for j in array:
        index_b = int(10 * j)
```

```
            bucket[index_b].append(j)

    # Sort the elements of each bucket
    for i in range(len(array)):
        bucket[i] = sorted(bucket[i])

    # Get the sorted elements
    k = 0
    for i in range(len(array)):
        for j in range(len(bucket[i])):
            array[k] = bucket[i][j]
            k += 1
    return array

array = [.42, .32, .33, .52, .37, .47, .51]
print("Sorted Array in descending order is")
print(bucketSort(array))
```

Output
Sorted Array in descending order is
[0.32, 0.33, 0.37, 0.42, 0.47, 0.51, 0.52]

Complexity

- Worst Case Complexity: O(n²)

When there are elements of close range in the array, they are likely to be placed in the same bucket. This may result in some buckets having more number of elements than others.

It makes the complexity depend on the sorting algorithm used to sort the elements of the bucket.

The complexity becomes even worse when the elements are in reverse order. If insertion sort is used to sort elements of the bucket, then the time complexity becomes O(n²).

- Best Case Complexity: O(n+k)

It occurs when the elements are uniformly distributed in the buckets with a nearly equal number of elements in each bucket.

The complexity becomes even better if the elements inside the buckets are already sorted.

If insertion sort is used to sort elements of a bucket then the overall complexity in the best case will be linear ie. O(n+k). O(n) is the complexity for making the buckets and O(k) is the complexity for sorting the elements of the bucket using algorithms having linear time complexity at the best case.

- Average Case Complexity: O(n)

It occurs when the elements are distributed randomly in the array. Even if the elements are not distributed uniformly, bucket sort runs in linear time. It holds true until the sum of the squares of the bucket sizes is linear in the total number of elements.

Bucket Sort Applications
Bucket sort is used when:
- input is uniformly distributed over a range.
- there are floating point values

Heap Sort

Heap Sort is a popular and efficient sorting algorithm in computer programming. Learning how to write the heap sort algorithm requires knowledge of two types of data structures - arrays and trees.

The initial set of numbers that we want to sort is stored in an array e.g. [10, 3, 76, 34, 23, 32] and after sorting, we get a sorted array [3,10,23,32,34,76]

Heap sort works by visualizing the elements of the array as a special kind of complete binary tree called a heap.

As a prerequisite, you must know about a complete binary tree and heap data structure.

Relationship between Array Indexes and Tree Elements
A complete binary tree has an interesting property that we can use to find the children and parents of any node.

If the index of any element in the array is i, the element in the index $2i+1$ will become the left child and element in $2i+2$ index will become the right child. Also, the parent of any element at index i is given by the lower bound of (i-1)/2.

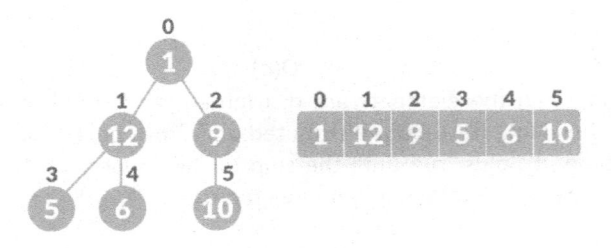

Relationship between array and heap indices

Let's test it out,

Left child of 1 (index 0)
= element in (2*0+1) index
= element in 1 index
= 12

Right child of 1
= element in (2*0+2) index
= element in 2 index
= 9

Similarly,
Left child of 12 (index 1)
= element in (2*1+1) index
= element in 3 index
= 5

Right child of 12
= element in (2*1+2) index
= element in 4 index
= 6

Let us also confirm that the rules hold for finding parent of any node

Parent of 9 (position 2)
= (2-1)/2
= ½

= 0.5
~ 0 index
= 1

Parent of 12 (position 1)
= (1-1)/2
= 0 index
= 1

Understanding this mapping of array indexes to tree positions is critical to understanding how the Heap Data Structure works and how it is used to implement Heap Sort.

What is Heap Data Structure?
Heap is a special tree-based data structure. A binary tree is said to follow a heap data structure if
- it is a complete binary tree
- All nodes in the tree follow the property that they are greater than their children i.e. the largest element is at the root and both its children and smaller than the root and so on. Such a heap is called a max-heap. If instead, all nodes are smaller than their children, it is called a min-heap

The following example diagram shows Max-Heap and Min-Heap.

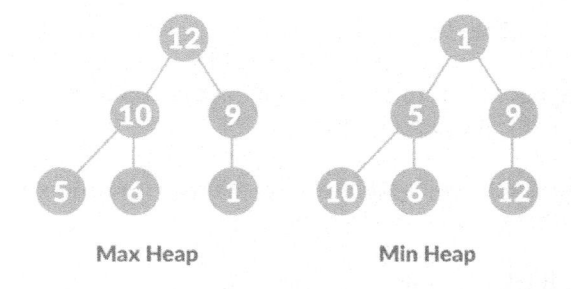

Max Heap and Min Heap

How to "heapify" a tree
Starting from a complete binary tree, we can modify it to become a Max-Heap by running a function called heapify on all the non-leaf elements of the heap.

Since heapify uses recursion, it can be difficult to grasp. So let's first think about how you would heapify a tree with just three elements.

```
heapify(array)
    Root = array[0]
    Largest = largest( array[0] , array [2*0 + 1]. array[2*0+2])
    if(Root != Largest)
        Swap(Root, Largest)
```

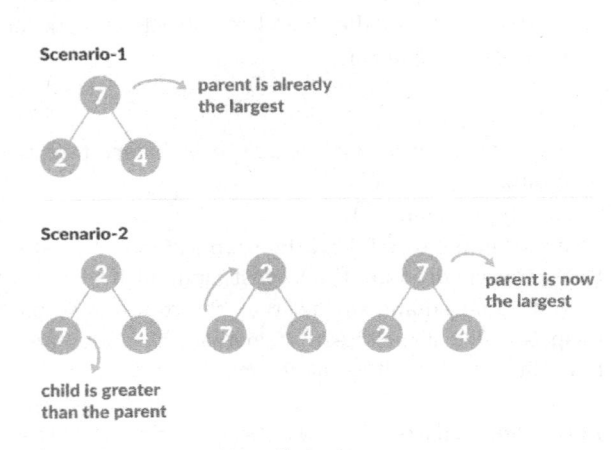

Scenario-1

parent is already the largest

Scenario-2

parent is now the largest

child is greater than the parent

Heapify base cases

The example above shows two scenarios - one in which the root is the largest element and we don't need to do anything. And another in which the root had a larger element as a child and we needed to swap to maintain max-heap property.

If you're worked with recursive algorithms before, you've probably identified that this must be the base case.

Now let's think of another scenario in which there is more than one level.

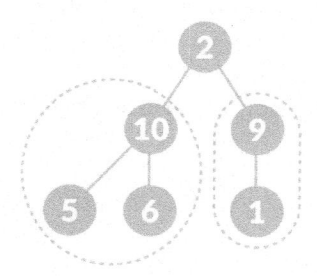

**both subtrees of the root
are already max-heaps**

How to heapify root element when its subtrees are already max heaps

The top element isn't a max-heap but all the sub-trees are max-heaps.

To maintain the max-heap property for the entire tree, we will have to keep pushing 2 downwards until it reaches its correct position.

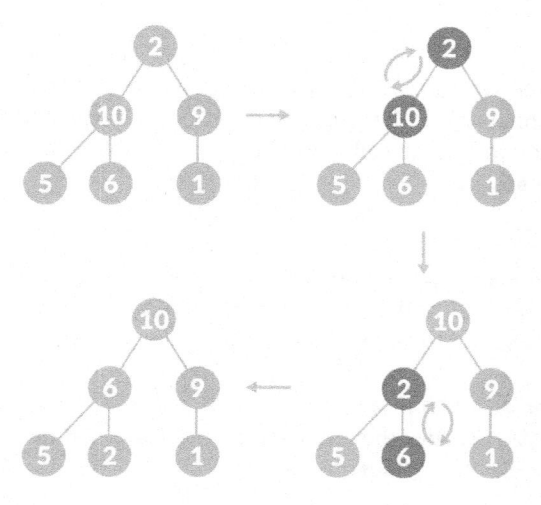

How to heapify root element when its subtrees are max-heaps

Thus, to maintain the max-heap property in a tree where both subtrees are max-heaps, we need to run heapify on the root element repeatedly until it is larger than its children or it becomes a leaf node.

We can combine both these conditions in one heapify function as

```
void heapify(int arr[], int n, int i) {
  // Find largest among root, left child and right child
  int largest = i;
  int left = 2 * i + 1;
  int right = 2 * i + 2;

  if (left < n && arr[left] > arr[largest])
    largest = left;

  if (right < n && arr[right] > arr[largest])
    largest = right;

  // Swap and continue heapifying if root is not largest
  if (largest != i) {
    swap(&arr[i], &arr[largest]);
    heapify(arr, n, largest);
  }
}
```

This function works for both the base case and for a tree of any size. We can thus move the root element to the correct position to maintain the max-heap status for any tree size as long as the sub-trees are max-heaps.

Build max-heap

To build a max-heap from any tree, we can thus start heapifying each sub-tree from the bottom up and end up with a max-heap after the function is applied to all the elements including the root element.

In the case of a complete tree, the first index of a non-leaf node is given by $n/2 - 1$. All other nodes after that are leaf-nodes and thus don't need to be heapified.

So, we can build a maximum heap as

```
// Build heap (rearrange array)
for (int i = n / 2 - 1; i >= 0; i--)
  heapify(arr, n, i);
```

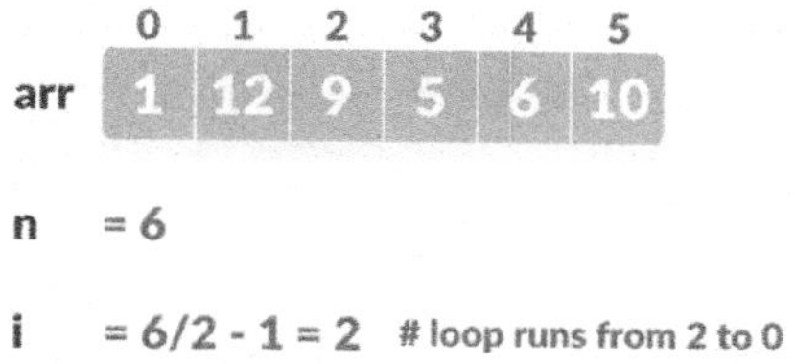

```
        0   1   2   3   4   5
arr     1  12   9   5   6  10

n   = 6

i   = 6/2 - 1 = 2   # loop runs from 2 to 0
```

Create array and calculate i

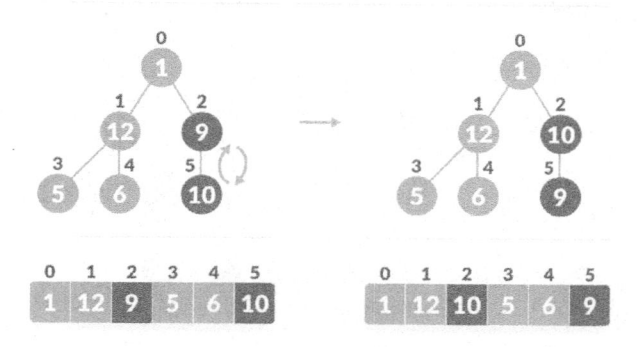

i = 2 ⟶ heapify(arr, 6, 2)

```
        0   1   2   3   4   5            0   1   2   3   4   5
        1  12   9   5   6  10            1  12  10   5   6   9
```

Steps to build max heap for heap sort

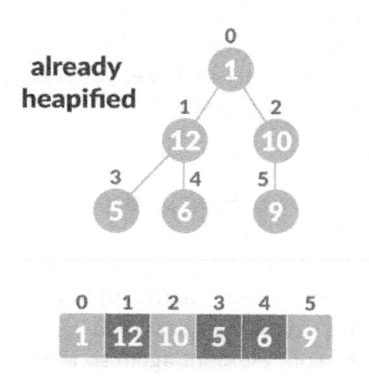

i = 1 ⟶ heapify(arr, 6, 1)

already heapified

```
        0   1   2   3   4   5
        1  12  10   5   6   9
```

Steps to build max heap for heap sort

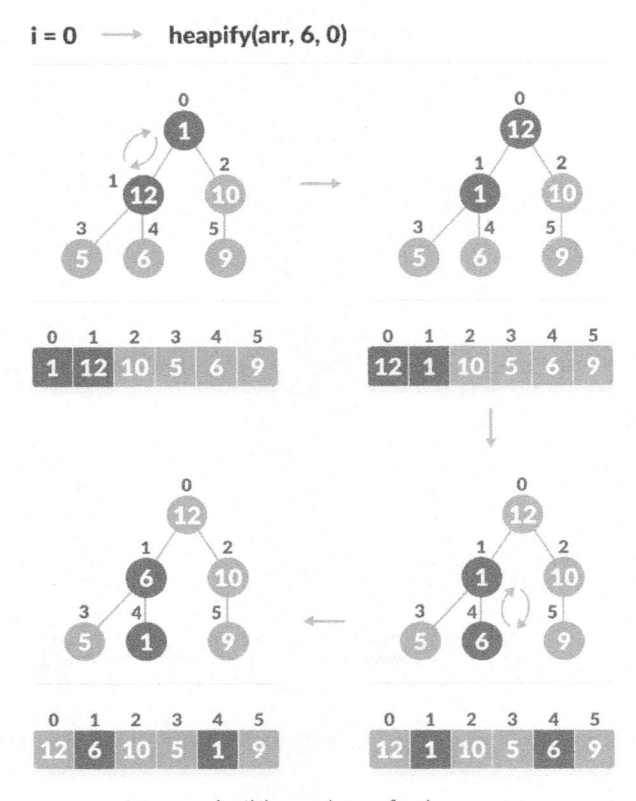

i = 0 ⟶ heapify(arr, 6, 0)

Steps to build max heap for heap sort

As shown in the above diagram, we start by heapifying the lowest smallest trees and gradually move up until we reach the root element. If you've understood everything till here, congratulations, you are on your way to mastering the Heap sort.

How Heap Sort Works?
1. Since the tree satisfies Max-Heap property, then the largest item is stored at the root node.
2. Swap: Remove the root element and put at the end of the array (nth position) Put the last item of the tree (heap) at the vacant place.
3. Remove: Reduce the size of the heap by 1.
4. Heapify: Heapify the root element again so that we have the highest element at root.

5. The process is repeated until all the items of the list are sorted.

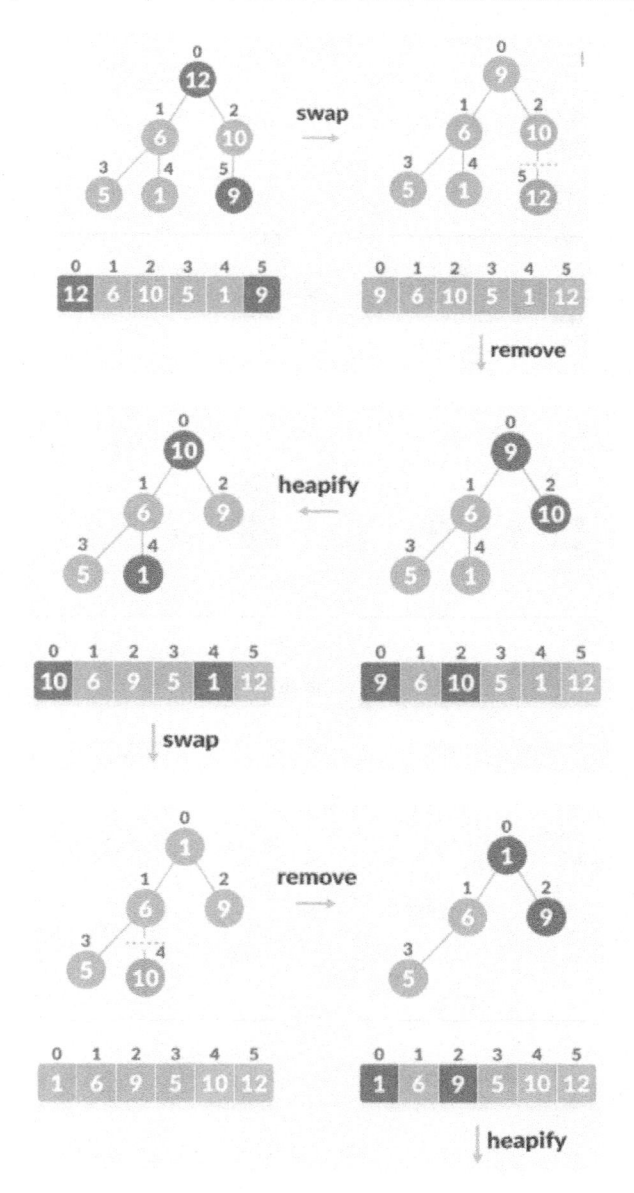

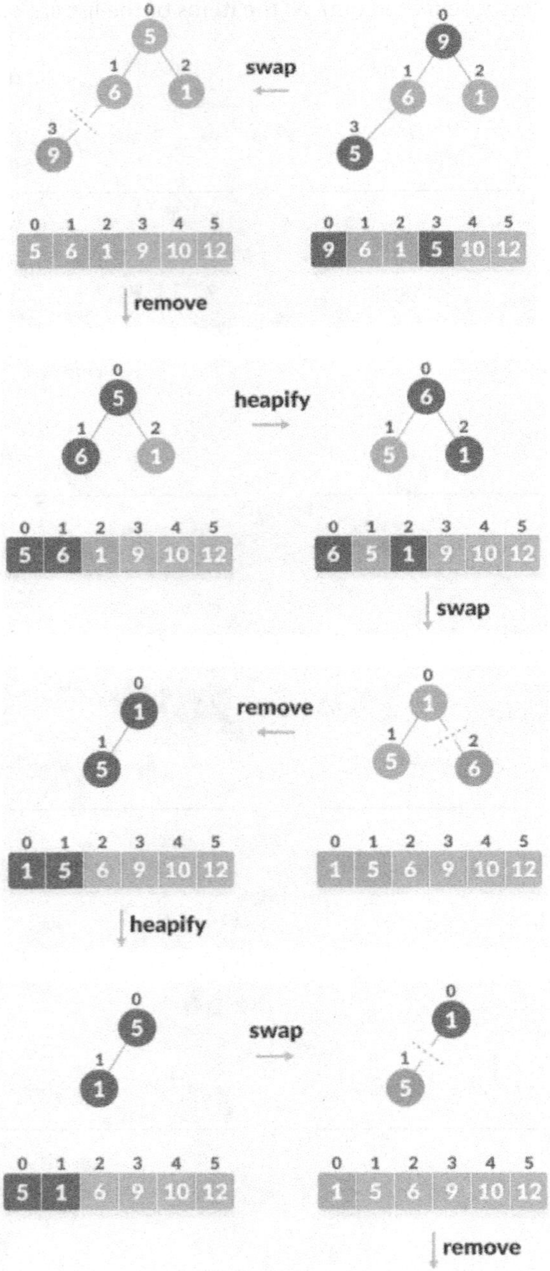
swap
5 6 1 9 10 12
9 6 1 5 10 12
remove
heapify
5 6 1 9 10 12
6 5 1 9 10 12
swap
remove
1 5 6 9 10 12
1 5 6 9 10 12
heapify
swap
5 1 6 9 10 12
1 5 6 9 10 12
remove

Swap, Remove, and Heapify

The code below shows the operation.

```
// Heap sort
for (int i = n - 1; i >= 0; i--) {
  swap(&arr[0], &arr[i]);

  // Heapify root element to get highest element at root again
  heapify(arr, i, 0);
}
```

```python
# Heap Sort in python

def heapify(arr, n, i):
    # Find largest among root and children
    largest = i
    l = 2 * i + 1
    r = 2 * i + 2

    if l < n and arr[i] < arr[l]:
        largest = l

    if r < n and arr[largest] < arr[r]:
        largest = r

    # If root is not largest, swap with largest and continue heapifying
    if largest != i:
        arr[i], arr[largest] = arr[largest], arr[i]
        heapify(arr, n, largest)

def heapSort(arr):
    n = len(arr)

    # Build max heap
    for i in range(n//2, -1, -1):
        heapify(arr, n, i)

    for i in range(n-1, 0, -1):
        # Swap
```

```
            arr[i], arr[0] = arr[0], arr[i]

            # Heapify root element
            heapify(arr, i, 0)
arr = [1, 12, 9, 5, 6, 10]
heapSort(arr)
n = len(arr)
print("Sorted array is")
for i in range(n):
    print("%d " % arr[i], end='')
```

Output
Sorted array is
1 5 6 9 10 12

Heap Sort Complexity
Heap Sort has $O(n \log n)$ time complexities for all the cases (best case, average case, and worst case).

Let us understand the reason why. The height of a complete binary tree
containing n elements is $\log n$

As we have seen earlier, to fully heapify an element whose subtrees are already max-heaps, we need to keep comparing the element with its left and right children and pushing it downwards until it reaches a point where both its children are smaller than it.

In the worst case scenario, we will need to move an element from the root to the leaf node making a multiple of $\log(n)$ comparisons and swaps.

During the build_max_heap stage, we do that for $n/2$ elements so the worst case complexity of the build_heap step is $n/2 * \log n \sim n \log n$.
During the sorting step, we exchange the root element with the last element and heapify the root element. For each element, this again takes $\log n$ worst time because we might have to bring the element all the way from the root to the leaf. Since we repeat this n times, the heap_sort step is also $n \log n$.

Also since the build_max_heap and heap_sort steps are executed one after another, the algorithmic complexity is not multiplied and it remains in the order of nlog n.

Also it performs sorting in O(1) space complexity. Compared with Quick Sort, it has a better worst case (O(nlog n)). Quick Sort has complexity O(n^2) for worst case. But in other cases, Quick Sort is fast. Introsort is an alternative to heapsort that combines quicksort and heapsort to retain advantages of both: worst case speed of heapsort and average speed of quicksort.

Heap Sort Applications
Systems concerned with security and embedded systems such as Linux Kernel use Heap Sort because of the O(n log n) upper bound on Heapsort's running time and constant O(1) upper bound on its auxiliary storage.

Although Heap Sort has O(n log n) time complexity even for the worst case, it doesn't have more applications (compared to other sorting algorithms like Quick Sort, Merge Sort). However, its underlying data structure, heap, can be efficiently used if we want to extract the smallest (or largest) from the list of items without the overhead of keeping the remaining items in the sorted order. For e.g Priority Queues.

Shell Sort

Shell sort is an algorithm that first sorts the elements far apart from each other and successively reduces the interval between the elements to be sorted. It is a generalized version of insertion sort.

In shell sort, elements at a specific interval are sorted. The interval between the elements is gradually decreased based on the sequence used. The performance of the shell sort depends on the type of sequence used for a given input array.

Some of the optimal sequences used are:
- Shell's original sequence: N/2 , N/4 , ..., 1

- Knuth's increments: 1, 4, 13, ..., (3k – 1) / 2
- Sedgewick's increments: 1, 8, 23, 77, 281, 1073, 4193, 16577...4j+1+ 3·2j+ 1
- Hibbard's increments: 1, 3, 7, 15, 31, 63, 127, 255, 511...
- Papernov & Stasevich increment: 1, 3, 5, 9, 17, 33, 65,...
- Pratt: 1, 2, 3, 4, 6, 9, 8, 12, 18, 27, 16, 24, 36, 54, 81....

How Shell Sort Works?

1. Suppose, we need to sort the following array.

| 9 | 8 | 3 | 7 | 5 | 6 | 4 | 1 |

Initial array

2. We are using the shell's original sequence (N/2, N/4, ...1) as intervals in our algorithm.

In the first loop, if the array size is N = 8 then, the elements lying at the interval of N/2 = 4 are compared and swapped if they are not in order.

- The 0th element is compared with the 4th element.
- If the 0th element is greater than the 4th one then, the 4th element is first stored in temp variable and the 0th element (ie. greater element) is stored in the 4th position and the element stored in temp is stored in the 0th position.

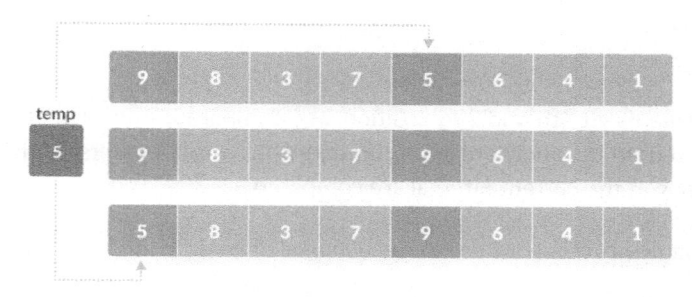

Rearrange the elements at n/2 interval

This process goes on for all the remaining elements.

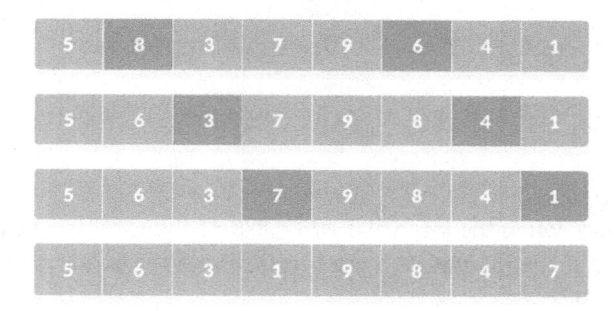

Rearrange all the elements at n/2 interval

3. In the second loop, an interval of N/4 = 8/4 = 2 is taken and again the elements lying at these intervals are sorted.

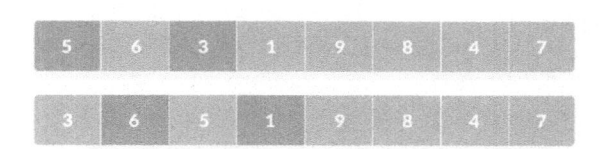

Rearrange the elements at n/4 interval

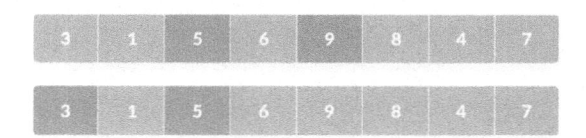

All the elements in the array lying at the current interval are compared.

The elements at 4th and 2nd position are compared. The elements at 2nd and 0th position are also compared. All the elements in the array lying at the current interval are compared.

4. The same process goes on for remaining elements.

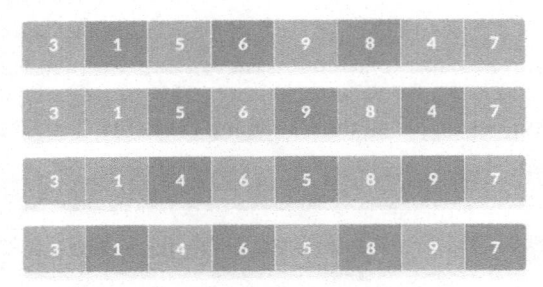

3	1	5	6	9	8	4	7
3	1	5	6	9	8	4	7
3	1	4	6	5	8	9	7
3	1	4	6	5	8	9	7

Rearrange all the elements at n/4 interval

5. Finally, when the interval is N/8 = 8/8 =1 then the array elements lying at the interval of 1 are sorted. The array is now completely sorted.

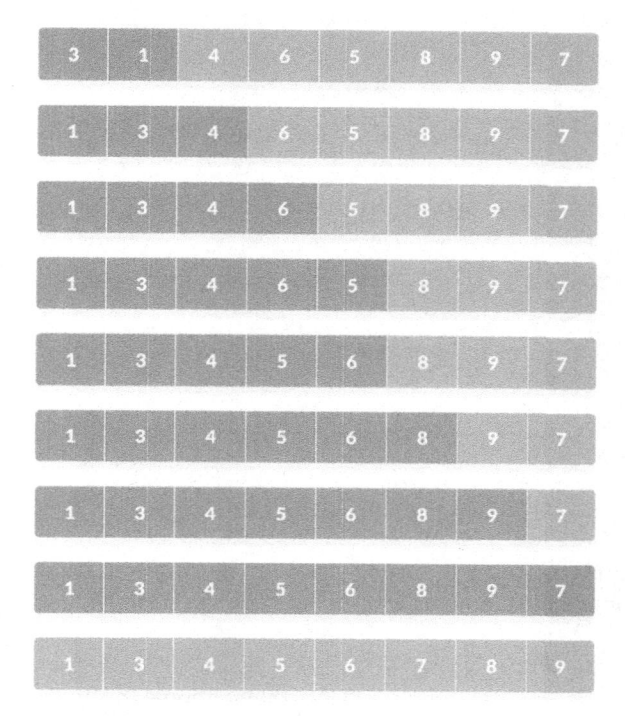

Rearrange the elements at n/8 interval

Shell Sort Algorithm

```
shellSort(array, size)
  for interval i <- size/2n down to 1
    for each interval "i" in array
      sort all the elements at interval "i"
end shellSort
```

```python
# Shell sort in python

def shellSort(array, n):

    # Rearrange elements at each n/2, n/4, n/8, ... interva
ls
    interval = n // 2
    while interval > 0:
```

305

```
            for i in range(interval, n):
                temp = array[i]
                j = i
                while j >= interval and array[j - interval] > t
emp:
                    array[j] = array[j - interval]
                    j -= interval

                array[j] = temp
            interval //= 2
data = [9, 8, 3, 7, 5, 6, 4, 1]
size = len(data)
shellSort(data, size)
print('Sorted Array in Ascending Order:')
print(data)
```

Output
```
Sorted Array in Ascending Order:
[1, 3, 4, 5, 6, 7, 8, 9]
```

Complexity
Shell sort is an unstable sorting algorithm because this algorithm does not examine the elements lying in between the intervals.

Time Complexity
- Worst Case Complexity: less than or equal to O(n2)

Worst case complexity for shell sort is always less than or equal to O(n2).

According to Poonen Theorem, worst case complexity for shell sort is $\Theta(N\log N)^2/(\log \log N)^2)$ or $\Theta(N\log N)^2/\log \log N)$ or $\Theta(N(\log N)^2)$ or something in between.

- Best Case Complexity: O(n*log n)

When the array is already sorted, the total number of comparisons for each interval (or increment) is equal to the size of the array.

- Average Case Complexity: O(n*log n)

It is around $O(n^{1.25})$.

The complexity depends on the interval chosen. The above complexities differ for different increment sequences chosen. Best increment sequence is unknown.

Space Complexity:
The space complexity for shell sort is O(1).

Shell Sort Applications
Shell sort is used when:
- calling a stack is overhead. uClibc library uses this sort.
- recursion exceeds a limit. bzip2 compressor uses it.
- Insertion sort does not perform well when the close elements are far apart. Shell sort helps in reducing the distance between the close elements. Thus, there will be less number of swappings to be performed.

Search

Linear Search

Linear search is the simplest searching algorithm that searches for an element in a list in sequential order. We start at one end and check every element until the desired element is not found.

How Linear Search Works?
The following steps are followed to search for an element k = 1 in the list below.

Array to be searched for

1. Start from the first element, compare k with each element x.

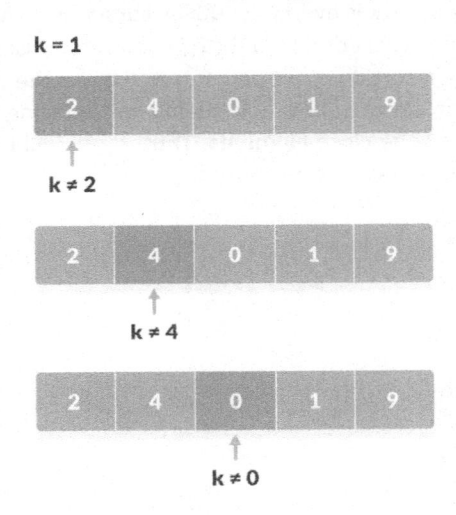

k = 1

k ≠ 2

k ≠ 4

k ≠ 0

Compare with each element

2. If x == k, return the index.

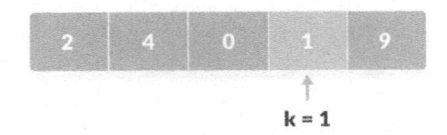

k = 1

Element found

3. Else, return not found.

Linear Search Algorithm

```
LinearSearch(array, key)
  for each item in the array
    if item == value
```

return its index

Linear Search Complexities
Time Complexity: O(n)
Space Complexity: O(1)

Linear Search Applications
1. For searching operations in smaller arrays (<100 items).

Binary Search

Binary Search is a searching algorithm for finding an element's position in a sorted array.

In this approach, the element is always searched in the middle of a portion of an array.

Binary search can be implemented only on a sorted list of items. If the elements are not sorted already, we need to sort them first.

Binary Search Working
Binary Search Algorithm can be implemented in two ways which are discussed below.
1. Iterative Method
2. Recursive Method

The recursive method follows the divide and conquer approach.

The general steps for both methods are discussed below.

1. The array in which searching is to be performed is:

| 3 | 4 | 5 | 6 | 7 | 8 | 9 |

Initial array

Let x = 4 be the element to be searched.

2. Set two pointers low and high at the lowest and the highest positions respectively.

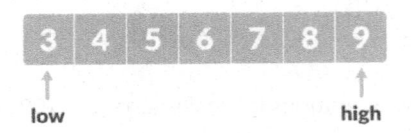

| 3 | 4 | 5 | 6 | 7 | 8 | 9 |
↑   ↑
low   high

Setting pointers

3. Find the middle element mid of the array ie. (arr[low + high]) / 2 = 6.

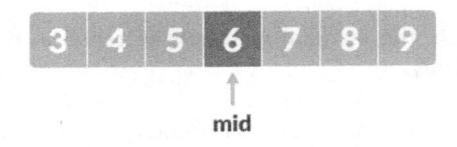

| 3 | 4 | 5 | 6 | 7 | 8 | 9 |
↑
mid

Mid element

4. If x == mid, then return mid. Else, compare the element to be searched with m.

5. If x > mid, compare x with the middle element of the elements on the right side of mid. This is done by setting low to low = mid + 1.

6. Else, compare x with the middle element of the elements on the left side of mid. This is done by setting high to high = mid - 1.

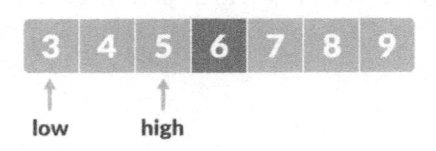

| 3 | 4 | 5 | 6 | 7 | 8 | 9 |
↑   ↑
low   high

Finding mid element

Repeat steps 3 to 6 until low meets high.

3	4	5

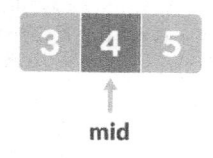

↑
mid

Mid element

x = 4 is found.

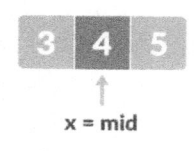

3	4	5

↑
x = mid

Found

Binary Search Algorithm

Iteration Method

do until the pointers low and high meet each other.
   mid = (low + high)/2
   if (x == arr[mid])
      return mid
   else if (x > A[mid]) // x is on the right side
      low = mid + 1
   else   // x is on the left side
      high = mid - 1

Recursive Method

binarySearch(arr, x, low, high)
   if low > high
      return False
   else
      mid = (low + high) / 2
      if x == arr[mid]
         return mid

```
        else if x < data[mid]      // x is on the right side
            return binarySearch(arr, x, mid + 1, high)
        else                       // x is on the right side
            return binarySearch(arr, x, low, mid - 1)
```

Iterative Method

```python
# Binary Search in python

def binarySearch(array, x, low, high):

    # Repeat until the pointers low and high meet each other
    while low <= high:

        mid = low + (high - low)//2

        if array[mid] == x:
            return mid

        elif array[mid] < x:
            low = mid + 1

        else:
            high = mid - 1

    return -1

array = [3, 4, 5, 6, 7, 8, 9]
x = 4

result = binarySearch(array, x, 0, len(array)-1)

if result != -1:
    print("Element is present at index " + str(result))
else:
    print("Not found")
```

Output
```
Element is present at index 1
```

Recursive Method

```python
# Binary Search in python

def binarySearch(array, x, low, high):

    if high >= low:

        mid = low + (high - low)//2
```

312

```
        # If found at mid, then return it
        if array[mid] == x:
            return mid

        # Search the left half
        elif array[mid] > x:
            return binarySearch(array, x, low, mid-1)

        # Search the right half
        else:
            return binarySearch(array, x, mid + 1, high)

    else:
        return -1

array = [3, 4, 5, 6, 7, 8, 9]
x = 4

result = binarySearch(array, x, 0, len(array)-1)

if result != -1:
    print("Element is present at index " + str(result))
else:
    print("Not found")
```

Output
Element is present at index 1

Binary Search Complexity

Time Complexities
- Best case complexity: O(1)
- Average case complexity: O(log n)
- Worst case complexity: O(log n)

Space Complexity
The space complexity of the binary search is O(n).

Binary Search Applications
- In libraries of Java, .Net, C++ STL
- While debugging, the binary search is used to pinpoint the place where the error happens.

Greedy Algorithm

A greedy algorithm is an approach for solving a problem by selecting the best option available at the moment, without worrying about the future result it would bring. In other words, the locally best choices aim at producing globally best results.

This algorithm may not be the best option for all the problems. It may produce wrong results in some cases.

This algorithm never goes back to reverse the decision made. This algorithm works in a top-down approach.
The main advantage of this algorithm is:

1. The algorithm is easier to describe.
2. This algorithm can perform better than other algorithms (but, not in all cases).

Feasible Solution
A feasible solution is the one that provides the optimal solution to the problem.

Greedy Algorithm
1. To begin with, the solution set (containing answers) is empty.
2. At each step, an item is added into the solution set.
3. If the solution set is feasible, the current item is kept.
4. Else, the item is rejected and never considered again.

Example - Greedy Approach
Problem: You have to make a change of an amount using the smallest possible number of coins.
Amount: $28
Available coins:
 $5 coin
 $2 coin
 $1 coin

Solution:
1. Create an empty solution-set = { }.
2. coins = {5, 2, 1}
3. sum = 0
4. While sum ≠ 28, do the following.
5. Select a coin C from coins such that sum + C < 28.
6. If C + sum > 28, return no solution.
7. Else, sum = sum + C.
8. Add C to solution-set.

Up to the first 5 iterations, the solution set contains 5 $5 coins. After that, we get 1 $2 coin and finally, 1 $1 coin.

Greedy Algorithm Applications
- Selection Sort
- Knapsack Problem

- Minimum Spanning Tree
- Single-Source Shortest Path Problem
- Job Scheduling Problem
- Prim's Minimal Spanning Tree Algorithm
- Kruskal's Minimal Spanning Tree Algorithm
- Dijkstra's Minimal Spanning Tree Algorithm
- Huffman Coding
- Ford-Fulkerson Algorithm

Ford-Fulkerson Algorithm

Ford-Fulkerson algorithm is a greedy approach for calculating the maximum possible flow in a network or a graph.

A term, flow network, is used to describe a network of vertices and edges with a source (S) and a sink (T). Each vertex, except S and T, can receive and send an equal amount of stuff through it. S can only send and T can only receive stuff.

We can visualize the understanding of the algorithm using a flow of liquid inside a network of pipes of different capacities. Each pipe has a certain capacity of liquid it can transfer at an instance. For this algorithm, we are going to find how much liquid can be flowed from the source to the sink at an instance using the network.

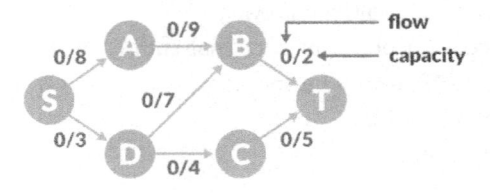

Flow network graph

Terminologies Used

Augmenting Path
It is the path available in a flow network.

Residual Graph
It represents the flow network that has additional possible flow.

Residual Capacity
It is the capacity of the edge after subtracting the flow from the maximum capacity.

How Ford-Fulkerson Algorithm works?

The algorithm follows:
1. Initialize the flow in all the edges to 0.
2. While there is an augmenting path between the source and the sink, add this path to the flow.
3. Update the residual graph.

We can also consider reverse-path if required because if we do not consider them, we may never find a maximum flow.

The above concepts can be understood with the example below.

Ford-Fulkerson Example

The flow of all the edges is 0 at the beginning.

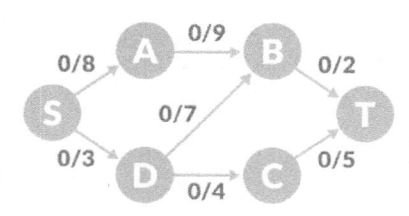

Flow network graph example

1. Select any arbitrary path from S to T. In this step, we have selected path S-A-B-T.

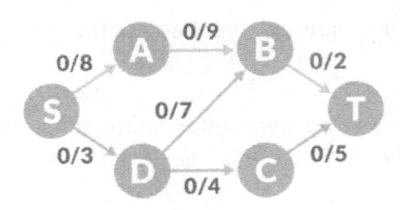

Find a path

The minimum capacity among the three edges is 2 (B-T). Based on this, update the flow/capacity for each path.

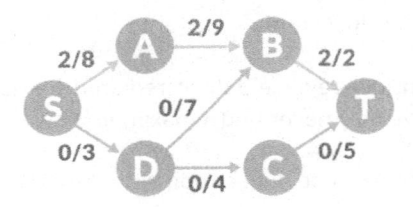

Update the capacities

2. Select another path S-D-C-T. The minimum capacity among these edges is 3 (S-D).

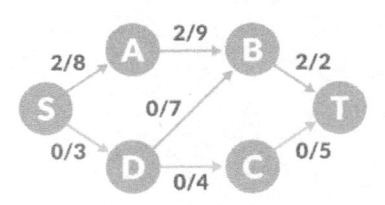

Find next path

Update the capacities according to this.

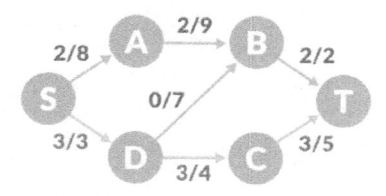

Update the capacities

3. Now, let us consider the reverse-path B-D as well. Selecting path S-A-B-D-C-T. The minimum residual capacity among the edges is 1 (D-C).

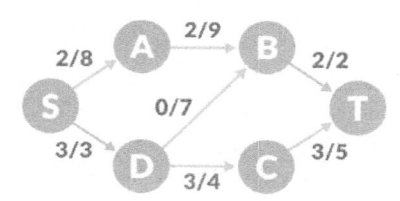

Find next path

Updating the capacities.

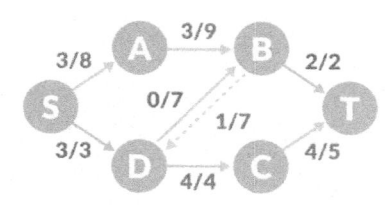

Update the capacities

The capacity for forward and reverse paths are considered separately.

4. Adding all the flows = 2 + 3 + 1 = 6, which is the maximum possible flow on the flow network.

Note that if the capacity for any edge is full, then that path cannot be used.

```
# Ford-Fulkerson algorith in Python
```

```python
from collections import defaultdict

class Graph:

    def __init__(self, graph):
        self.graph = graph
        self.ROW = len(graph)


    # Using BFS as a searching algorithm
    def searching_algo_BFS(self, s, t, parent):

        visited = [False] * (self.ROW)
        queue = []

        queue.append(s)
        visited[s] = True

        while queue:

            u = queue.pop(0)

            for ind, val in enumerate(self.graph[u]):
                if visited[ind] == False and val > 0:
                    queue.append(ind)
                    visited[ind] = True
                    parent[ind] = u

        return True if visited[t] else False

    # Applying fordfulkerson algorithm
    def ford_fulkerson(self, source, sink):
        parent = [-1] * (self.ROW)
        max_flow = 0

        while self.searching_algo_BFS(source, sink, parent):

            path_flow = float("Inf")
            s = sink
            while(s != source):
                path_flow = min(path_flow, self.graph[parent[s]][s])
                s = parent[s]

            # Adding the path flows
            max_flow += path_flow

            # Updating the residual values of edges
            v = sink
            while(v != source):
                u = parent[v]
                self.graph[u][v] -= path_flow
                self.graph[v][u] += path_flow
```

```
                v = parent[v]

        return max_flow
graph = [[0, 8, 0, 0, 3, 0],
         [0, 0, 9, 0, 0, 0],
         [0, 0, 0, 0, 7, 2],
         [0, 0, 0, 0, 0, 5],
         [0, 0, 7, 4, 0, 0],
         [0, 0, 0, 0, 0, 0]]

g = Graph(graph)

source = 0
sink = 5

print("Max Flow: %d " % g.ford_fulkerson(source, sink))
```

Output
Max Flow: 6

Ford-Fulkerson Applications
- Water distribution pipeline
- Bipartite matching problem
- Circulation with demands

Dijkstra's Algorithm

Dijkstra's algorithm allows us to find the shortest path between any two vertices of a graph.

It differs from the minimum spanning tree because the shortest distance between two vertices might not include all the vertices of the graph.

How Dijkstra's Algorithm works
Dijkstra's Algorithm works on the basis that any subpath B -> D of the shortest path A -> D between vertices A and D is also the shortest path between vertices B and D.

the shortest path between the source and destination
a subpath which is also the shortest path between its source and destination

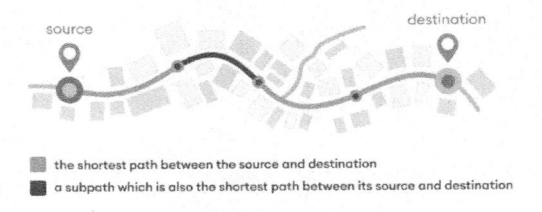

Each subpath is the shortest path

Djikstra used this property in the opposite direction i.e we overestimate the distance of each vertex from the starting vertex. Then we visit each node and its neighbors to find the shortest subpath to those neighbors.

The algorithm uses a greedy approach in the sense that we find the next best solution hoping that the end result is the best solution for the whole problem.

Example of Dijkstra's algorithm

It is easier to start with an example and then think about the algorithm.

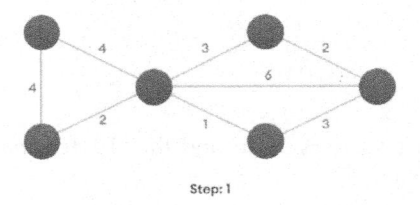

Step: 1

Start with a weighted graph

Step: 2

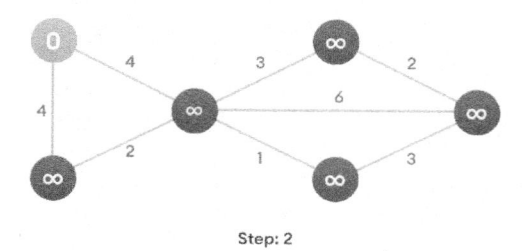

Choose a starting vertex and assign infinity path values to all other devices

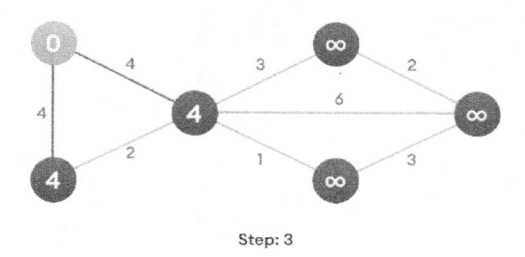

Step: 3

Go to each vertex and update its path length

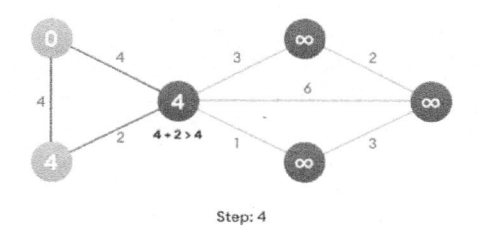

Step: 4

If the path length of the adjacent vertex is lesser than new path length, don't update it

323

Step: 5

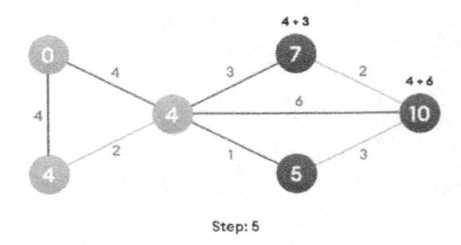

Avoid updating path lengths of already visited vertices

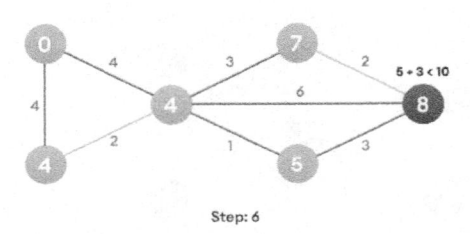

Step: 6

After each iteration, we pick the unvisited vertex with the least path length. So we choose 5 before 7

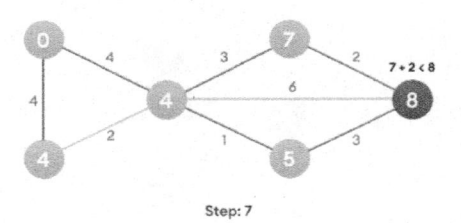

Step: 7

Notice how the rightmost vertex has its path length updated twice

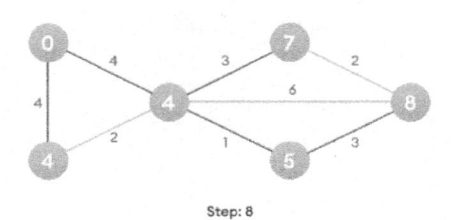

Step: 8

Repeat until all the vertices have been visited

Djikstra's algorithm pseudocode

We need to maintain the path distance of every vertex. We can store that in an array of size v, where v is the number of vertices.

We also want to be able to get the shortest path, not only know the length of the shortest path. For this, we map each vertex to the vertex that last updated its path length.

Once the algorithm is over, we can backtrack from the destination vertex to the source vertex to find the path.

A minimum priority queue can be used to efficiently receive the vertex with least path distance.

```
function dijkstra(G, S)
    for each vertex V in G
        distance[V] <- infinite
        previous[V] <- NULL
        If V != S, add V to Priority Queue Q
    distance[S] <- 0

    while Q IS NOT EMPTY
        U <- Extract MIN from Q
        for each unvisited neighbour V of U
            tempDistance <- distance[U] + edge_weight(U, V)
            if tempDistance < distance[V]
                distance[V] <- tempDistance
                previous[V] <- U
    return distance[], previous[]
```

Code for Dijkstra's Algorithm

```python
# Dijkstra's Algorithm in Python

import sys

# Providing the graph
vertices = [[0, 0, 1, 1, 0, 0, 0],
            [0, 0, 1, 0, 0, 1, 0],
            [1, 1, 0, 1, 1, 0, 0],
            [1, 0, 1, 0, 0, 0, 1],
```

```
                [0, 0, 1, 0, 0, 1, 0],
                [0, 1, 0, 0, 1, 0, 1],
                [0, 0, 0, 1, 0, 1, 0]]

edges = [[0, 0, 1, 2, 0, 0, 0],
         [0, 0, 2, 0, 0, 3, 0],
         [1, 2, 0, 1, 3, 0, 0],
         [2, 0, 1, 0, 0, 0, 1],
         [0, 0, 3, 0, 0, 2, 0],
         [0, 3, 0, 0, 2, 0, 1],
         [0, 0, 0, 1, 0, 1, 0]]

# Find which vertex is to be visited next
def to_be_visited():
    global visited_and_distance
    v = -10
    for index in range(num_of_vertices):
        if visited_and_distance[index][0] == 0 \
            and (v < 0 or visited_and_distance[index][1] <=
                    visited_and_distance[v][1]):
            v = index
    return v

num_of_vertices = len(vertices[0])

visited_and_distance = [[0, 0]]
for i in range(num_of_vertices-1):
    visited_and_distance.append([0, sys.maxsize])

for vertex in range(num_of_vertices):

    # Find next vertex to be visited
    to_visit = to_be_visited()
    for neighbor_index in range(num_of_vertices):

        # Updating new distances
        if vertices[to_visit][neighbor_index] == 1 and \
            visited_and_distance[neighbor_index][0] == 0:
            new_distance = visited_and_distance[to_visit][1] \
                + edges[to_visit][neighbor_index]
            if visited_and_distance[neighbor_index][1] > new_distance:
                visited_and_distance[neighbor_index][1] = new_distance

        visited_and_distance[to_visit][0] = 1

i = 0

# Printing the distance
for distance in visited_and_distance:
    print("Distance of ", chr(ord('a') + i),
        " from source vertex: ", distance[1])
```

```
i = i + 1
```

Output
```
Distance of  a  from source vertex:  0
Distance of  b  from source vertex:  3
Distance of  c  from source vertex:  1
Distance of  d  from source vertex:  2
Distance of  e  from source vertex:  4
Distance of  f  from source vertex:  4
Distance of  g  from source vertex:  3
```

Dijkstra's Algorithm Complexity
Time Complexity: O(E Log V)
where, E is the number of edges and V is the number of vertices.

Space Complexity: O(V)

Dijkstra's Algorithm Applications
- To find the shortest path
- In social networking applications
- In a telephone network
- To find the locations in the map

Kruskal's Algorithm

Kruskal's algorithm is a minimum spanning tree algorithm that takes a graph as input and finds the subset of the edges of that graph which
- form a tree that includes every vertex
- has the minimum sum of weights among all the trees that can be formed from the graph

How Kruskal's algorithm works
It falls under a class of algorithms called greedy algorithms that find the local optimum in the hopes of finding a global optimum.

We start from the edges with the lowest weight and keep adding edges until we reach our goal.

The steps for implementing Kruskal's algorithm are as follows:

1. Sort all the edges from low weight to high
2. Take the edge with the lowest weight and add it to the spanning tree. If adding the edge created a cycle, then reject this edge.
3. Keep adding edges until we reach all vertices.

Example of Kruskal's algorithm

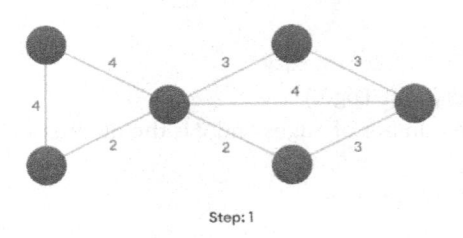

Step: 1

Start with a weighted graph

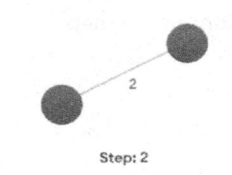

Step: 2

Choose the edge with the least weight, if there are more than 1, choose anyone

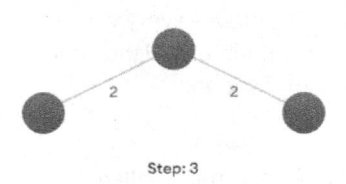

Step: 3

Choose the next shortest edge and add it

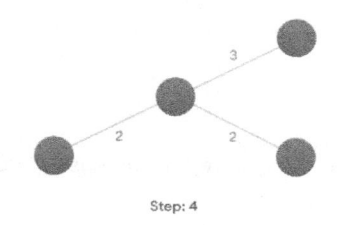

Step: 4

Choose the next shortest edge that doesn't create a cycle and add it

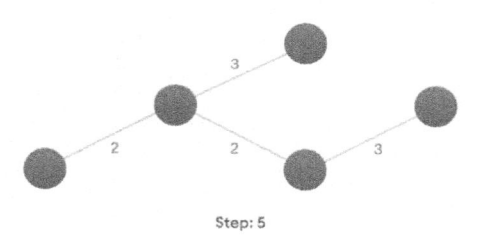

Step: 5

Choose the next shortest edge that doesn't create a cycle and add it

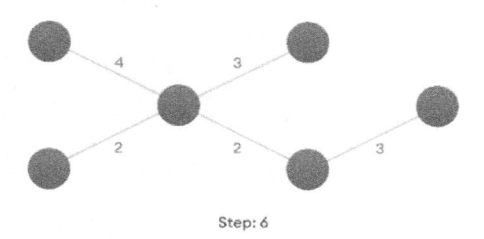

Step: 6

Repeat until you have a spanning tree

Kruskal Algorithm Pseudocode
Any minimum spanning tree algorithm revolves around checking if adding an edge creates a loop or not.

The most common way to find this out is an algorithm called Union FInd. The Union-Find algorithm divides the vertices into clusters and allows us to check if two vertices belong to the same cluster or not and hence decide whether adding an edge creates a cycle.

KRUSKAL(G):
A = ∅
For each vertex v ∈ G.V:
    MAKE-SET(v)
For each edge (u, v) ∈ G.E ordered by increasing order by weight(u, v):
    if FIND-SET(u) ≠ FIND-SET(v):
    A = A ∪ {(u, v)}
    UNION(u, v)
return A

```python
# Kruskal's algorithm in Python

class Graph:
    def __init__(self, vertices):
        self.V = vertices
        self.graph = []

    def add_edge(self, u, v, w):
        self.graph.append([u, v, w])

    # Search function

    def find(self, parent, i):
        if parent[i] == i:
            return i
        return self.find(parent, parent[i])

    def apply_union(self, parent, rank, x, y):
        xroot = self.find(parent, x)
        yroot = self.find(parent, y)
        if rank[xroot] < rank[yroot]:
            parent[xroot] = yroot
        elif rank[xroot] > rank[yroot]:
            parent[yroot] = xroot
        else:
            parent[yroot] = xroot
            rank[xroot] += 1

    #  Applying Kruskal algorithm
    def kruskal_algo(self):
        result = []
        i, e = 0, 0
        self.graph = sorted(self.graph, key=lambda item: item[2])
        parent = []
        rank = []
        for node in range(self.V):
            parent.append(node)
            rank.append(0)
        while e < self.V - 1:
```

```
            u, v, w = self.graph[i]
            i = i + 1
            x = self.find(parent, u)
            y = self.find(parent, v)
            if x != y:
                e = e + 1
                result.append([u, v, w])
                self.apply_union(parent, rank, x, y)
        for u, v, weight in result:
            print("%d - %d: %d" % (u, v, weight))
g = Graph(6)
g.add_edge(0, 1, 4)
g.add_edge(0, 2, 4)
g.add_edge(1, 2, 2)
g.add_edge(1, 0, 4)
g.add_edge(2, 0, 4)
g.add_edge(2, 1, 2)
g.add_edge(2, 3, 3)
g.add_edge(2, 5, 2)
g.add_edge(2, 4, 4)
g.add_edge(3, 2, 3)
g.add_edge(3, 4, 3)
g.add_edge(4, 2, 4)
g.add_edge(4, 3, 3)
g.add_edge(5, 2, 2)
g.add_edge(5, 4, 3)
g.kruskal_algo()
```

Output
1 - 2: 2
2 - 5: 2
2 - 3: 3
3 - 4: 3
0 - 1: 4

Kruskal's vs Prim's Algorithm
Prim's algorithm is another popular minimum spanning tree algorithm that uses a different logic to find the MST of a graph. Instead of starting from an edge, Prim's algorithm starts from a vertex and keeps adding lowest-weight edges which aren't in the tree, until all vertices have been covered.

Kruskal's Algorithm Complexity
The time complexity Of Kruskal's Algorithm is: O(E log E).

Kruskal's Algorithm Applications
- In order to layout electrical wiring
- In computer network (LAN connection)

Prim's Algorithm

Prim's algorithm is a minimum spanning tree algorithm that takes a graph as input and finds the subset of the edges of that graph which
- form a tree that includes every vertex
- has the minimum sum of weights among all the trees that can be formed from the graph

Professor Robert Clay Prim

How Prim's algorithm works
It falls under a class of algorithms called greedy algorithms that find the local optimum in the hopes of finding a global optimum.

We start from one vertex and keep adding edges with the lowest weight until we reach our goal.

The steps for implementing Prim's algorithm are as follows:
1. Initialize the minimum spanning tree with a vertex chosen at random.
2. Find all the edges that connect the tree to new vertices, find the minimum and add it to the tree
3. Keep repeating step 2 until we get a minimum spanning tree

Example of Prim's algorithm

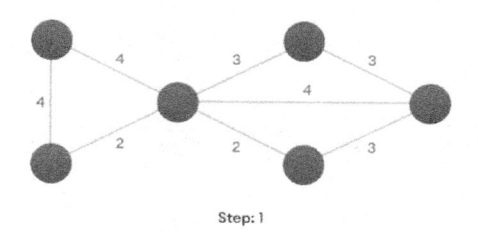

Step: 1

Start with a weighted graph

Step: 2

Choose a vertex

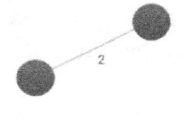

Step: 3

Choose the shortest edge from this vertex and add it

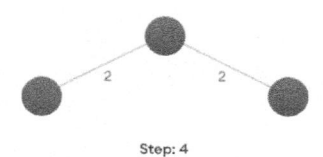

Step: 4

Choose the nearest vertex not yet in the solution

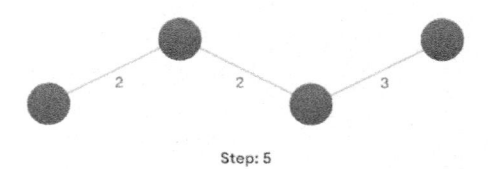

Step: 5

Choose the nearest edge not yet in the solution, if there are multiple choices, choose one at random

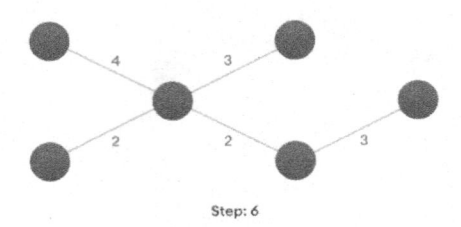

Step: 6

Repeat until you have a spanning tree

Prim's Algorithm pseudocode

The pseudocode for prim's algorithm shows how we create two sets of vertices U and V-U. U contains the list of vertices that have been visited and V-U the list of vertices that haven't. One by one, we move vertices from set V-U to set U by connecting the least weight edge.

```
T = ∅;
U = { 1 };
while (U ≠ V)
    let (u, v) be the lowest cost edge such that u ∈ U and v ∈ V - U;
    T = T ∪ {(u, v)}
    U = U ∪ {v}
```

```python
# Prim's Algorithm in Python

INF = 9999999
# number of vertices in graph
V = 5
# create a 2d array of size 5x5
# for adjacency matrix to represent graph
G = [[0, 9, 75, 0, 0],
     [9, 0, 95, 19, 42],
     [75, 95, 0, 51, 66],
     [0, 19, 51, 0, 31],
     [0, 42, 66, 31, 0]]
# create a array to track selected vertex
# selected will become true otherwise false
selected = [0, 0, 0, 0, 0]
# set number of edge to 0
no_edge = 0
# the number of egde in minimum spanning tree will be
```

```
# always less than(V - 1), where V is number of vertices in
# graph
# choose 0th vertex and make it true
selected[0] = True
# print for edge and weight
print("Edge : Weight\n")
while (no_edge < V - 1):
    # For every vertex in the set S, find the all adjacent
vertices
    #, calculate the distance from the vertex selected at s
tep 1.
    # if the vertex is already in the set S, discard it oth
erwise
    # choose another vertex nearest to selected vertex  at
step 1.
    minimum = INF
    x = 0
    y = 0
    for i in range(V):
        if selected[i]:
            for j in range(V):
                if ((not selected[j]) and G[i][j]):
                    # not in selected and there is an edge
                    if minimum > G[i][j]:
                        minimum = G[i][j]
                        x = i
                        y = j
    print(str(x) + "-" + str(y) + ":" + str(G[x][y]))
    selected[y] = True
    no_edge += 1
```

Output
Edge : Weight

0-1:9
1-3:19
3-4:31
3-2:51

Prim's vs Kruskal's Algorithm
Kruskal's algorithm is another popular minimum spanning tree algorithm that uses a different logic to find the MST of a graph. Instead of starting from a vertex, Kruskal's algorithm sorts all the edges from low weight to high and keeps adding the lowest edges, ignoring those edges that create a cycle.

Prim's Algorithm Complexity
The time complexity of Prim's algorithm is O(E log V).

Prim's Algorithm Application
- Laying cables of electrical wiring
- In network designed
- To make protocols in network cycles

Huffman Coding

Huffman Coding is a technique of compressing data to reduce its size without losing any of the details. It was first developed by David Huffman.

Huffman Coding is generally useful to compress the data in which there are frequently occurring characters.

How Huffman Coding works?
Suppose the string below is to be sent over a network.

| B | C | A | A | D | D | D | C | C | A | C | A | C | A | C |

Initial string

Each character occupies 8 bits. There are a total of 15 characters in the above string. Thus, a total of 8 * 15 = 120 bits are required to send this string.

Using the Huffman Coding technique, we can compress the string to a smaller size.

Huffman coding first creates a tree using the frequencies of the character and then generates code for each character.

Once the data is encoded, it has to be decoded. Decoding is done using the same tree.

Huffman Coding prevents any ambiguity in the decoding process using the concept of prefix code ie. a code associated with a character should not be present in the prefix of any other code. The tree created above helps in maintaining the property.

Huffman coding is done with the help of the following steps.

1. Calculate the frequency of each character in the string.

1	6	5	3
B	C	A	D

Frequency of string

2. Sort the characters in increasing order of the frequency. These are stored in a priority queue Q.

1	3	5	6
B	D	A	C

Characters sorted according to the frequency

3. Make each unique character as a leaf node.

4. Create an empty node z. Assign the minimum frequency to the left child of z and assign the second minimum frequency to the right child of z. Set the value of the z as the sum of the above two minimum frequencies.

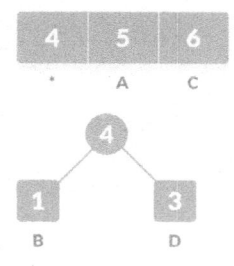

4	5	6
*	A	C

```
        4
       / \
      1   3
      B   D
```

Getting the sum of the least numbers

5. Remove these two minimum frequencies from Q and add the sum into the list of frequencies (* denote the internal nodes in the figure above).

6. Insert node z into the tree.

7. Repeat steps 3 to 5 for all the characters.

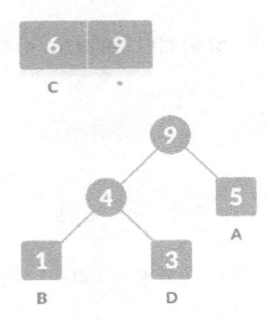

Repeat steps 3 to 5 for all the characters.

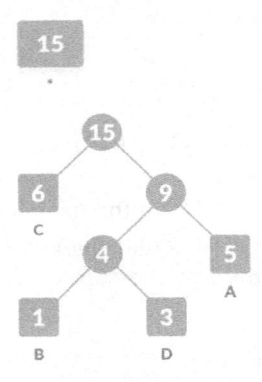

Repeat steps 3 to 5 for all the characters.

8. For each non-leaf node, assign 0 to the left edge and 1 to the right edge.

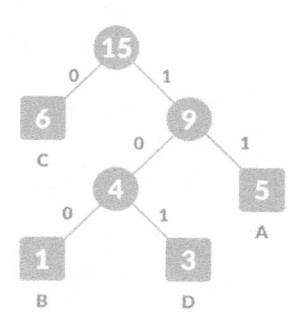

Assign 0 to the left edge and 1 to the right edge

For sending the above string over a network, we have to send the tree as well as the above compressed-code. The total size is given by the table below.

Character	Frequency	Code	Size
A	5	11	5*2 = 10
B	1	100	1*3 = 3
C	6	0	6*1 = 6
D	3	101	3*3 = 9
4 * 8 = 32 bits		15 bits	28 bits

Without encoding, the total size of the string was 120 bits. After encoding the size is reduced to 32 + 15 + 28 = 75.

Decoding the code

For decoding the code, we can take the code and traverse through the tree to find the character.

Let 101 is to be decoded, we can traverse from the root as in the figure below.

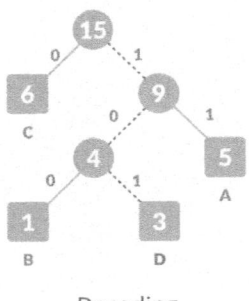

Decoding

Huffman Coding Algorithm

create a priority queue Q consisting of each unique character.
sort then in ascending order of their frequencies.
for all the unique characters:
    create a newNode
    extract minimum value from Q and assign it to leftChild of newNode
    extract minimum value from Q and assign it to rightChild of newNode
    calculate the sum of these two minimum values and assign it to the value of newNode
    insert this newNode into the tree
return rootNode

```python
# Huffman Coding in python

string = 'BCAADDDCCACACAC'

# Creating tree nodes
class NodeTree(object):

    def __init__(self, left=None, right=None):
        self.left = left
        self.right = right

    def children(self):
        return (self.left, self.right)

    def nodes(self):
        return (self.left, self.right)

    def __str__(self):
        return '%s_%s' % (self.left, self.right)
```

```python
# Main function implementing huffman coding
def huffman_code_tree(node, left=True, binString=''):
    if type(node) is str:
        return {node: binString}
    (l, r) = node.children()
    d = dict()
    d.update(huffman_code_tree(l, True, binString + '0'))
    d.update(huffman_code_tree(r, False, binString + '1'))
    return d

# Calculating frequency
freq = {}
for c in string:
    if c in freq:
        freq[c] += 1
    else:
        freq[c] = 1

freq = sorted(freq.items(), key=lambda x: x[1], reverse=True)

nodes = freq

while len(nodes) > 1:
    (key1, c1) = nodes[-1]
    (key2, c2) = nodes[-2]
    nodes = nodes[:-2]
    node = NodeTree(key1, key2)
    nodes.append((node, c1 + c2))

    nodes = sorted(nodes, key=lambda x: x[1], reverse=True)

huffmanCode = huffman_code_tree(nodes[0][0])

print(' Char | Huffman code ')
print('----------------------')
for (char, frequency) in freq:
    print(' %-4r |%12s' % (char, huffmanCode[char]))
```

Output
Char | Huffman code

 'C' | 0
 'A' | 11
 'D' | 101
 'B' | 100

Huffman Coding Complexity

The time complexity for encoding each unique character based on its frequency is O(nlog n).

Extracting minimum frequency from the priority queue takes place 2*(n-1) times and its complexity is O(log n). Thus the overall complexity is O(nlog n).

Huffman Coding Applications
- Huffman coding is used in conventional compression formats like GZIP, BZIP2, PKZIP, etc.
- For text and fax transmissions.

Dynamic Programming

Dynamic Programming is a technique in computer programming that helps to efficiently solve a class of problems that have overlapping subproblems and optimal substructure property.

Such problems involve repeatedly calculating the value of the same subproblems to find the optimum solution.

Dynamic Programming Example
Take the case of generating the fibonacci sequence.

If the sequence is F(1) F(2) F(3)........F(50), it follows the rule
F(n) = F(n-1) + F(n-2)

F(50) = F(49) + F(48)
F(49) = F(48) + F(47)
F(48) = F(47) + F(46)
...

Notice how there are overlapping subproblems, we need to calculate F(48) to calculate both F(50) and F(49). This is exactly the kind of algorithm where Dynamic Programming shines.

How Dynamic Programming Works
Dynamic programming works by storing the result of subproblems so that when their solutions are required, they are at hand and we do not need to recalculate them.

This technique of storing the value of subproblems is called memoization. By saving the values in the array, we save time for computations of sub-problems we have already come across.

```
var m = map(0 → 0, 1 → 1)
function fib(n)
   if key n is not in map m
      m[n] = fib(n – 1) + fib(n – 2)
   return m[n]
```

Dynamic programming by memoization is a top-down approach to dynamic programming. By reversing the direction in which the algorithm works i.e. by starting from the base case and working towards the solution, we can also implement dynamic programming in a bottom-up manner.

```
function fib(n)
```

```
if n = 0
   return 0
else
   var prevFib = 0, currFib = 1
   repeat n - 1 times
      var newFib = prevFib + currFib
      prevFib = currFib
      currFib = newFib
return currentFib
```

Recursion vs Dynamic Programming

Dynamic programming is mostly applied to recursive algorithms. This is not a coincidence, most optimization problems require recursion and dynamic programming is used for optimization.

But not all problems that use recursion can use Dynamic Programming. Unless there is a presence of overlapping subproblems like in the fibonacci sequence problem, a recursion can only reach the solution using a divide and conquer approach.

That is the reason why a recursive algorithm like Merge Sort cannot use Dynamic Programming, because the subproblems are not overlapping in any way.

Greedy Algorithms vs Dynamic Programming

Greedy Algorithms are similar to dynamic programming in the sense that they are both tools for optimization.

However, greedy algorithms look for locally optimum solutions or in other words, a greedy choice, in the hopes of finding a global optimum. Hence greedy algorithms can make a guess that looks optimum at the time but becomes costly down the line and do not guarantee a globally optimum.

Dynamic programming, on the other hand, finds the optimal solution to subproblems and then makes an informed choice to combine the results of those subproblems to find the most optimum solution.

Floyd-Warshall Algorithm

Floyd-Warshall Algorithm is an algorithm for finding the shortest path between all the pairs of vertices in a weighted graph. This algorithm works for both the directed and undirected weighted graphs. But, it does not work for the graphs with negative cycles (where the sum of the edges in a cycle is negative).

A weighted graph is a graph in which each edge has a numerical value associated with it.

Floyd-Warhshall algorithm is also called as Floyd's algorithm, Roy-Floyd algorithm, Roy-Warshall algorithm, or WFI algorithm.

This algorithm follows the dynamic programming approach to find the shortest paths.

How Floyd-Warshall Algorithm Works?

Let the given graph be:

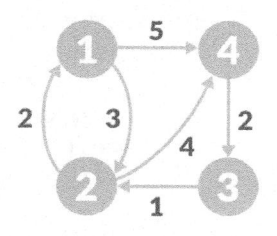

Initial graph

Follow the steps below to find the shortest path between all the pairs of vertices.

1. Create a matrix A^1 of dimension n*n where n is the number of vertices. The row and the column are indexed as i and j respectively. i and j are the vertices of the graph.

Each cell A[i][j] is filled with the distance from the ith vertex to the jth vertex. If there is no path from i^{th} vertex to j^{th} vertex, the cell is left as infinity.

$$A^0 = \begin{array}{c} \\ 1 \\ 2 \\ 3 \\ 4 \end{array} \begin{array}{cccc} 1 & 2 & 3 & 4 \\ \left[\begin{matrix} 0 & 3 & \infty & 5 \\ 2 & 0 & \infty & 4 \\ \infty & 1 & 0 & \infty \\ \infty & \infty & 2 & 0 \end{matrix}\right] \end{array}$$

Fill each cell with the distance between ith and jth vertex

2. Now, create a matrix A^1 using matrix A^0. The elements in the first column and the first row are left as they are. The remaining cells are filled in the following way.

Let k be the intermediate vertex in the shortest path from source to destination. In this step, k is the first vertex. A[i][j] is filled with (A[i][k] + A[k][j]) if (A[i][j] > A[i][k] + A[k][j]).

That is, if the direct distance from the source to the destination is greater than the path through the vertex k, then the cell is filled with A[i][k] + A[k][j].

In this step, k is vertex 1. We calculate the distance from source vertex to destination vertex through this vertex k.

$$A^1 = \begin{array}{c} \\ 1 \\ 2 \\ 3 \\ 4 \end{array} \begin{array}{cccc} 1 & 2 & 3 & 4 \\ \left[\begin{matrix} 0 & 3 & \infty & 5 \\ 2 & 0 & & \\ \infty & & 0 & \\ \infty & & & 0 \end{matrix}\right] \end{array} \longrightarrow \begin{array}{c} \\ 1 \\ 2 \\ 3 \\ 4 \end{array} \begin{array}{cccc} 1 & 2 & 3 & 4 \\ \left[\begin{matrix} 0 & 3 & \infty & 5 \\ 2 & 0 & 9 & 4 \\ \infty & 1 & 0 & 8 \\ \infty & \infty & 2 & 0 \end{matrix}\right] \end{array}$$

Calculate the distance from the source vertex to destination vertex through this vertex k

For example: For $A^1[2, 4]$, the direct distance from vertex 2 to 4 is 4 and the sum of the distance from vertex 2 to 4 through vertex (ie. from vertex 2 to 1 and from vertex 1 to 4) is 7. Since 4 < 7, $A^0[2, 4]$ is filled with 4.

3. Similarly, A² is created using A³. The elements in the second column and the second row are left as they are.

In this step, k is the second vertex (i.e. vertex 2). The remaining steps are the same as in step 2.

$$A^2 = \begin{array}{c} \\ 1 \\ 2 \\ 3 \\ 4 \end{array} \begin{array}{cccc} 1 & 2 & 3 & 4 \\ \left[\begin{array}{cccc} 0 & 3 & & \\ 2 & 0 & 9 & 4 \\ & 1 & 0 & \\ & \infty & & 0 \end{array} \right] \end{array} \longrightarrow \begin{array}{c} \\ 1 \\ 2 \\ 3 \\ 4 \end{array} \begin{array}{cccc} 1 & 2 & 3 & 4 \\ \left[\begin{array}{cccc} 0 & 3 & 9 & 5 \\ 2 & 0 & 9 & 4 \\ 3 & 1 & 0 & 5 \\ \infty & \infty & 2 & 0 \end{array} \right] \end{array}$$

Calculate the distance from the source vertex to destination vertex through this vertex 2

4. Similarly, A³ and A⁴ is also created.

$$A^3 = \begin{array}{c} \\ 1 \\ 2 \\ 3 \\ 4 \end{array} \begin{array}{cccc} 1 & 2 & 3 & 4 \\ \left[\begin{array}{cccc} 0 & & & \infty \\ & 0 & 9 & \\ \infty & 1 & 0 & 8 \\ & & 2 & 0 \end{array} \right] \end{array} \longrightarrow \begin{array}{c} \\ 1 \\ 2 \\ 3 \\ 4 \end{array} \begin{array}{cccc} 1 & 2 & 3 & 4 \\ \left[\begin{array}{cccc} 0 & 3 & 9 & 5 \\ 2 & 0 & 9 & 4 \\ 3 & 1 & 0 & 5 \\ 5 & 3 & 2 & 0 \end{array} \right] \end{array}$$

Calculate the distance from the source vertex to destination vertex through this vertex 3

$$A^4 = \begin{array}{c} \\ 1 \\ 2 \\ 3 \\ 4 \end{array} \begin{array}{cccc} 1 & 2 & 3 & 4 \\ \left[\begin{array}{cccc} 0 & & & 5 \\ & 0 & & 4 \\ & & 0 & 5 \\ 5 & 3 & 2 & 0 \end{array} \right] \end{array} \longrightarrow \begin{array}{c} \\ 1 \\ 2 \\ 3 \\ 4 \end{array} \begin{array}{cccc} 1 & 2 & 3 & 4 \\ \left[\begin{array}{cccc} 0 & 3 & 7 & 5 \\ 2 & 0 & 6 & 4 \\ 3 & 1 & 0 & 5 \\ 5 & 3 & 2 & 0 \end{array} \right] \end{array}$$

Calculate the distance from the source vertex to destination vertex through this vertex 4

A^4 gives the shortest path between each pair of vertices.

Floyd-Warshall Algorithm

n = no of vertices
A = matrix of dimension n*n
for k = 1 to n
  for i = 1 to n
    for j = 1 to n
      $A^k[i, j]$ = min ($A^{k-1}[i, j]$, $A^{k-1}[i, k]$ + $A^{k-1}[k, j]$)
return A

```
# Floyd Warshall Algorithm in python

# The number of vertices
nV = 4

INF = 999

# Algorithm implementation
def floyd_warshall(G):
    distance = list(map(lambda i: list(map(lambda j: j, i))
, G))

    # Adding vertices individually
    for k in range(nV):
        for i in range(nV):
            for j in range(nV):
                distance[i][j] = min(distance[i][j], distan
ce[i][k] + distance[k][j])
    print_solution(distance)

# Printing the solution
def print_solution(distance):
    for i in range(nV):
        for j in range(nV):
            if(distance[i][j] == INF):
                print("INF", end=" ")
            else:
                print(distance[i][j], end="  ")
        print(" ")

G = [[0, 3, INF, 5],
     [2, 0, INF, 4],
     [INF, 1, 0, INF],
     [INF, INF, 2, 0]]
floyd_warshall(G)
```

Output
```
0 3 7 5
2 0 6 4
3 1 0 5
5 3 2 0
```

Floyd Warshall Algorithm Complexity

Time Complexity
There are three loops. Each loop has constant complexities. So, the time complexity of the Floyd-Warshall algorithm is $O(n^3)$.

Space Complexity
The space complexity of the Floyd-Warshall algorithm is $O(n^2)$.

Floyd Warshall Algorithm Applications
- To find the shortest path is a directed graph
- To find the transitive closure of directed graphs
- To find the Inversion of real matrices
- For testing whether an undirected graph is bipartite

Longest Common Subsequence

The longest common subsequence (LCS) is defined as the longest subsequence that is common to all the given sequences, provided that the elements of the subsequence are not required to occupy consecutive positions within the original sequences.

If S1 and S2 are the two given sequences then, Z is the common subsequence of S1 and S2 if Z is a subsequence of both S1 and S2.

Furthermore, Z must be a strictly increasing sequence of the indices of both S1 and S2.

In a strictly increasing sequence, the indices of the elements chosen from the original sequences must be in ascending order in Z.

If
S1 = {B, C, D, A, A, C, D}

Then, {A, D, B} cannot be a subsequence of S1 as the order of the elements is not the same (ie. not strictly increasing sequence).

Let us understand LCS with an example.

If
S1 = {B, C, D, A, A, C, D}
S2 = {A, C, D, B, A, C}

Then, common subsequences are
{B, C}, {C, D, A, C}, {D, A, C}, {A, A, C}, {A, C}, {C, D}, ...

Among these subsequences, {C, D, A, C} is the longest common subsequence. We are going to find this longest common subsequence using dynamic programming.

Before proceeding further, if you do not already know about dynamic programming, please go through dynamic programming.

Using Dynamic Programming to find the LCS

Let us take two sequences:

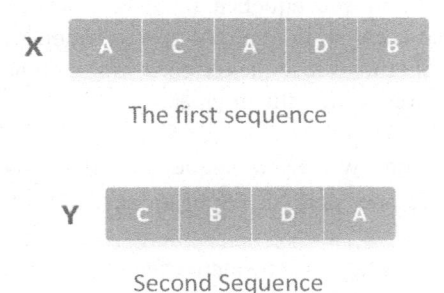

| X | A | C | A | D | B |

The first sequence

| Y | C | B | D | A |

Second Sequence

The following steps are followed for finding the longest common subsequence.

1. Create a table of dimension n+1*m+1 where n and m are the lengths of X and Y respectively. The first row and the first column are filled with zeros.

350

	C	B	D	A
	0	0	0	0	0
A	0				
C	0				
A	0				
D	0				
B	0				

Initialise a table

2. Fill each cell of the table using the following logic.

3. If the character correspoding to the current row and current column are matching, then fill the current cell by adding one to the diagonal element. Point an arrow to the diagonal cell.

4. Else take the maximum value from the previous column and previous row element for filling the current cell. Point an arrow to the cell with maximum value. If they are equal, point to any of them.

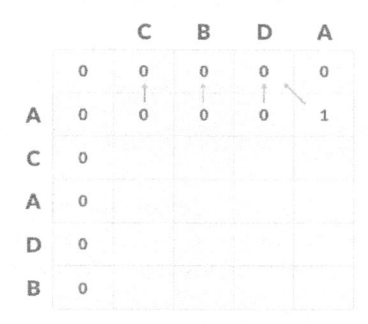

		C	B	D	A
	0	0	0	0	0
A	0	0	0	0	1
C	0				
A	0				
D	0				
B	0				

Fill the values

5. Step 2 is repeated until the table is filled.

	C	B	D	A
	0	0	0	0	0
A	0	0	0	0	1
C	0	1 ← 1 ← 1	1
A	0	1	1	1	2
D	0	1	1	2	2
B	0	1	2	2	2

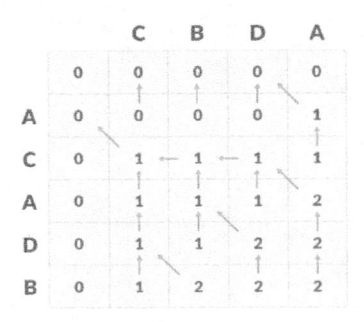

Fill all the values

6. The value in the last row and the last column is the length of the longest common subsequence.

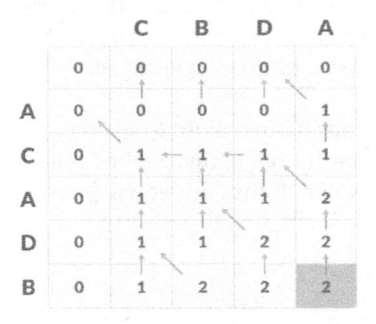

	C	B	D	A
	0	0	0	0	0
A	0	0	0	0	1
C	0	1 ← 1 ← 1	1
A	0	1	1	1	2
D	0	1	1	2	2
B	0	1	2	2	**2**

The bottom right corner is the length of the LCS

7. In order to find the longest common subsequence, start from the last element and follow the direction of the arrow. The elements corresponding to () symbol form the longest common subsequence.

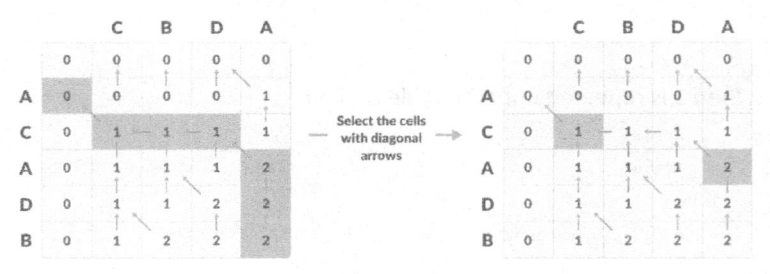

Select the cells with diagonal arrows →

Create a path according to the arrows

352

Thus, the longest common subsequence is CD.

C	A

LCS

How is a dynamic programming algorithm more efficient than the recursive algorithm while solving an LCS problem?

The method of dynamic programming reduces the number of function calls. It stores the result of each function call so that it can be used in future calls without the need for redundant calls.

In the above dynamic algorithm, the results obtained from each comparison between elements of X and the elements of Y are stored in a table so that they can be used in future computations.

So, the time taken by a dynamic approach is the time taken to fill the table (ie. O(mn)). Whereas, the recursion algorithm has the complexity of $2^{max(m, n)}$.

Longest Common Subsequence Algorithm

```
X and Y be two given sequences
Initialize a table LCS of dimension X.length * Y.length
X.label = X
Y.label = Y
LCS[0][] = 0
LCS[][0] = 0
Start from LCS[1][1]
Compare X[i] and Y[j]
    If X[i] = Y[j]
        LCS[i][j] = 1 + LCS[i-1, j-1]
        Point an arrow to LCS[i][j]
    Else
        LCS[i][j] = max(LCS[i-1][j], LCS[i][j-1])
        Point an arrow to max(LCS[i-1][j], LCS[i][j-1])
```

```python
# The longest common subsequence in Python

# Function to find lcs_algo
def lcs_algo(S1, S2, m, n):
    L = [[0 for x in range(n+1)] for x in range(m+1)]

    # Building the mtrix in bottom-up way
    for i in range(m+1):
        for j in range(n+1):
            if i == 0 or j == 0:
                L[i][j] = 0
            elif S1[i-1] == S2[j-1]:
                L[i][j] = L[i-1][j-1] + 1
            else:
                L[i][j] = max(L[i-1][j], L[i][j-1])

    index = L[m][n]

    lcs_algo = [""] * (index+1)
    lcs_algo[index] = ""

    i = m
    j = n
    while i > 0 and j > 0:

        if S1[i-1] == S2[j-1]:
            lcs_algo[index-1] = S1[i-1]
            i -= 1
            j -= 1
            index -= 1

        elif L[i-1][j] > L[i][j-1]:
            i -= 1
        else:
            j -= 1

    # Printing the sub sequences
    print("S1 : " + S1 + "\nS2 : " + S2)
    print("LCS: " + "".join(lcs_algo))

S1 = "ACADB"
S2 = "CBDA"
m = len(S1)
n = len(S2)
lcs_algo(S1, S2, m, n)
```

Output
S1 : ACADB
S2 : CBDA
LCS: CB

Longest Common Subsequence Applications
1. in compressing genome resequencing data

2. to authenticate users within their mobile phone through in-air signatures

Backtracking Algorithm

A backtracking algorithm is a problem-solving algorithm that uses a brute force approach for finding the desired output.

The Brute force approach tries out all the possible solutions and chooses the desired/best solutions.

The term backtracking suggests that if the current solution is not suitable, then backtrack and try other solutions. Thus, recursion is used in this approach.

This approach is used to solve problems that have multiple solutions. If you want an optimal solution, you must go for dynamic programming.

State Space Tree
A space state tree is a tree representing all the possible states (solution or nonsolution) of the problem from the root as an initial state to the leaf as a terminal state.

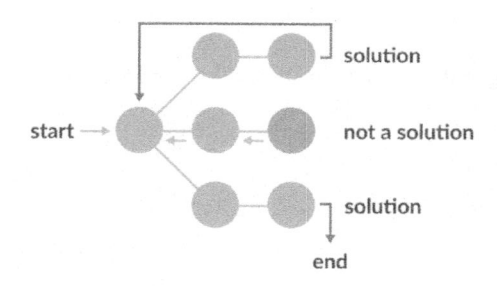

State Space Tree

Backtracking Algorithm

Backtrack(x)

    if x is not a solution
        return false
    if x is a new solution
        add to list of solutions
    backtrack(expand x)

Example Backtracking Approach

Problem: You want to find all the possible ways of arranging 2 boys and 1 girl on 3 benches. Constraint: Girl should not be on the middle bench.

Solution: There are a total of 3! = 6 possibilities. We will try all the possibilities and get the possible solutions. We recursively try all the possibilities.

All the possibilities are:

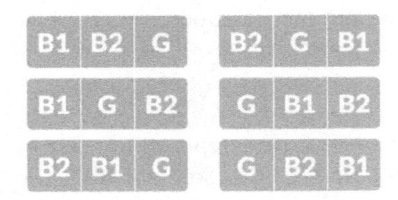

B1	B2	G		B2	G	B1
B1	G	B2		G	B1	B2
B2	B1	G		G	B2	B1

All the possibilities

The following state space tree shows the possible solutions.

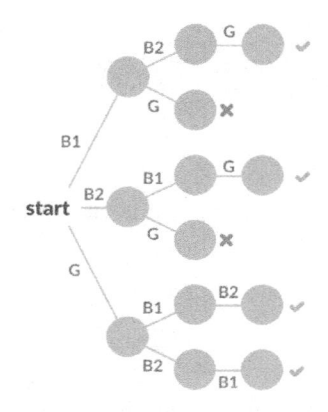

State tree with all the solutions

Backtracking Algorithm Applications
1. To find all Hamiltonian Paths present in a graph.
2. To solve the N Queen problem.
3. Maze solving problem.
4. The Knight's tour problem.

Rabin-Karp Algorithm

Rabin-Karp algorithm is an algorithm used for searching/matching patterns in the text using a hash function. Unlike Naive string matching algorithm, it does not travel through every character in the initial phase rather it filters the characters that do not match and then performs the comparison.

A hash function is a tool to map a larger input value to a smaller output value. This output value is called the hash value.

How Rabin-Karp Algorithm Works?
A sequence of characters is taken and checked for the possibility of the presence of the required string. If the possibility is found then, character matching is performed.

Let us understand the algorithm with the following steps:

Let the text be:

A	B	C	D	D	A	E	F	G

Text

And the string to be searched in the above text be:

C	D	D

Pattern

Let us assign a numerical value(v)/weight for the characters we will be using in the problem. Here, we have taken first ten alphabets only (i.e. A to J).

A	B	C	D	E	F	G	H	I	J
1	2	3	4	5	6	7	8	9	10

Text Weights

m be the length of the pattern and n be the length of the text. Here, m = 10 and n = 3.

Let d be the number of characters in the input set. Here, we have taken input set {A, B, C, ..., J}. So, d = 10. You can assume any suitable value for d.

Let us calculate the hash value of the pattern.

C	D	D

hash value = 6

Hash value of text

hash value for pattern(p) = Σ(v * dm-1) mod 13
$\qquad$ = ((3 * 10^2) + (4 * 10^1) + (4 * 10^0)) mod 13
$\qquad$ = 344 mod 13
$\qquad$ = 6

In the calculation above, choose a prime number (here, 13) in such a way that we can perform all the calculations with single-precision arithmetic.

The reason for calculating the modulus is given below.

Calculate the hash value for the text-window of size m.

For the first window ABC,
hash value for text(t) = Σ(v * d^{n-1}) mod 13
= ((1 * 10^2) + (2 * 10^1) + (3 * 10^0)) mod 13
= 123 mod 13
= 6

Compare the hash value of the pattern with the hash value of the text. If they match then, character-matching is performed.

In the above examples, the hash value of the first window (i.e. t) matches with p so, go for character matching between ABC and CDD. Since they do not match so, go for the next window.

We calculate the hash value of the next window by subtracting the first term and adding the next term as shown below.

t = ((1 * 10^2) + ((2 * 10^1) + (3 * 10^0)) * 10 + (3 * 10^0)) mod 13
 = 233 mod 13
 = 12

In order to optimize this process, we make use of the previous hash value in the following way.

t = ((d * (t - v[character to be removed] * h) + v[character to be added]) mod 13
 = ((10 * (6 - 1 * 9) + 3)mod 13
 = 12

Where, h = d^{m-1} = 10^{3-1} = 100.

For BCC, t = 12 (≠6). Therefore, go for the next window. After a few searches, we will get the match for the window CDA in the text.

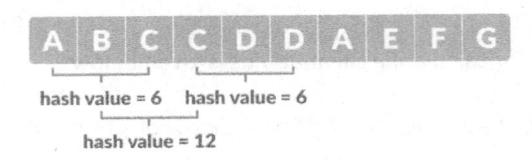

| A | B | C | C | D | D | A | E | F | G |

hash value = 6   hash value = 6
hash value = 12

Hash value of different windows

Algorithm

n = t.length
m = p.length
h = dm-1 mod q
p = 0
t0 = 0
for i = 1 to m
   p = (dp + p[i]) mod q
   t0 = (dt0 + t[i]) mod q
for s = 0 to n - m
   if p = ts
      if p[1.....m] = t[s + 1..... s + m]
         print "pattern found at position" s
   If s < n-m
      ts + 1 = (d (ts - t[s + 1]h) + t[s + m + 1]) mod q

```python
# Rabin-Karp algorithm in python

d = 10

def search(pattern, text, q):
    m = len(pattern)
    n = len(text)
    p = 0
    t = 0
    h = 1
    i = 0
    j = 0

    for i in range(m-1):
        h = (h*d) % q

    # Calculate hash value for pattern and text
```

```
        for i in range(m):
            p = (d*p + ord(pattern[i])) % q
            t = (d*t + ord(text[i])) % q

        # Find the match
        for i in range(n-m+1):
            if p == t:
                for j in range(m):
                    if text[i+j] != pattern[j]:
                        break

                j += 1
                if j == m:
                    print("Pattern is found at position: " + str(i+1))

            if i < n-m:
                t = (d*(t-ord(text[i])*h) + ord(text[i+m])) % q

                if t < 0:
                    t = t+q

text = "ABCCDDAEFG"
pattern = "CDD"
q = 13
search(pattern, text, q)
```

Output
Pattern is found at position: 4

Limitations of Rabin-Karp Algorithm

Spurious Hit
When the hash value of the pattern matches with the hash value of a window of the text but the window is not the actual pattern then it is called a spurious hit.

Spurious hit increases the time complexity of the algorithm. In order to minimize spurious hit, we use modulus. It greatly reduces the spurious hit.

Rabin-Karp Algorithm Complexity
The average case and best case complexity of Rabin-Karp algorithm is $O(m + n)$ and the worst case complexity is $O(mn)$.

The worst-case complexity occurs when spurious hits occur a number for all the windows.

Rabin-Karp Algorithm Applications
- For pattern matching
- For searching string in a bigger text

Made in the USA
Coppell, TX
02 January 2025

43843536R00203